Educational Action Research

Becoming Practically Critical

D0037453

Educational Action Research

Becoming Practically Critical

Susan E. Noffke
Robert B. Stevenson
EDITORS

Foreword by Susan Lytle
and Marilyn Cochran-Smith

Teachers College • Columbia University
New York and London

Published by Teachers College Press, 1234 Amsterdam Avenue, New York, NY 10027

Library of Congress Cataloging-in-Publication Data

Educational action research : becoming practically critical / edited
  by Susan E. Noffke, Robert B. Stevenson.
    p.   cm.
  Includes bibliographical references and index.
  ISBN 0-8077-3441-1. – ISBN 0-8077-3440-3 (pbk.)
    1. Action research in education – Case studies. 2. Teachers –
Training of – Case studies.   3. School management and organization –
Case studies.   I. Noffke, Susan E.   II. Stevenson,
Robert B.
LB1028.24.E38 1995
370'.78 – dc20   94-47335

ISBN 0-8077-3440-3 (paper)
ISBN 0-8077-3441-1 (cloth)

Printed on acid-free paper
Manufactured in the United States of America
01 00 99 98 97 96 95   8 7 6 5 4 3 2 1

Contents

Foreword by Marilyn Cochran-Smith and Susan L. Lytle   vii

1   Action Research and Democratic Schooling: Problematics
    and Potentials   1
         Susan E. Noffke

Part I   Action Research in Teacher Education

2   Using Action Research as a Vehicle for Student Teacher Reflection:
    A Social Reconstructionist Approach   13
         Kenneth M. Zeichner and Jennifer M. Gore

3   The Death of Idealism? Or, Issues of Empowerment in the
    Preservice Setting   31
         Lynn Brunner

4   Preservice Teacher Supervision and Reflective Practice   43
         Pat Schuyler and David Sitterley

5   Teaching Action Research: A Case Study   60
         Robert B. Stevenson, Susan E. Noffke, Eduardo Flores, and Susan Granger

6   Confused on a Higher Level About More Important Things!   74
         Catherine Battaglia

Part II   Action Research in Schools

7   Putting the "P" into a Participation in Government Course   95
         Gregory Bronson

8   The Principal as Action Researcher: A Study of Disciplinary Practice   115
         Elizabeth Soffer

9   Embedding Action Research in Professional Practice   127
         Allan Feldman and J. Myron Atkin

Part III   Supporting Action Research

10   Developing Discourses and Structures to Support Action Research
     for Educational Reform: Working Both Ends   141
                    David Hursh

11   What Happens When a School District Supports Action Research?   154
                    Cathy Caro-Bruce and Jennifer McCreadie

12   The Role of the Collaborator in Action Research   165
                    Eduardo Flores and Susan Granger

13   The Institutionalization of Action Research: The California
     "100 Schools" Project   180
                    Allan Feldman

14   Action Research and Supportive School Contexts: Exploring the
     Possibilities for Transformation   197
                    Robert B. Stevenson

References   211
About the Editors and the Contributors   219
Index   223

Foreword

Over the past decade, a new generation of educators in both schools and universities has been pressing a set of challenging and often unsettling questions about practice and the power of collective action in educational reform. Reformers have been contesting common assumptions about fundamental processes of educational change and about the central players in these processes, and at the same time imagining and developing radically different approaches to teaching, learning, and schooling. Action research and other modes of practitioner inquiry have emerged as particularly promising vehicles for politically strategic action and in some settings have come to play a galvanizing role in collaborative efforts to rethink the relationships of theory and practice, school and university, and local and wider agendas for social change. In the current era of reform, a book that situates action research theoretically and historically and also reveals how it plays out on a practical level is both provocative and timely.

Noffke and Stevenson's edited volume is true to both halves of its compelling title—*Educational Action Research: Becoming Practically Critical*. In their framing of the volume, the editors argue persuasively for action research as a process that itself embodies fundamental democratic principles and promises a radically reconstructed role for practitioners as actors in the larger emancipatory project. They suggest that the distinguishing feature of this form of inquiry is its intentional and continuous engagement in an ethical and political discourse. It is no small task, however, to show readers what this endeavor really entails. To do so, and to emphasize the power of action research to unpack the ideological underpinnings of everyday educational practice, the editors have collected a set of rich and detailed accounts. These narratives demonstrate palpably how action research improves practice and the understanding of practice as well as alters the circumstances under which educational practice occurs. What is most impressive is that the book captures what happens when practitioners struggle to become *practically* critical, demystifying the practices and consequences of action research and offering us a refreshing reversal of the tendency to advocate critical theory rather than to live it.

We find this collection of essays unusual in its range, offering us perspectives of differently positioned practitioners including teachers and teacher educators, student teachers, fieldwork supervisors, staff developers, principals, consultants, and graduate students. The skillful juxtaposition of these multiple vantage points within a single volume enables readers to envision a transfigured educational scene wherein all the players struggle to reinvent their lives and work along more ethical and democratic lines. Across these quite diverse texts, we also find a remarkable consistency of stance and focus. Each contributor unflinchingly calls attention to the tensions, contradictions, and complexities of actually doing action research from inside his or her own imperfect but familiar educational setting. And each implicitly helps make the case that to change educational practice, it is essential to interrogate and change relationships between and among students, teachers, administrators, and university partners. Taken together, these 14 chapters show what it means to develop and sustain an agenda for reflective action that transforms—individually and collectively—relationships of power, voice, and participation in teaching and learning.

We feel confident that this volume will provoke questions that are germane to the most important conversations in education today. Noffke, Stevenson, and their collaborators invite us to reconsider research itself, particularly the ways that the cyclical nature of action research can interrupt narrow notions of purposes and outcomes. The book also contributes to the ongoing discussion of what it means to generate and use knowledge in teaching, particularly the problems inherent in trying to separate knowledge from the knower or from the political and social context in which it is generated. Implicit in this work are questions about professional development in an era of reform, especially the role and relative importance of individual change in the larger project of bringing about social justice. Perhaps most importantly, this volume poses troubling but necessary questions about what we as educators are doing to affect the material conditions of children's and teachers' lives and argues passionately that supporting action research—as both stance and method—can further enhance the emancipatory agenda.

—Marilyn Cochran-Smith and Susan L. Lytle
University of Pennsylvania

Educational Action Research

Becoming Practically Critical

1

Action Research and Democratic Schooling

Problematics and Potentials

Susan E. Noffke

> I am done with great things and big plans, great institutions and big success. I am
> for those tiny, invisible loving human forces that work from individual to individ-
> ual, creeping through the crannies of the world like so many rootlets, or like the
> capillary oozing of water, yet which, if given time, will rend the hardest monu-
> ments of human pride.
>
> —William James, cited in Lackey & Walker, 1994, p. 3

A chapter with a title like this one, especially in a book that announces itself as *Becoming Practically Critical*, must address some basic questions: What is action research and what does it have to do with democratic schooling? And, most fundamentally, what does it have to do with making the lives of children and the people who care for them any better? Critical scholarship has long established itself in educational thinking. Works that identify the ways in which education within social democracy does not fulfill its promises are well documented. Yet it is often hard to find clarity about the practical implications of critical thought, the continuous interplay between doing something and revising our thought about what ought to be done, which is often called praxis. Indeed, a major impetus for this book has been the desire to see works that address action research both in terms of what it ought to be able to do and in stories of how it occurs and what it creates.

Here, I want to explore some of the problematics as well as the potentials involved in trying to work toward democracy in education through action research. While the origins of action research can be seen as intertwined at times with social action toward greater social justice, it is also clear that this has not always been the case. First, I explore the question, "What is action research?" with particular attention to the ways in which issues of democratizing schooling are addressed. A historical case is made for linkages between action research and notions of democracy. Next, I consider ways in which understanding action research in conjunction with democracy must continue to be addressed if its work is to be seen as making life in educational situations better. Finally, some comments are offered on how the chapters of this book relate to action research and democratic schooling and the task of *Becoming Practically Critical*.

WHAT IS ACTION RESEARCH AND WHAT DOES IT HAVE TO DO WITH CREATING DEMOCRACY IN SCHOOLING?

The question, "What is action research?" is not easily answered. Frequently, differences in conceptions and activities have been characterized as emphasizing either the technical, the moral/ethical, or the emancipatory aspects to action research (e.g., Grundy, 1982). While such categories are indeed useful in terms of ease of recognition of potential interests represented in the research process, they also tend to obscure the various ways in which interests are seldom one-dimensional, but rather interconnected and all essential to educational practice (Noffke, 1990). There is the additional danger that the categories may be seen not only as distinct and discrete, but also as hierarchical in nature, with the lowest being the practical. As has been argued elsewhere (Noffke & Brennan, 1988; Somekh, 1989; Zeichner, 1993a), this implicit ordering in significance, along with the use of academic discourses, not only acts to devalue the activities and deliberations of practitioners, but also serves to potentially alienate the "doers" of action research (most of whom, in the United States at least, have been female teachers) from those who theorize about it (primarily male academics). Clearly, an understanding of action research that transcends the traditional divisions between practitioners and scholars is needed.

Understanding Action Research Historically

Action research has been part of educational work for over 50 years. In the United States during the 1930s, the term was used both by John Collier, the U.S. Commissioner of Indian Affairs, to describe his work in democratic forms of agricultural planning and by Kurt Lewin, a social psychologist who, with his associates, focused on understanding and changing human action, often around issues of reducing prejudice and increasing democratic behaviors. The topics chosen for study matched the needs and contexts under study, and the process was seen as cyclical, involving a nonlinear pattern of planning, acting, observing, and reflecting on changes in the social situations. This work is particularly important, not only in understanding action research in education, but also in seeing its relationship to such fields as organizational development, especially the current work on "quality circles." Lewin's efforts can be seen as integrally related to others that emphasized issues of greater productivity and efficiency rather than the "democratic agenda." Action research was and continues to be used to explore the role of social science in initiating changes not only in education, but in, for example, industry, community development, and the military.

In education, the history of action research can be situated within broad, but differing, traditions. In the United States, for example, action research efforts can be loosely associated with "progressive education." However, it is important to remember that label often is applied to projects with very different assumptions. Some parts of progressive education were focused on scientific management orientations, while other attempted to work toward "child-centered" schooling. A "social meliorist" position, which recognized social (primarily economic) injustices, and worked toward rectifying them, is also a recognizable part of that movement (Kliebard, 1986). Early efforts in action research at the Horace Mann–Lincoln Institute at Teachers College, especially the work of Stephen Corey (1953) and A. W. Foshay (Foshay et al., 1954) reflected that diversity of views. Some of these projects focused on creating democracy in classrooms by involving children in the action research process, while others highlighted children's social values. Somewhat later, a declining salience of issues relating to democratic schooling and an increasing attention to issues of personal and profession growth are apparent in the efforts of Hilda Taba (Taba & Noel, 1957) and Abraham Shumsky (1958). Whether due to the rise of McCarthyism or to the growth in federally funded research projects to develop more discipline-based curricula, action research not only changed in meaning and focus, but moved out of the national spotlight.

Over the past 2 decades, action research efforts have returned to visibility and are even enjoying a new degree of acceptance. However, with this has also come a further proliferation of meanings and uses of the term. Sometimes there are clear connections with efforts to develop pedagogical and curricular reforms that bring students' involvement in their own learning to the center of education. Present, too, at times are glimpses of educators working in the midst of social change. The work in the United Kingdom in the 1970s and early 1980s (Elliott & Adelman, 1973; Stenhouse, 1975), for example, clearly reflects these characteristics. From this family of action researchers also emerged a conception of teachers as professionals whose practice includes not only curriculum development but moral, yet not necessarily political, deliberation (Elliott, 1987). The projects that developed in those years have influenced the institutionalization of action research in some parts of inservice teacher education and have led to the formation of the Classroom Action Research Network (CARN) and the launching of *Educational Action Research*, a new journal that is international in scope and ecumenical in its approach to action research.

The work of Kemmis and McTaggart and others in Australia, built on a broad-based effort for collaborative curriculum planning and social justice agendas, articulates a vision of action research, through the use of critical theory, in which teachers are participants in the project of human emancipation (Carr & Kemmis, 1986; Kemmis & McTaggart, 1988). These works have enjoyed wide dissemination, and the ideas are used in initial teacher education programs as well as staff development. This same articulation of action research to social justice efforts can be seen clearly in areas outside of education. Maria Mies's (1983) efforts to create shelters for women who have been battered and participatory action research efforts in postcolonial societies as well as in the United States over issues such as land ownership and economic self-determination (Fals Borda & Rahman, 1991; Park, Brydon-Miller, Hall, & Jackson, 1993) are but two examples.

Yet it is also true that work in action research does not automatically bring with it ideals of economic and social democracy (Noffke, 1989, 1994). Widely distributed works in the United States (e.g., Oja & Smulyan, 1989; Sagor, 1992) certainly reflect more of the professional development and knowledge base orientation noted earlier. The relative absence in the literature of examples of work by practitioners addressing social justice, and the relative preponderance of examples in which questions of personal development and professional knowledge supplant political and ethical discourse are well noted (Weiner, 1989; Zeichner, 1993a). While historical and contemporary links between action research and efforts to create more democratic schools can be found, they clearly are not always compelling enough to establish firm connections.

Toward a Definition of Action Research

As shown in the historical discussion, multiple definitions of action research have been and continue to be developed. Yet to say this does not excuse one from offering some sort of synthesis, from taking a position. Action research is, at once, a technology—that is, a set of things one can do, a set of political commitments that acknowledges, however tacitly, that educational (and other) lives are filled with injustices—and a moral and ethical stance that recognizes the improvement of human life as a goal. To say this requires recognizing that people in schools live in a world in which the question "What will I do?" lives alongside, "What is going on?" and "What shall I do?"

As a research method, action research is cyclical, that is, it does not progress from an initial question to the formulation of data collection, analysis, and conclusion. Rather, it assumes that understandings and actions emerge in a constant cycle, one that always highlights the ways in which educators are partially correct, yet in continual need of revision, in their thoughts and actions. The process does not end, as with traditional notions of research, with richer understandings of education for others to implement; rather it aids in the ongoing process of identifying contradictions, which, in turn, help to locate spaces for ethically defensible, politically strategic action.

While the original, Lewinian cycles of plan, act, observe, reflect may not always occur in neat cycles, but rather intermingle "where I went" with "where I should go," there are points at which the logic of one's actions and the time one has to think things over impose fairly arbitrary distinctions. In general, though, action research in education proceeds along lines compatible with the ongoing rhythms of life in schools, while at the same time not taking those rhythms for granted.

Action research, then, is about taking everyday things in the life of education and unpacking them for their historical and ideological baggage. It is similar to, but not the same as, the everyday process of improvement, in that it is public and collaborative. It highlights process with content, rather than content alone. It allows for a focus on teaching, in addition to student outcomes, and on the interplay between the two.

In the collection of data, or evidence, related to practice, action research emphasizes the educator's own, often intuitive, judgments of teaching and helps to locate one's vision of good teaching within those of others involved in the educative process (parents, children, teacher educators, the community, the state, etc.). In so doing it helps to make the educational process continually problematic. This continual revisiting of issues and practices builds a new kind of theory-practice relationship, one in which our understanding of education is always partially correct and partially in need of revision.

A result of this process can be the recognition of the power of working together, across the myriad of differences, in building new networks of communication. A major part of this, then, must be a continuous process of clarification of our vision in the area of social justice, of recognizing the constraints on practice, and of developing the capabilities necessary to realize those visions, while at the same time holding all three as problematic. It is in this sense that action research involves the improvement of practice, of the understanding of practice, and of the situations in which practice occurs (Kemmis & McTaggart, 1988).

CAN ACTION RESEARCH MAKE SCHOOLS BETTER?

The quote that begins this chapter, taken from a 1994 collaborative issue of *Democracy and Education* and *Hands On: A Journal for Teachers*, asserts a position common among at least some advocates of action research. The pages of these journals, as well as of other publications such as *Rethinking Schools*, are filled with reminders both of the legacy of attempts to create schools in which both teachers and educators learn about democracy by living it and of the contemporary struggles to make these visions a reality in the face of undeniable evidence of the tremendous inequalities in American education (Kozol, 1991; Shujaa, 1994). Such publications and the dozens of groups they represent are parts of long-standing traditions, in the United States as well as most other nations, of efforts, often very similar to action research, to create and sustain schools that work for social justice, at both an interpersonal as well as an institutional level.

I took a copy of the *Democracy and Education/Hands On* journal issue to a recent meeting with a group of teachers and an administrator. Their immediate reaction upon seeing the title of the journal, *Democracy and Education*, was, "Is there such a thing?" These are teachers who are committed to improving the lives of the children with whom they work by engaging in action research projects in their classrooms and schools. Working in a context where over 60% of school-aged children live in poverty, where there has been no implemented teachers' contract for over 4 years, where district and state exams exert powerful influences on their lives, even such teachers sometimes find that democracy and education seem like a contradiction in terms.

Many educators are working in projects that like the description by James quoted earlier, seek educational change by working from a grass-roots base as individuals and in groups. This belief in the power of communities participating in social change is often regarded as a fundamental component of democratic living as well as of action research. But it also may be, as Zeichner (1991) has indicated, that democratization in education is not without its contradictions and tensions, especially when there are no clear linkages to broader social change.

One could address the question of action research in relation to democratic schooling in several ways. One would be to look at the various definitions of democratic education that in recent years have become more prominent in educational writings. Works by Bastian, Gittell, Greer, and Haskins (1986), Gutmann (1987), Jensen and Walker (1989), Weiler and Mitchell (1992), and Weis and Fine (1993) have greatly increased our understandings of the various ways to think about the meaning of democratic education and have pointed the way toward its realization. Many of these works, of course, build on the continuingly useful thoughts of John Dewey, Paulo Freire, Henry Giroux, Herb Kohl, and Ira Shor. Examination of these would give greater clarity to the kinds of tasks that might be undertaken within an action research framework.

One could, instead, examine the implications of educators engaging in action research in schools that historically have been undemocratic and that are increasingly controlled, albeit in more subtle ways (Apple, 1993). Understanding action research in the political economy of knowledge production, understanding the contradictions between the moves for more "site-based management" and the push for "standards," and understanding efforts for the creation of separate schools for African Americans are only a few of the topics with direct implications for the possibility of engaging in action research for more democratic schooling.

Both of those approaches would be helpful in identifying possible tensions and contradictions in the practices of action research in relation to democratic schooling. In this section, however, I focus on something that to me remains the "bottom line" in any discussions of educational change, namely, what (if anything) action research in conjunction with visions of greater democracy in schooling has to contribute to real instances of improving the lives of children and the people who care for them. Along with this, of course, come the questions, "What is meant by improving?" and "For whom?"

In 1954, Stephen Corey argued that a major advantage to engaging in action research by teachers resided in their "beginning to know" rather than just "hoping" (p. 208) that their work was successful. Indeed, the systematic inquiry associated with action research may help practitioners "to know" that their practice is successful. Yet, as with other forms of research, it may reveal only those parts of education that they are positioned to see. Identities and the experiences that help to construct them affect visions of what ought to be.

Action research, then, carries with it the dual potential of helping preservice and inservice teachers to seek alternatives to current practice and also of helping them reproduce what already exists. As action research struggles to gain legitimacy within academic circles as well as in school districts and state certification boards, there is both the potential of new and more just educational practice and the problematic that such research may be used to create a new authority of practice (Gore, 1991b). For those who would facilitate and support action research efforts, come the tasks of helping to create conditions where action research can take place and also of ensuring that their practice, intertwined as it is with that of other educators, is always held equally problematic.

If action research is to aid in creating schools that improve the lives of children and the people who care for them, some minimal characteristics must be present, addressing both the substance of action research as well as the process. Action research must not be seen as only a staff development strategy; it must also serve as a means to make public the understandings of practitioners and the contexts in which they work. This has several implications for how reports of action research, especially those offered in conjunction with efforts to create more democratic schooling, are to be addressed. First, "findings" of research must be provisional. This reflects not only issues of "validity" or alternative interpretation of events recounted, but also the cyclical, ongoing nature of action research and the tremendous power the status quo has over us all. Reports, including those offered in this book, are offered as the best narrative of what has occurred thus far. Writing them (and rereading them) often reveals tensions and contradictions to the authors, in common with their readers. The illusion of the meritocratic system; the patterns of race, gender, and class inequities in society;

and the ways in which children are regarded have tremendous holds, often rooted in culture and economics, which only continual examination can reveal. As many action researchers have noted, there are no "ends" to the cycles, points at which others can implement what they have found. There are only points at which researchers share, deliberate, and move on, hoping that others will gain new ideas from what they have recounted.

Second, schooling for democracy must not be held out as some immutable truth that cannot itself be interrogated. After all, as Pateman (1989) and Young (1990) have asserted, democracy can be claimed to exist and community to be achieved, when the voices of many are excluded and the pressures to conform exceed those of dissidence and difference. What many who advocate greater democracy in schooling share is a sense that what exists is not what ought to be. What is of issue here is not greater efficiency or closer alignment with the economic sector, although these are not unimportant. Rather, there is a probing beyond what has been learned about such notions as "ability" and the illusion of the individualist meritocracy it supports, into areas that affirm each child's worth, each potential contribution to the building of a society in which the current rhetoric of "all children learning" becomes a reality.

Finally, the seemingly mundane concerns of educators, of children, and of parents, must be seen as reminding us that democracy develops not only in the realms of theories, but also in the everyday practices of lives with children. Whether it is in looking at the ways in which lunch count proceeds, in the supervision of recess, in the curriculum, or in disciplinary actions, action research can be a tool for the development of more democratic schooling. Without the concurrent examination of notions of emerging and constantly changing visions of social justice embedded in such activities, however, that potential may become part of the problem.

EXPLORATIONS IN EDUCATIONAL ACTION RESEARCH

The chapters included in this volume reflect various images of what action research might be and how it might be articulated with visions of democratic schooling. The chapters are divided into three parts: Action Research in Teacher Education, Action Research in Schools, and Supporting Action Research. These sections reflect concerns with how action research occurs within the overall context of teacher education, how it evolves in practice, and how those outside of classrooms and schools might facilitate and enhance its work. The relationships between what is recounted here and the analysis of action research and democratic schooling are by no means to be seen as presented unproblematically. Rather, the substance of the chapters as well as the process reported are assumed to be tentative and contradictory, providing spaces for both the authors and readers to plan new inquiries, new actions, and new reflections.

In Part I, issues and practices of action research in both pre- and inservice teacher education are addressed. In Chapter 2, "Using Action Research as a Vehicle for Student Teacher Reflection," Kenneth Zeichner and Jennifer Gore examine action research in teacher education. Their outline of a "social reconstructionist" approach seeks to resist the imposition of a particular model of educational reform, opting instead for a continuous reflection on their own and others' social agendas in the preparation of teachers. Chapter 3, "The Death of Idealism," examines Lynn Brunner's experiences in a teacher education program, raising many questions about not only the content but also the context of learning to teach. In Chapter 4, written by supervisors of student teachers, the authors address not only the process of helping students to become more reflective about a broad range of educational issues, but also the institutional context in which they, as graduate students, work. Chapter 5, "Teaching Action Research: A Case Study," focuses attention on the ways in which Bob Stevenson and I attempted to improve the teaching in our class in action research, in particular in how we attempted to address the great diversity of students, especially in terms of authority, and to create "democratic communities" within the class. In Chapter 6, Catherine Battaglia writes about being "Confused on a Higher Level." Her experiences as a staff developer raise very useful questions about the meaning of practice in a context in which so much of what she does impinges on the lives and work of others.

Part II focuses attention on the work of educational practitioners in the field. In Chapter 7, "Putting the 'P' into a Participation in Government Course," Gregory Bronson explores his efforts to live out the course title in his classes. Elizabeth Soffer, in Chapter 8, "The Principal as Action Researcher," recounts her efforts to examine her own actions as a school administrator, ending with her understanding of how she needs to create a broader sense of community over issues of discipline in her school. Concluding the part, Allan Feldman and J. Myron Atkin address questions of "Embedding Action Research in Professional Practice" (Chapter 9). Their comments, while foreshadowing issues raised in Part III, focus on the qualities of action research embodied in the chapters by Bronson and Soffer. Feldman and Atkin argue for a conceptualization of action research that is self-sustaining, one that builds on the nature of teaching and of the questions that teachers (and presumably others involved in education) raise. Such a conception, they argue, sustains itself through the personal and professional fulfillment of the practitioner's goals and through the sharing with other practitioners of the fruits of their labors.

In Part III, "Supporting Action Research," issues of institutional as well as personal conditions for action research are addressed. In Chapter 10, David

Hursh recounts his experiences in "Developing Discourses and Structures to Support Action Research for Educational Reform." He is "Working both ends," in the schools and in teacher education, to support action research in the interests of democratic school reform. Chapter 11 focuses attention on "What Happens When a School District Supports Action Research." In this chapter, Cathy Caro-Bruce and Jennifer McCreadie describe their efforts to develop action research within the framework of staff development in their school district. In Chapter 12, "The Role of the Collaborator in Action Research," Eduardo Flores and Susan Granger illustrate the ways in which the "democratic agenda" of their university course instructors (Bob Stevenson and myself) is perceived by students who have been enlisted to help collaborate in the process of action research. Written in the form of letters, it explores the ways in which collaborators see themselves as both distant from and integrated with the concerns of the people whose work they facilitate. In Chapter 13, by Allan Feldman, "The Institutional-ization of Action Research," issues related to work with teachers in an action research project are juxtaposed against the goals of the funding agent.

Part III concludes with Chapter 14 by Robert Stevenson, "Action Research and Supportive School Contexts: Exploring the Possibilities for Transformation," in which he addresses both the situations in which action research takes place and the need for constant revision of the form and purposes of educational research.

In all the chapters in this book, the tentative nature of action research is present, both in the definition of its processes as well as in its goals. These chapters are beginning points as well as narratives, instances of explorations in educational action research. They are also examples of educational research in action, ones in which the "tiny, invisible loving human forces," as part of the project of understanding and constructing democracy in schooling, are gradually becoming visible. They are offered as the opportunities for further critique, of both the substance and the process, in the hope that both senses of the "practi-cally" of the subtitle of the book will be furthered.

Part I

ACTION RESEARCH IN TEACHER EDUCATION

2

Using Action Research as a Vehicle for Student Teacher Reflection

A Social Reconstructionist Approach

Kenneth M. Zeichner & Jennifer M. Gore

The use of action research as a strategy for encouraging more reflective teaching practice by prospective teachers in the United States is not a new idea. During the 1950s when many experienced teachers throughout the United States were encouraged to participate in various kinds of action research work (e.g., Corey, 1953; Shumsky, 1958), there were also efforts to introduce action research to students in preservice teacher education programs (e.g., Beckman, 1957; Perrodin, 1959). Teacher educators who have argued for the introduction of action research into the preservice teacher education curriculum have stressed the importance of establishing habits of "self-monitoring" during initial training so that teachers can enter the profession with the dispositions and skills that will enable them to continue to learn from experience and become better at teaching throughout their careers (Biott, 1983; Rudduck, 1985).

Teacher educators at several teacher education institutions in the United States and elsewhere, such as the University of Florida, the University of Pennsylvania, and the University of Houston, have reported using action research as a part of their preservice teacher education curriculum (e.g., Clift, Veal, Johnson, & Holland, 1990; Cochran-Smith, 1988; Ross, 1987).[1] The recent re-emergence of action research in U.S. preservice teacher education has paralleled the increased influence of constructivist approaches in the U.S. educational research community (Posner, Strike, Hewson, & Gertzog, 1982) and teacher education community (Fosnot, 1989), the rapidly growing body of research on teacher thinking (Clark, 1988), and the increased attention to teachers' "practical knowledge" (Fenstermacher, 1986).

In the past decade, "action research," "reflective teaching," "reflection in action," "teacher research," and "research-based or inquiry-oriented teacher education" have become fashionable slogans throughout all segments of the U.S. teacher education community. Among the signs of this ascendancy are two national conferences focused primarily on reflective inquiry in teacher education (e.g., Clift, Houston, & Pugach, 1990), a special issue of the *Journal of Teacher Education* (1989) devoted to "Critical Reflection in Teacher Education," the popularity of the labels reflective teaching and action research at American Educational Research Association (AERA) conferences, and the recent proliferation of books and monographs on reflective practice in teaching and teacher education (e.g., Grimmett & Erickson, 1988; Henderson, 1992; Posner, 1989; Valli, 1992).

Since 1985, teacher educators in the elementary student teaching program at the University of Wisconsin–Madison also have used action research as a vehicle for facilitating student teacher reflection.[2] In this chapter, we aim to provide a framework for thinking about action research and to argue for a social reconstructionist approach. First, we elaborate the social reconstructionist approach to action research that guided our work together, distinguishing it from other orientations and practices in contemporary teacher education. Next, we outline issues in the enactment of social reconstructionist action research, offering a detailed consideration of its complexities. To highlight some of these issues, we then present a brief analysis of the action research reports of one group of student teachers. Finally, we conclude the chapter with a reconsideration of the approach we have taken.

DISTINGUISHING A SOCIAL RECONSTRUCTIONIST APPROACH TO ACTION RESEARCH

Given the diverse approaches now evident throughout the teacher education community, we do not know very much at all about a practice, such as action research, if it is merely described as something aimed at facilitating the development of reflective teachers. We agree with Calderhead's (1989) assessment that the full range of beliefs within the teacher education community about teaching, schooling, teacher education, and the social order has now been incorporated into the discourse about reflective practice. Indeed, it would be rare to find a teacher educator who would say that he or she wasn't concerned about preparing teachers who are reflective. The criteria that have become attached to reflective practice are so diverse, however, that important differences between specific practices are masked by the use of the common signifier.

On the one hand, the recent work of teacher educators such as Cruickshank (1987), who has drawn upon Dewey (1933) for inspiration, gives us some guidance. The distinction that often is made between reflective and routine practice is not trivial and enables us to make some important qualitative distinctions among different teachers and teaching practices. Similarly, the enormously popular work of Schön (1983, 1987, 1988), which has challenged the dominant technical rationality in professional education and argued for more attention to promoting artistry in teaching by encouraging "reflection in action" and "reflection on action" among teachers, also directs our attention to the preparation of particular kinds of teachers and not others. These generic approaches to reflective teaching lose their heuristic value, however, after a certain point and begin to hide more than they reveal.

After we have agreed with Cruickshank and Schön, for example, that thoughtful teachers who reflect about their practice on and in action are more desirable than thoughtless teachers, who are ruled by tradition, authority, and circumstance, there are still many unanswered questions. Neither Cruickshank nor Schön has much to say, for example, about what it is that teachers ought to be reflecting about, the kinds of criteria that should come into play during the process of reflection (e.g., what distinguishes good from unacceptable educational practice), and the degree to which teachers' deliberations should incorporate a critique of the institutional contexts in which they work. In some extreme cases, the impression is given that as long as teachers reflect about something, in some manner, whatever they decide to do is okay, since they have reflected about it (see Zeichner, 1993a).

One of the reasons that these generic conceptions of reflection have been so popular is that they can be employed by teacher educators of every ideological persuasion. Everyone can identify with them and they offend no one, except those who would seek to tightly control teachers' actions through external prescription. There are important distinctions between reflective and routine practice on the one hand and between technical rationality and an epistemology of practice on the other (Schön, 1983), both of which affirm the value of teachers' practical knowledge. We do not think, however, that it makes much sense to seek to promote or assess reflective practice in general, and action research in particular, without establishing clear priorities for the reflections that emerge from a reasoned educational and social philosophy. We do not accept the implication that exists throughout much of the literature, that teachers' actions are necessarily better just because they are more deliberate and intentional.

Distinguishing Among Versions of Reflective Teaching

There are various ways in which we can distinguish particular proposals for reflective teaching from one another. Liston and Zeichner (1991) have used various traditions of reform in twentieth-century U.S. teacher education to distinguish four varieties of reflective teaching practice: (1) an academic version that stresses the representation and translation of subject matter knowledge to promote student understanding (e.g., Shulman, 1987); (2) a social efficiency version that emphasizes the thoughtful application of particular teaching strategies that have been suggested by research on teaching (Ross & Kyle, 1987); (3) a developmentalist version that prioritizes teaching that is sensitive to students' interests, thinking, and patterns of developmental growth (Duckworth, 1987); and (4) a social reconstructionist version that stresses reflection about the social and political context of schooling and the assessment of classroom actions for their ability to contribute toward greater equity, social justice, and humane conditions in schooling and society (Beyer, 1988). In each of these views of reflective teaching practice, certain priorities are established about schooling and society that emerge from particular historical traditions and educational and social philosophies.

None of these elements is sufficient by itself for providing a moral basis for teaching and teacher education. Good teaching and teacher education need to attend to all of the elements that are brought into focus by the various traditions: the representation of subject matter, student thinking and understanding, teaching strategies suggested by research conducted by academics and classroom teachers, and educational equity and the social contexts of teaching. These elements, however, do not take the same form or receive the same emphasis within each tradition (see Zeichner & Tabachnick, 1991).

This problematizing of the social context of teaching is often missing from many of the attempts within the United States to incorporate action research into the preservice teacher education curriculum. Reflection is often encouraged as an end in itself and as a purely individual activity unconnected to any democratic educational and/or political project. While action research has the potential of disturbing the "deep structures" (Holly, 1987) of schooling, what we have seen most often in the U.S. action research literature is a purely individualist version of action research that largely ignores the social conditions of schooling and society (see Valli, 1990b; Zeichner, 1992a). We also have seen frequently the encouragement by teacher educators of recipe-driven and mechanical application of the steps in the action research spiral and a failure by teacher educators to make distinctions about the quality of the work that is produced through teacher research.

Locating Action Research Within a Social Reconstructionist Tradition

We see our work together, and the ongoing work at the University of Wisconsin–Madison, as located within the social reconstructionist tradition in U.S. teacher education. This tradition brings the social and political context into focus and considers whether our work in teacher education is contributing toward the elimination of inequalities and injustices in schooling and society. While educational projects alone, no matter how well conceived and implemented, can play only contributory roles in transforming unjust and inhumane social, economic, and political conditions, they can play an important part. Contrary to the popular view that teacher educators somehow should maintain political neutrality, it is our belief that every plan for teacher education takes a position, at least implicitly, on the current institutional form and social context of schooling (Crittenden, 1973).

In situating our work within the social reconstructionist tradition, we are not suggesting that it is unimportant for teacher education programs to be concerned with the priorities emphasized in the other reform traditions (teachers' subject matter knowledge and their ability to represent this knowledge to their students in ways that promote understanding; a liberal education that empowers students to be active participants in the democratic deliberations of society; familiarity with knowledge about teaching and learning generated through the research of academics and teachers). We care deeply about academic literacy, technical competence, and developmentally appropriate schooling, but we want to see these benefits of schooling shared equally by all students.

The central axis around which our work in teacher education revolves is a commitment to social justice. Sirotnik (1990) argues that a moral code for teaching and teacher education that includes a commitment to social justice

> demands that schools provide equal access to and equal receipt of a quality education for all students. Any structures or practices that interfere with the simultaneous goals of equity and excellence, that perpetuate preexisting social and economic inequalities are subject to critique and elimination. (p. 310)

This commitment to social justice underlies what we have done in our teacher education program, including our work with action research. We also have maintained a commitment to our students and to the establishment of relationships in our program that are based on fidelity to persons (Noddings, 1986).

This dual commitment to caring and social justice has presented certain difficulties when the goal is to promote reflective teaching through the incorporation of action research into the preservice teacher education curriculum. While it is not within the scope of this chapter to fully articulate an argument about our own commitments to social justice *and* an ethic of care, the following brief comments are offered as a summary of our position.

Our commitment to social justice is broader than an ethic of rights, and our commitment to an ethic of care is broader than our relationship to "the one cared for." Moreover, we believe that both "ethics" are necessary in the practice of teacher education. In short, we reject the dualism. To explain: In our work with individual student teachers, especially in the one-to-one supervisory relationship, we have attempted to adopt the caring attitude that Noddings (1984) defines by "engrossment," "motivational displacement," and "dual perspective." At another level, in our concern for the moral responsibilities of teachers and teacher educators, our commitment is to social justice. Thus, while we care for the student teachers in our care, we also care for *their* students (present and future), *and* we care for ourselves in trying not to compromise our own moralities. Noddings might say we are confusing "natural caring" with "ethical caring," but we also draw on a different notion of ethics, namely, Foucault's (1978, 1984) ethical concern for one's relation with oneself; that is, concern not only with what we say and do to others but with what we say and do to ourselves. Here lies the source of our difficulties when it comes to our commitment to caring and to social justice in the use of action research in preservice teacher education. In attempting to care for the individual student teacher's interests and to fulfill our commitment to "everybody's children," we have sometimes been at odds with ourselves. In condoning the student teacher's chosen "action research" topic of, for example, "comparing discipline techniques" in a classroom where we see enormous problems of racism or sexism, whose agenda is to dominate? To date, especially in less blatantly inequitable situations, we have privileged our caring for individuals and so refrained from manipulating students to adopt our agendas. The consequences of this decision are presented briefly in an analysis of student teacher reports outlined later in the chapter.

ENACTING A SOCIAL RECONSTRUCTIONIST APPROACH TO ACTION RESEARCH

For the past 8 years, experimentation with the use of action research in the student teaching component of the University of Wisconsin–Madison elementary teacher education program has been proceeding.[3] The student teaching experience is usually completed by students during the fifth year of a 5-year preservice teacher education program and consists of 20 weeks of work, usually in one school, with a weekly seminar. Although we probably do not go as far in emphasizing the collaborative aspects of action research as Kemmis and McTaggart (1988) suggest (we and our students work collaboratively in groups but usually on individual projects), our use of action research at Wisconsin probably comes closest to the Deakin University notion of "emancipatory action research" than to any of the existing alternatives.[4]

> Action research is a form of collective self reflective inquiry undertaken by participants in a social situation in order to improve the rationality and justice of their own social practices, as well as their understanding of these practices and the situations in which these practices are carried out. (Kemmis & McTaggart, 1988, p. 5)[5]

We see our work with action research in teacher education as emancipatory in intent because of its focus on both the individual and social dimensions of schooling, and because of the program context in which the action research is embedded (i.e., a teacher education program that deliberately draws students' attention to issues of equity and social justice through readings and other course activities; see Zeichner, 1993b). Although we are interested in facilitating reflection about teaching practices and the elaboration of student teachers' practical theories (Handal & Lauvas, 1987), we also are concerned with encouraging action research that contributes toward the elimination of the social conditions that distort the self-understandings of teachers and undermine the educative potential and moral basis of schooling and teacher education. [6]

Realistically, we cannot expect institutional change to be a primary outcome of action research conducted by preservice student teachers. [7] The experience of the National Teacher Corps in the United States should have taught us that we can't expect to change schools that are failing, by relying primarily on the most vulnerable and least experienced members of the occupation. While recognizing that preservice student teachers have been able to exercise the least formal power of any group in the educational arena, possibly with the exception of their pupils, and that the incorporation of the critical domain of rationality into teacher education programs may end up putting students in more vulnerable positions (if they indeed choose to act on certain of the critical insights gained during the process of conducting research), we still believe that it is important to incorporate a critical dimension into our teacher education programs.

Critical Action Research: Spaces Between Manipulation and Relativism

How one goes about incorporating the critical dimension of a social reconstructionist approach is extremely important. While we reject the view that student teachers need to be "enlightened" about the true meaning of reality and manipulated toward acceptance of the "correct" solutions to our problems (i.e., indoctrination), we also reject the moral relativism that would lead us to be satisfied with *any* knowledge that has been generated by student teacher research, merely because the research was conducted by student teachers (see Zeichner, 1992c). One way in which, with students, we have highlighted the critical dimension in our orientation to reflective teaching is through the lens provided by the tripartite distinction among technical, practical, and critical rationality. Van Manen (1977) has described these three different domains of reflection as follows. [8] First, in technical reflection, the concern is with the efficiency and effectiveness of the means used to attain ends that themselves remain unexamined. Second, in practical reflection, the task is one of explicating and clarifying the assumptions and predispositions underlying teaching activity and of assessing the adequacy of the educational goals toward which the activity leads. Here every action is seen as linked to particular value commitments, and the actor considers the worth of competing educational ends as well as how well the particular learning goals that he or she is working toward are achieved by students. Finally, critical reflection incorporates moral and ethical criteria into the discourse about practical action.

Here the major concern is with whether educational goals, activities, and experiences lead toward forms of life that are characterized by justice, equity, caring, and compassion. In our work with teacher education students, we emphasize the importance of reflecting across all three of these domains.

Indeed, we think that there is an obligation on the part of teacher educators to focus students' attention on the moral and ethical implications of practices and structures in their everyday classroom realities. This would mean, for example, that instead of merely being concerned with whether the classroom is orderly (technical rationality), and with whether particular activities are consistent with such an educational goal as encouraging student understanding (practical rationality), student teachers also would be assessing things like which students are gaining increased understanding and whose perspectives are represented in what is being understood (critical rationality).

At the same time as we reject moral relativism, however, we also reject universalized notions of emancipation and oppression, which function to legislate particular notions of the appropriate content for emancipatory action research. We want to avoid the dogmatism that class, gender, and race formations (and often only one of these) are *the* appropriate issues for all contexts. Although action research is said to proceed from the particular concerns of those who conduct it, there has been a general tendency to prescribe a moral basis that is generalized rather than specific to particular contexts. Encouraging student teachers to recognize the particular relationships that characterize their situations at the same time as we promote a contemporary critical approach to understanding schooling remains a tension we seek to balance in our work with action research.

Seeing the Critical as Embedded in the Technical and Practical

We reject the view that the "critical" is somehow separate from the "technical" and "practical" classroom-based reality of student teachers, and that when broaching the critical, teacher educators are necessarily violating alleged "laws" of student teacher development. In our experience the "critical" is embedded in the very essence of the student teacher's classroom reality. The problem is one of helping student teachers develop dispositions and capabilities to see and act upon the connections between the classroom and the social and political contexts in which it is embedded.

For example, an issue that is confronted regularly by our student teachers is the disproportionate assignment of pupils of color to the lower tracks of school programs and to such remedial categories as "learning disabled." In the Madison area, pupils of color also have higher than average school suspension rates and lower than average high school graduation rates. All of this is very common across the United States. These so called "facts" of our student teachers' realities often are taken by students at first to be either natural elements of their situation (i.e., as background) or a result of some deficit in the children or their parents. An examination of the ways in which the school and classroom actively contribute to these inequities in access to and the receipt of a quality education for certain children, requires deliberate intervention on our part in the ways in which we structure our teacher education courses.[9] These relationships between inequality and schooling are also present, however, in the classrooms and schools in which our students complete their practicums and student teaching, in the everyday reality of student teachers.[10]

We believe that it is important for teacher educators to maintain a critical focus while using action research within the preservice teacher education curriculum, despite the difficulties that are involved. While we must be very careful not to romanticize about what can be accomplished by using action research, we also should not succumb to the widely accepted myth that a focus on the critical domain of rationality during preservice teacher education is "premature" or inevitably part of a process of political indoctrination (see Zeichner & Teitelbaum, 1982, and Feiman-Nemser & Floden, 1980). Although it has been clearly documented that the vast majority of prospective teachers in the United States (including most of our own students) do not come into teacher education programs disposed toward the reconstruction of schooling and society (Lanier & Little, 1986), it does not automatically follow that teacher educators should exclude the consideration of critical perspectives (e.g., a focus on gender and racial inequalities in schooling) from the preservice teacher education curriculum. Nor should critical perspectives be excluded simply because of the norms that are dominant in the schools and colleges in which learning to teach takes place.

When action research is the vehicle for structuring the reflections of student teachers, a major problem is that of encouraging "relational" thinking while maintaining students' ownership of their research projects. Our commitment to an ethic of care and a fidelity to persons has caused us to refrain from trying to manipulate students to work on our agendas through their action research. In the end, we have taken the stance that our students own their action research projects and we have resisted the deliberate "politicization" of student teachers' research that has been described in other programs (Robottom, 1988). At the same time we recognize that the authority of persons who initiate the action research cannot be underestimated in the context of teacher education. Pedagogy within educational institutions has always functioned, in part, to regulate groups of people. Emancipatory action research, as a course requirement, struggles to maintain any emancipatory effect within such a context (Gore, 1991b). Our strategy has been to create, in the overall teacher education program, a learning environment that reflects our commitment to social reconstructionist values.

At the preservice level, we aim for the creation of a learning environment in our programs that, through the issues that it draws students' attention to and the way in which it is conducted, reflects a commitment to certain fundamental values (e.g., social justice and fidelity to persons). We are aiming for an impact on individual students that involves the loss of innocence about inequalities and injustices in society and that helps individual students see themselves as part of a community of people working for greater educational equity. In the following section we outline specific contextual and strategic considerations we made in the enactment of action research with one group of student teachers. While referring specifically to this one group, we should point out that many of these considerations continue to shape the use of action research in the student teaching curriculum at the University of Wisconsin–Madison.

ACTION RESEARCH IN THE STUDENT TEACHING CURRICULUM

The question of strategies for the introduction of action research to preservice student teachers is not one we have considered outside of the context in which that introduction is to take place. While student teachers are now introduced to action research during their introductory course in teacher education, the students whose projects we refer to here were not introduced to action research until their final "student teaching" semester. Nevertheless, the introduction of action research took place in the context of a teacher education program oriented toward "reflective teaching practice." Throughout the program, there was an emphasis on the student teacher as learner, and attention to issues of inequity and injustice in schooling and society. The final practicum experience continued the reflective teaching theme, which was presented as an investigation of teaching and its social conditions. As such, action research was linked with the other tasks and goals of the student teaching semester. Students were asked to keep journals; conduct some formal observations of other classes; prepare, teach, and evaluate a unit of work; and conduct action research. The short-term goal of all these tasks was to assist students to understand and improve their situation and their practice: a goal consistent with our affiliation with "emancipatory" action research.

We also took context into account at other levels. The majority of the students were white, middle class women. Most held an unpoliticized view of teaching and schools. The issues of concern to this group were expected to differ from the concerns of students who are already committed to social change. The student teaching semester, placed at the end of their university career, meant that some students experienced competing demands on their time, such as the need to take courses to finish their other requirements in addition to the continuing need of many to work to sustain themselves (McCarthy, 1986). Thus, we needed to have realistic expectations of the students' commitment to action research. In this regard, we tried to construct the action research project as a "natural" extension of their student teaching experience rather than as an additional task. The action research provided a focus and a systematic element to their reflection in order to help them work through or work within the "problems" they experienced.

Because this introduction to action research was located in a university-based teacher education program, we also tried to remain cognizant of the relations of power, which are difficult to escape given the historical development of teacher education programs. That is, we needed to acknowledge the power relations of university supervisor, cooperating teacher, and student teacher, and the way these are played out in various contexts. For instance, while several cooperating teachers are engaged in action research of their own (e.g., Madison Metropolitan School District, 1992; Wood, 1988), for many cooperating teachers action research was new. Some felt uncomfortable or excluded by the university supervisor and student teacher in their supposedly shared understanding of the process. Clearly, more needed to be done within the program to better inform teachers about action research and to include them in the process.[11] Moreover, the relation of university to schools in the process of teacher education could not be ignored. It was our experience that some teachers see all "assignments" as peripheral to the central task of learning to teach through practical classroom experience. We needed to be careful to explain that the purpose of action research is the improvement of the student teacher's own practice or situation.

Clearly, some choices had to be made about what to emphasize in a semester-long preservice experience of action research. We can think of action research as having several components—(1) researching one's own practice and situation; (2) collaboratively; and (3) with emancipatory/democratic intent. We tended to emphasize the first: researching one's own practice and situation. We could have emphasized collaboration by, for example, making the seminar itself the focus of the action research and working collaboratively to improve that practice/situation (e.g., Altrichter, 1988). We could have emphasized the democratic intent by rather stringently controlling the topics students could research, either by prescribing topics in advance or by redirecting students' focus through some kind of "approval" mechanism. Making the seminar the focus would have taken away from our central concern with facilitating reflective teaching practice during the student teaching semester and would have ignored the concerns addressed above about the triadic power relations of student teaching. Overdirecting students' choice of topic would have risked losing the responsiveness of the research approach to classroom events and conditions. Robottom (1988) reports that the setting of specific and detailed tasks in a research-based course in science education, "while justified by an interest in directing attention to the relationship of understanding, situation and practice, in the event [was] seen as suggestive of an impositional directive that is contrary to the alleged responsiveness of participatory research" (p. 112).

Our emphasis made central the student's own practice/situation. At the same time, we tried to keep the other elements alive by situating the action research within a whole semester of related experiences—seminar, readings, journals—many of which made explicit the democratic commitment of the program, and by asking students to share their projects with others by at least seeking their responses and occasionally their help. In this way, it was our intention that even if the project itself became rather individualistic and technical, the readings and interactions with other students prevented too narrow a focus during the student teaching semester. Thus, in the Wisconsin program, action research did not, and still does not, exist in isolation. In the remainder of this section we refer to our analysis of the written reports of the action research projects conducted by 18 student teachers during the 1988–89 academic year (see Gore & Zeichner, 1991).

The Student Teachers' Research Projects

These student teachers' reports were analyzed to explore the extent to which action research seemed to be contributing to reflective teaching practice as we have defined it; that is, reflection within all three domains of rationality.

Our analysis of the written reports revealed three broad categories of projects. One small group of projects revealed a clear concern for moral and political issues as integral to the project. A larger second group of projects showed some concern for these issues but did not develop the ideas. The third group of projects, more than half of them, revealed no explicit concern for moral and political issues at all.

While the written reports of action research may be limited in their ability to convey the breadth of students' thoughts about their action research experiences, the findings of this study regarding the types of thinking evident in the projects and factors influencing the action research experience are consistent with other analyses of action research projects produced in the elementary teacher education program at the University of Wisconsin–Madison. These earlier analyses of action research projects also revealed some evidence that during the process of conducting action research, students made the social conditions of schooling problematic and considered the moral and ethical implications of their work.

Even where we have found evidence of "reflective teaching" in the reports of student teachers' research, however, we do not claim that the action research itself generated the reflective teaching. In some cases where reflective teaching was evident, students came into the student teaching experience with dispositions to examine their teaching *and* the social context, and were willing and able to reflect in all three domains of rationality. The action research enabled these student teachers, who were already reflective, to pursue issues and gain capabilities in their preferred directions. In some other cases where there was some evidence of the incorporation of the critical domain during student teaching, we would attribute this "success" to the overall teacher education program rather than merely to the action research.

However, examples of reflective teaching have not been dominant in the students' projects. Several different responses have been given by students when asked to assess the impact of their action research: (1) that it helped them be more thoughtful in general about their teaching; (2) it helped them become more aware of their own practices and of the gaps between their beliefs and their practices; and (3) it helped them become more aware of their pupils' thinking and learning. While we value these gains, we remain concerned about the relative lack of reflective teaching in the way we have defined it.

In short, reasons for the lack of reflective teaching include: biographical factors such as the generally unpoliticized view of schooling held by most students, and the relative (un)importance of academic work in their lives; situational factors such as their placement in schools and classrooms in which few students were confronted with explicit discussions of the moral aspects of teaching, and their temporary status in these locations; and cultural factors such as the technical rationality, individualism, and instrumentalism that dominate educational thinking. Although our focus in this chapter has been on issues of curriculum and program change, this outline of factors impeding reflective teaching points also to issues of selection in the facilitation of reflective teaching. That is, program selection criteria also may have to be adjusted if the composition of the learning community in teacher education programs is to be more conducive to reflective teaching. Specifically, social consciousness and racial and ethnic diversity need to be considered in both faculty and student selection.

While some critics of action research have argued that preservice teachers cannot take on "critical" issues because they are not ready or because their focus is narrowly and understandably on the classrooms in which they are placed, we disagree. There *are* features of university education, of students' placements and biographies, of contemporary U.S. culture that militate against the development of reflective teaching practice, but these are not entirely insurmountable. Political and moral issues are not separate from classrooms. Consider our earlier example of the disproportionate placement of pupils of color in such remedial categories as "learning disabled." Many of the students whose projects we have been analyzing were in classrooms where this was true and yet most "received" it as background. Bringing such conditions of classrooms to the foreground certainly could help our students to learn from, or in some cases get through, their student teaching experience (see Zeichner, 1992c).

Despite the constraints, we believe that all action research projects have the potential to raise and address moral and political questions. Hence, the lack of "critical" reflection in many of the reports is not so much a question of the topic as it is a question of the way the topic is framed. As an example, let us consider

Melinda's project in which she documented her struggle for authority in her cooperating teacher's domain. After observations about a mother–child relationship intersecting with the teacher–student relationship of her cooperating teacher and students, and her own reluctance to intervene in that relationship, Melinda proceeded to a focus on her classroom management as the means to asserting her authority in the classroom. She might have explored issues of gender and teaching and the construction of nurturing as the role of the elementary teacher. She might have proceeded by interviewing her own cooperating teacher and others in the school about their perceptions of these relationships. She might have focused on exploring with her teacher their interventions in each other's authority. They might have worked together to improve the ways in which they shared the classroom. Instead, Melinda framed the problem around what she interpreted as her own inadequacies with confidence and classroom management. This tendency to personalize the "problem," in an individualistic manner, seems a common response among our student teachers, when instead they might extend their own experience to its connection to broader relations of power in schools and society more generally.

In the concluding section of the chapter we discuss ways to help students to move to these kinds of considerations in their action research projects—ways that are consistent with our position on the use of action research at the preservice level.

CONCLUSION

Given present conditions, it is clear that we need to do more in terms of helping students to frame their action research topics more broadly. We have tried carefully to avoid imposing or manipulating students toward our own agendas and have avoided some of the more directive practices of action research facilitation evident in some of the Deakin University work (Di Chiro, Robottom, & Tinning, 1988). We believe that the projects should be the students' and that manipulating students to adopt our agendas would be inconsistent with our commitment to fidelity to persons and to a fundamental premise of action research—that it should be the researchers' own interests and concerns that drive the project.

But what of emancipatory intent? We could do more in terms of helping students to bring to the foreground what is often assumed as background, challenging students to observe more carefully and to ask more questions about what they see. As indicated earlier, journals, readings, seminars, and supervisory conferences appear to be critical in broadening the scope of the inquiry. It is important that the supervisor talk frequently with each student about her or his project, so that appropriate resources can be provided throughout the process. These changes require little revision to our present construction and use of action research in student teaching.

In rethinking our construction of action research, we have identified two changes that might help us more fully realize the potential of action research in our social reconstructionist-oriented teacher education program. First, although we have regularly shared with students the action research projects completed by students during previous semesters as examples of action research in student teaching, we have not placed enough value on the knowledge that has been produced (and the specific insights gained) in these projects. As we have explored various issues in student teaching seminars, such as ability grouping and racism and sexism in the classroom, we have relied too much in our selection of readings on papers written by university academics and have largely ignored the writings of classroom teachers and student teachers, including some of our own former students who explored aspects of these same issues in their action research reports. This failure to make use of the action research reports and writings of our own graduates and classroom teachers in general, in the curriculum of the student teaching seminar, undermines our efforts to convince students of the value of action research and reinforces the separation of action research from teaching that we have tried to counteract in our program.

Although the majority of students' action research reports do not reflect attention to the moral and political implications of teaching as we would have hoped for, we do (as was pointed out above) have examples in graduates' action research reports of "critical analysis" of some of the very issues that are dealt with in the seminar. Additionally, other publication sources, such as *Rethinking Schools* and *Democracy & Education*, contain examples of the writings of public school teachers who have engaged in this kind of "relational" analysis of classroom issues. We need to focus much more attention in the future on helping our students gain access to these examples of reflective teaching by classroom teachers.

Another area that we need to address is related to the problem of the lack of time for group discussion of the students' research in the seminar. Our student teaching program, like many others in the United States, has invested a considerable amount of resources in supporting a clinical supervision program that involves university supervisors observing and conferring with student teachers in dyads or in triads that also include the student's cooperating teacher. While our approach to clinical supervision has emphasized attention to the kinds of issues and a quality of analysis that is consistent with our social reconstructionist orientation, and while we have made deliberate efforts to connect with students' ongoing research in this supervision, the clinical supervision process within our program is still structurally distinct from both the seminar and the action research projects.

One possible way to deal with the problem of time to discuss, in a group, the students' research projects is to give less emphasis to clinical supervision and more attention to the building of research communities within the schools involving the student teachers and their cooperating teachers. We have been very intrigued by the descriptions of Project START at the University of Pennsylvania where preservice students become part of communities of researchers in their schools that also include teacher educators and experienced teachers (Cochran-Smith, 1991). School districts in the Madison area, like many others throughout the United States (Cochran-Smith & Lytle, 1993), recently have given support to teacher research. In fact, some staff development personnel in the district recently have expressed interest in focusing some of the teacher research that the district supports on issues related to educational equity. We need to do a better job of linking the action research in our program to these efforts and of involving cooperating teachers in the student teachers' inquiries. We are beginning to question the degree to which our continuing commitment to a clinical supervision model has made it more difficult for us to do so.[12] As we have begun to look at whole schools rather than individual classrooms as sites for student teaching (Zeichner, 1992b), we have started to think about the need to broaden the learning community for student teachers beyond what exists in the clinical supervision conference. It may be that there is not room for both clinical supervision and the collaborative research group during student teaching. We want to begin to explore, more than we have done in the past, how we can transcend the limits that may be inherent in the structure of clinical supervision.

Finally, while we have strong personal commitments to the transformation of schools and society, our focus in our student teaching program has been on assisting individual students to acquire a broader perspective. At the preservice level, our major concern is realistically with the dispositions, skills, and knowledge of individuals as opposed to institutional change initiated by student teachers. As one of the student teachers, Jo, realized:

> No matter what, I was always aware that this still was not *my* classroom, nor were these *my* students. Worse still, was always knowing that the changes I made were only temporary influences in the lives of these students, as was I. That awareness had a discouraging effect on me, at times.

On the other hand, though, many students commented on the support they gained from action research. For example, Jo again:

> Whereas this semester could have potentially "damaged" me as a student teacher, due to the many conflicts which never seemed to reach resolution, the action research process itself became a mechanism of support. I was able to channel personal feelings of frustration, doubt, and disgust as well as "professional" feelings of disagreement—with practices and issues in education—into my action research, rather than just suffering with them/suffer-

ing through them. The action research proved to be a much relied upon and much valued learning medium for me.

Our long-term goal is that these students will use the dispositions, skills, and knowledge gained from their teacher education program to work, in consort with others, toward the making of a more just and humane society.

NOTES

1. For examples outside of the United States, see Lucas (1988) and Robottom (1988).

2. Jennifer Gore was a university supervisor in this program during 1988 and 1989, and Ken Zeichner has co-directed the program since 1976.

3. We use the term *experimentation* because of the second-order action research work that we have conducted on our use of action research in our program (see Noffke & Zeichner, 1987; Brennan & Noffke, 1988; Liston & Zeichner, 1990; Noffke & Brennan, 1991; Gore, 1991a; Gore & Zeichner, 1991, and Tabachnick & Zeichner, in press).

4. See Grundy (1982) and Carr and Kemmis (1986) for a discussion of three different modes of action research that correspond to the three domains of rationality discussed later in the chapter: technical, practical, and emancipatory.

5. It is important to recognize that action research occurs naturally in the work of teachers. The difference is that in action research, teachers conduct these activities more carefully and more systematically than they normally would (Boomer, 1987). As one of our students, Kate, put it, "the difference between having a specific action research project and simply being a reflective teacher was that I was forced to draw all of my individual thoughts and ideas together. In pulling these ideas together, I was able to see things I wouldn't have seen through individual and isolated ideas or observations." Also, in action research, no conceptual distinction is drawn between the practice being researched and the process of researching. It is not so much a matter of doing action research *on* teaching as it is of viewing teaching itself as a form of inquiry or experimentation (Elliott, 1985).

6. By educative potential, we are referring to whether "teaching for understanding" is present (see Holmes Group, 1990). By moral basis, we are referring to whether what exists reflects a commitment to certain values such as social justice and caring (see Sirotnik, 1990).

7. This is not to say, however, that student teachers are incapable of instituting changes in their classrooms and schools. Many do. However, even when students are successful in "strategic redefinition" of their situations (Lacey, 1977), the changes are often temporary and disappear when the student leaves.

8. Van Manen (1977) presents these as "levels of reflection." The hierarchical notion of levels conveys the mistaken impression, however, of a developmental framework where technical and practical reflection are eventually transcended and critical reflection prevails. This devalues technical skill and the position of the teacher and increases the odds that teacher educators will neglect the vulnerable condition of their students (Lucas, 1988) and aim straight at their goals over the heads of those whom they

teach (Noddings, 1986). Our view is that reflection by teachers should involve all three of these domains of rationality. From this perspective, technical issues are not transcended, but become linked to considerations of the nature of and justification for educational ends and goals.

9. See Tabachnick and Zeichner (1991) for examples of this in relation to foundations courses, methods courses, and practicums.

10. The relationships between educational inequality and other forms of inequality and oppression beyond the school also require deliberate attention in our teacher education program. It is just plain foolish or dishonest to speak about the restructuring of schools and teacher education programs without explicitly dealing with the need for broader social, economic, and political transformations. Remaining silent on issues related to the social preconditions for educational reform, is to lend support to the view so successfully ingrained in the public consciousness in these times of conservative restoration, that what is wrong with society is the fault of the schools and is amenable to correction by the schools.

11. The program faculty and Madison school district staff collaborated in offering a Teacher Research conference that was held in Madison in April 1993. One of the purposes of this conference (which provided a forum for student teacher and teacher action researchers to present their work) was to encourage more teachers to become involved in action research.

12. In an experimental action research seminar, we have devoted more time to discussion of students' research and have dropped discussion of readings and issues that do not emerge directly from student teachers' inquiries (Tabachnick & Zeichner, in press).

3

The Death of Idealism? Or, Issues of Empowerment in the Preservice Setting

Lynn Brunner

We think by feeling. What is there to know?
                                            —T. Roethke, "The Waking"

In the spring of 1992, I began the student teaching phase of my teacher education program at a northeastern state university. Through this program I had been working concurrently toward certification in secondary social studies and a master's degree in social studies education. I had had a variety of teaching experiences before and during the program, including substitute teaching in a local city school and tutoring in the city campus of the local community college. The problems that I witnessed and encountered in these experiences made me eager to apply to my own practice as a teacher some of the theories about empowering practices that I had learned in my graduate studies. I expressed this desire to my graduate advisor and with her support I decided to attempt an action research project during my student teaching.

I had already done some research on empowering practices and I set out to "empower" my students by employing such practices. My efforts, however, were not nearly as successful as I had hoped. My cooperating teacher, seeing my visible disappointment, at one point commented that I was experiencing "the death of idealism," and I somewhat reluctantly accepted that she might be right. However, through the reflective analysis of my difficulties that the action re-search project demanded, and with the patient encouragement of my advisor, I discovered that my experience was not that different from that of other student teachers and that the "empowering" change I had worked for in my students still might be achieved—although slowly and with considerable negotiation.

DEFINING EMPOWERMENT

Empowerment, as Sleeter (1991) points out, can be conceptualized in a variety of ways ranging from an emphasis on the individual's recognition that he or she may have power—that is, the ability to act with effect—to a more collective recognition on the part of oppressed groups that they may act to transform society. I conceptualize empowerment in the narrower sense, as an individual's belief that he or she may act with effect. This is not because I wish to ignore the collective aspect of empowerment, but because I believe the individual aspect is crucial to achieving the collective aspect.

I care about empowerment in education for two reasons. First, I feel that my own public school education left me ill equipped for higher education and the work world. We students sat passively in neat rows without, for the most part, interacting. Knowledge was primarily dispensed in the traditional manner, in fragmented and decontextualized pieces that were to be memorized and reproduced on tests. This kind of education, in my opinion, encouraged obedience and passivity, rather than an ability to think critically, to integrate knowledge with lived experience, and to act on learning. It left me feeling disempowered. As a teacher, I do not want to perpetuate those practices that I found hurtful.

Second, I became aware, through my work as a tutor at a local community college, of a particular kind of disempowerment suffered by some students. It seemed that many of the students who sought help with assignments did not complete them successfully or learn from them. Their failure, as I saw it, had less to do with intelligence or ability and more to do with attitudes and feelings about school. These students tended to view an assignment not as a learning opportunity but as an obstacle to overcome. Success for them meant simply completing an assignment, rather than completing it well. Also, they tended to look at instructors with fear and suspicion, regarding them as all knowing and all powerful, mysterious adversaries whose wishes were to be guessed at rather than questioned. Not surprisingly, I observed, as has Takata (1991), that students seemed often "bored, scared or confused by their schooling" (p. 269).

Coulter (1989) says that "the purpose of education is to empower learners to make considered choices about their personal lives and to encourage students to engage in socially conscious activities with others" (p. 26). If one agrees with this statement, as I do, then as a teacher one should learn to avoid practices that produce fear, confusion, and boredom in students and learn to develop practices that empower, that is, encourage the belief in students that they may act with effect.

Because I was preparing to student teach, I was in a potential position to work on becoming an empowering teacher. Initially I was not so hopeful that my student teaching experience would help me to become the kind of teacher I wished to be. I had observed classes at a local city high school; it was a magnet school accepting students from all over the city and had been named a national school of excellence. What I saw there was very similar to what I had experienced in public school. However, I was encouraged by an article entitled "The Power to Empower" (Martin, 1991) to seek out a placement with a teacher who might have developed empowering practices and could help me to do so. Believing that multicultural education is the key to empowering education, Martin asserted that "the classroom setting, climate, and tone as determined by the administration and the classroom teacher, are of paramount importance" (p. 293) in enabling and influencing the student teacher to become an empowering educator.

Interested in becoming an empowering educator, I discussed my concerns with my advisor. She suggested that I might do an action research project in my student teaching experience in which I could work at trying out my ideas about empowerment in practice, possibly with the help of the cooperating teacher. I was eager to do this.

Because I was interested in the subject, I had already surveyed some of the relevant literature on practices that are conducive to empowering students (e.g., Coulter, 1989; Fagan, 1989; Freire, 1972; Shor & Freire, 1987; Sleeter, 1991; Takata, 1991; Wood, 1989). I identified six major practices that are considered empowering. Four of those practices deal with how the teacher treats the curriculum knowledge that he or she provides for students, and two others deal with the attitude with which the teacher approaches his or her role as teacher. A teacher may help to empower students if he or she:

1. Contextualizes knowledge (Fagan, 1989; Sleeter, 1991; Wood, 1989);
2. Includes knowledge that reflects multiple perspectives (Coulter, 1989; Sleeter, 1991);
3. Treats knowledge as open-ended and constructed, and teaches the students how to think, not what to think (Freire, 1972; Shor & Freire, 1987);
4. Focuses not on job training but on active involvement in society (Cornbleth, 1990; Wood, 1989);
5. Is the "empowering helper" (Sleeter, 1991); or
6. Engages the students in active learning (Shor & Freire, 1987; Takata, 1991; Wood, 1989).

It is interesting to note that not a few of these practices were identified in the negative; that is, they were not directly stated but were implied through discussion of disempowering practices.

So, I approached the teacher education program's coordinator to express my wish to be placed with a teacher who employed empowering practices, preferably cooperative learning, in a setting that was culturally diverse.

THE STUDENT TEACHING PLACEMENT

I was placed at an urban magnet school that serves grades 5–12 and is located in what is considered the poorest, most violent, and most crime ridden area in the city. This section of the city is predominantly African American, and many of the students in the school are drawn from the surrounding neighborhood. Also attending the school are students of various European ethnic backgrounds, including Italian, Polish, Irish, and German, predominantly poor or working class. The culture within the school is marked by its emphasis on structure and discipline. The school employs a dress code. No students are allowed in the halls between classes for any reason. If students violate school rules, they are punished with a type of in-school suspension referred to as ILC or "ice," where they spend the day writing school pledges on puzzle-like grids.

I was assigned to teach twelfth grade social studies. My cooperating teacher, it turned out, was not entirely proficient in the practices I had identified as empowering, but rather often employed those practices I had identified as contributing to student disempowerment. Also, because of personal difficulties she experienced during the year, I found it difficult to find time to adequately explain my ideas to her or have her observe me. However, she seemed to be open to my experimental ideas, and, despite the disempowering activities I observed, she occasionally had lively discussions with the students, indicating that they had the ability and disposition to become engaged in schoolwork. In addition, I felt that in my university supervisor I had found a trusted observer with whom to discuss my efforts; so, I decided to proceed.

I followed the action research model presented by Kemmis and McTaggart (1988), which consists of a cycle of four basic steps of planning, enacting, observing the plan, and reflection. Prior to beginning the cycle there is an initial phase that can be thought of as having three different but related parts: an open-ended and speculative preliminary review of one's situation, the identification of an area of concern that one wishes to improve, and a reconnaissance of the circumstances related to the thematic concern.

TRYING OUT EMPOWERING PRACTICES

The events that followed were filled with confusion, contradiction, and frustration, as well as a small measure of success. My preliminary review consisted of an examination of the larger context of the school, the classroom, and the teaching practices of my cooperating teacher rather than my own, since I was a preservice teacher. In this review I identified not only disempowering practices, but also the possibility for lively discussion in the classroom. Based on what I observed in my review, I identified as my thematic concern the notion of "banking education" described by Freire (1972) in which students passively receive education that is "deposited" in them by the teacher. I decided that I wanted students to interact actively. So, when I began to teach I organized the class around group activities in which students would work together to examine aspects of public policy. I provided articles that discussed societal problems and attempts to address them through some sort of governmental involvement. I selected articles from newspapers and magazines, including a school newsletter, in which students could identify the problem, the members of society affected, and the level of government involved with its solution. I thought that this would be a good way to contextualize knowledge, to relate curriculum knowledge to events happening in the "real world." I also organized the analysis of articles around topics that would need to be discussed in public policy papers students had to write in order to graduate. Several students had approached me for help with their papers and seemed concerned about completing the papers successfully. I felt that organizing the curriculum around the paper might make the tasks relevant to the students.

My initial attempts at creating empowering practice floundered when students did not readily accept my efforts. I felt threatened and out of control. I wrote in my journal, "I got the impression that they were not taking me seriously, giggling and rolling their eyes." I felt that the class was chaotic; a few students listened while many chattered or listened halfheartedly, misunderstanding what they did hear. Finally, a student angrily challenged me on classroom rules, claiming that the way I did things was not the way the cooperating teacher did things, and others expressed similar resentment at my having changed things. I took my cooperating teacher's advice and gave the students what they seemed to want, lots of rote work. I converted all of my group lesson material to overhead notes from which I lectured, and which the students copied in their notebooks. The students behaved much better and seemed overall to be happier. I had reproduced, against my will, those disempowering practices that had been employed in the context of the classroom before my arrival.

Realizing what had happened, I was at first very disappointed. However, I thought I would give my project one more try. I realized that I could not attempt to incorporate all of the practices deemed empowering, but I needed to focus on one or two. I observed the students become engrossed sporadically in conversation with me, a neighbor, or the cooperating teacher about a topic of class discussion, indicating that they were capable of active engagement with the subject matter. However, they tended not to remain engaged and were easily distracted. So, I created a lesson patterned after a cooperative jigsaw activity in which each student was responsible for a unique piece of information. It was my hope that making each student responsible to the group would require them to actively engage with each other over the subject matter. When I enacted the plan, my university supervisor and I observed quite a bit of interaction among students over the subject matter. This worked well while the groups were highly structured. However, when students finished earlier than I had expected and I stood in front of the room and attempted to lead a whole class discussion, things fell apart. Students fell into old habits of disengaging and chattering off the subject, although discussion became lively on the issue of school choice, which was directly related to the students' experience in a magnet school.

REFLECTIONS ON THE PROJECT

So, I did achieve a small amount of what I'd hoped for, active engaged learning. However, I was baffled and disappointed by my setbacks and struggles. I was aware of things in the context of the classroom that I did not wish to reproduce, and I strove to create different practices. How had I ended up becoming what I had worked so hard to avoid?

In her book, *Practice Makes Practice*, Deborah Britzman (1991) suggests that my experience may not be uncommon to student teachers and attributes this phenomenon to institutional pressures to conform. She says:

> Student teachers do not set out to collude with authoritarian pedagogy. Nor do they desire to suppress their own subjectivity or those of their students. Just the opposite: they usually begin with intentions of enhancing student potential and find this intention thwarted by socially patterned school routines. (p. 237)

She goes on to make the case that teachers are not self-made, but that learning to teach is, rather, a process of social negotiation. She, therefore, conceptualizes learning to teach "as a struggle for voice and discursive practices amid a cacophony of past and present voices, lived experience and available practices" and states that "tensions among what has preceded, what is confronted, and what one desires shape the contradictory realities of learning to teach" (p. 8).

Understanding Experiences Contextually

My own experience of learning to teach, I feel, was a struggle to be true to my desire to develop practices conducive to student empowerment. This struggle was shaped by the tensions among what preceded my experience, what I confronted, and what I desired to accomplish as I acted within the context of socially patterned school routines.

Catherine Cornbleth (1990) provides a theoretical framework for discussing how the tensions between what preceded, what was confronted, and what was desired may have interacted to shape the contradictions that characterized my student teaching experience. She describes the development and change of curriculum as an ongoing social process that occurs in a set of nested, interacting contexts. These contexts consist of the biographical context, which includes personal and professional histories and beliefs; the structural context of the school, defined as "established roles and relationships, including operating procedures, shared beliefs and norms" (p. 6); and the sociocultural context, which includes the social, political, and economic environment beyond the education system. Each of these contexts, in complex ways, may interact, cooperating or conflicting, to work for or against attempts at change.

I believe the contradictory realities of my student teaching experience may be described as tensions among the biographical context, the structural context, and the sociocultural context that were present in my preservice setting. These contexts interacted at times to impede and at times to facilitate my attempts to develop an empowering practice.

The biographical context of my cooperating teacher and the structural context of the school, I believe, cooperated to make my attempts at change more difficult. The coop's beliefs about education as depositing knowledge, her role as a benevolent helper, as well as her level of expectations for behavior and work, created a classroom climate, part of the structural context, in which students were resistant to the interaction, participation, and engagement I desired. For example, when I held a student responsible for participating in class, he told me that I could not do this because the cooperating teacher never held such rules. The class, palpably hostile, was quiet and someone muttered, "Who do they think they are coming in here and telling us what to do." Some of them, anyway, resented my changing things. And, even though I felt that I was not asking much of them, they felt that I was expecting too much. At other times I gave them assignments to bring in articles regarding their own papers, but they showed no interest; a great majority did not do the assignment at all despite my extension of deadlines.

The structural context of the school reinforced this classroom climate. With its emphasis on conformity, obedience, and control, efforts to create a climate of questioning and active learning where students might appear to be out of control and become noisy were discouraged. For example, the principal, who is noted for his controlling style of management, requires teachers to keep their doors open at all times and may come to the door to reprimand students and teacher if the class becomes too loud. I had heard from a few teachers that the principal dislikes cooperative learning because he perceives it as disorderly and noisy.

However, I saw teachers occasionally close the classroom door when students became noisy or when they wished to put students in groups. Also, despite the seeming strictness of these rules, there were occasions when I saw students in the halls or wearing clothes that appeared to violate the dress code. It seemed to me that the principal enforced rules inconsistently, at times harshly and at other times not at all. As a result, the atmosphere in the school seemed restrained and cautious, but not overly fearful.

Personal Biography in Context

A surprising aspect of my own biographical context had acted to impede my desire for change when I encountered the sociocultural context from which the students came. Despite my critical perspectives on education and my desire to act on that theory to become an empowering teacher, I was amazed at my own desire to maintain authority and control. After reflecting on my written accounts of events in the classroom, I realized that I felt threatened, frustrated, and angry over students' noncompliance with my demands and their challenges to authority. I also noticed that at times having students quiet was my goal. I often interpreted quiet from students as cooperating with my demands, and quiet, on several occasions, constituted a good day.

I grew up in a family, with its roots in the working class, that had certain assumptions about children, obedience, and authority. Adults had authority and "children were meant to be seen but not heard." My father, a teacher, expected quiet and obedience from his students as well as his children. Quiet and obedience he did not always receive, however, from his troubled inner-city students or his children, and to this he reacted with anger.

Also, in the suburban, White, primarily middle class school system, the one in which I had received a "banking" style education, students, for the most part, were quiet and obedient, not questioning the authority of the teacher. This behavior was very unlike that of my students, who came primarily from the violent and crime ridden neighborhood surrounding the school. They were more inclined to say what they thought and seemed to have less fear of authority. Perhaps I, despite myself, expected the same quiet, obedience, and passivity that had been expected of me at home and at school.

I discovered what Britzman (1991) asserts, that "learning to teach constitutes a time of biographical crisis as it simultaneously invokes one's autobiography" (p. 8). These attitudes about authority and obedience I had never considered to be my own, yet here they appeared despite my wish to empower rather than to expect obedience from students.

My cooperating teacher had developed a "defensive teaching" style (McNeil, 1988). Teachers who teach defensively, says McNeil, choose "methods of presentation and evaluation that they hope will make their workload more efficient and create as little student resistance as possible" (p. 174). She offered success to students in exchange for minimal effort, compliance, and "doing the work." For example, homework, often done by the students during the class period when there were no worksheets to do, consisted of writing the definitions of chapter vocabulary words and summarizing the accounts of lives of famous economists presented in the text. These written tasks were to be kept in a notebook, which, at the end of a unit of study, would be checked and awarded points for each task completed. The quality of the work was not examined; the work was merely looked at to see if it had been done. If it had been completed, the student would receive the full number of points, which would be added for a grade.

My coop had developed this style partly out of benevolence, creating a system whereby all students could succeed regardless of ability as long as they did the work. She explained to me that not every student could be smart, but each student could keep a notebook and memorize vocabulary, and in this way, by working and trying, each could succeed. However, she also used this style to foster control. She feared that unsuccessful students would become discipline problems. She asserted that if the students felt that they could not succeed, many would give up and then they could become disruptive.

When I felt my authority threatened, I too created a kind of defensive teaching style to maintain control. I chose methods of presentation, that is, overhead notes rather than cooperative learning groups, to create as little resistance from students as possible and thereby control their behavior. I wrote in my journal:

> I asked the sixth-period class to copy the notes I was writing on the overhead as we discussed the branches of government on each level of government. To tell the truth, I think I had them write it down, not necessarily because they really needed to, but because it would keep them busy and shut them up. (3/17)

However, there were reasons other than anger over students' disobedience that compelled me to create a defensive teaching style. First, I feared that my coop, or perhaps some member of the administration drawn by the noise in the room, would consider these confrontations and seeming lack of control as evidence that I did not have what it takes to teach. I could not be certain that my coop felt this way, but she told me that she had learned to teach on her own when her cooperating teacher had handed over his classes and left. Also, she had counseled me that my disappointments were the death of my idealism, indicating to me that perhaps she saw my ideas and attempts to create an empowering environment as unrealistic or wishful thinking. I needed her ultimate approval of my teaching to allow me to continue as a teacher. If she judged that I didn't have what it takes to teach and failed to recommend me, she could ruin my chances in a career in which I had already invested much time and effort and ultimately wanted to pursue. So, I made sure to get control of the class to prove that I could teach.

When I felt the students were resistant to my demands that they work in groups, I expressed in my journal a need to "do some regular teaching." I wrote:

> I also feel like they (or is it me?) are getting tired of the group thing. I feel like I have to do some regular teaching. (3/17)

By "regular teaching," I meant the kind of banking education that I had witnessed in my life as a student. When I felt threatened and the need to control, I resorted to that regular teaching, which, if not desirable to me, was at least easy to reproduce given my experience with it. In addition, because my coop had not developed empowering practices, she could not model or assist me in developing alternative ways of teaching.

Britzman (1991) says that the myth that the teacher is self-made, that everything depends on the teacher as an isolated individual, "requires an overreliance on the self, which in actuality mandates an overdependence on one's institutional biography, since this part of one's biography is most familiar to the school context" (p. 238). In keeping with her assertion that learning to teach is a process of social negotiation, she says:

> The fact is, not everything depends upon the teacher, and when the teaching stance is constructed as if it did, the teacher's work becomes confined to controlling classroom life and exerting institutional control. (p. 225)

In these ways, my own biographical context, as well as my coop's, the structural context of the school, and the sociocultural context from which the students came worked to impede my efforts at developing empowering practices.

Small Spaces for Change: Contextual Contradictions

However, biographical and structural contexts also cooperated to, if not help shape, then at least facilitate my attempts to develop empowering practices. For example, my coop had no real agenda for me as her student teacher. She felt that being left alone by her cooperating teacher had been a difficult experience, but that it had allowed her to develop her own style. She would allow me to do as I wished so that I could develop my own style. While I felt that this approach did not assist me in shaping the kind of practice that I wished to develop, at least it left me free to try to make changes.

Also, because my coop had a personal dislike of the principal and other administrators, and resented any intrusion into her classroom, she devised ways to minimize their appearances.

She related to me one occasion on which an administrator had observed her and had criticized a particular practice. She, in a pleasant way, invited the administrator to come to her class and demonstrate the practice in question so that she might learn. She told me that the administrator never came back to her classroom again.

She would also argue with the principal so that, it seemed, he would stay away in order to avoid conflict. Another teacher told me privately that the principal was annoyed with her but would make no attempt to remove her from the school because she could get a significant number of students to pass their exams.

Her ability to keep administrators at bay allowed her a measure of freedom in her own classroom. This, in turn, allowed me a measure of freedom to experiment. During one attempt at cooperative learning in which the class had gotten quite chaotic and noisy, the principal did put his head in the door, and, with a menacing look, surveyed the room. My coop quickly moved to the door, and, in a chastising manner, pointed out that this was cooperative learning. Looking as if he dreaded a confrontation with her, he surveyed the room once more and left.

In addition, within the structural context of the school, school rules were not consistently adhered to or enforced. The principal was not always prowling halls, and teachers did not always leave doors open or avoid such activities as cooperative learning. Such inconsistency also allowed for a little room to try methods not necessarily favored by school policy.

In these ways the various contexts, if not providing models for empowering practices, at least allowed me small spaces in which to negotiate my practice. However, Martin's (1991) assertion seems even more relevant to me. He stated that in the student teaching experience,

> The classroom, setting, climate and tone, as determined by the administration and classroom teacher, are of paramount importance. Setting the stage and creating an appropriate atmosphere influence the ability of a student-teacher to become a talented multicultural [empowering] educator. (p. 293)

CONCLUSION

Although I did achieve a small part of my goal to develop empowering practices, there was a good amount of failure in my efforts. This could have been expected in any setting in which I had attempted to change practice. Kemmis and McTaggart warn: "Do not expect immediate and substantial 'success'—remember that real change usually breeds a certain amount of incompetence" (p. 87). However, I feel that I could have achieved greater competence in a setting more conducive to and supportive of my aims.

The question is, then, Did this experience constitute the "death of my idealism"? The answer is yes and no. Yes, in that I have learned, as Kemmis and McTaggart suggest, "how resilient institutions are to change" (p. 87). They quote the educational evaluator, Barry McDonald, who said, "The citadel of established practice will not fall to the polite knock of a good idea" (p. 87). Also, I have learned that the practice that I develop cannot be determined only by me but will be shaped by and negotiated within the setting in which I teach. With these lessons, I have lost a bit of my hope that I could become entirely the kind of teacher I wish to be.

Although my idealism may have been tempered, it was not entirely extinguished in that I saw, even in a setting that was largely antithetical to my goals, that I could negotiate a small amount of success in developing empowering practices. I still hope to become an empowering teacher.

In a sense, I was disempowered in my attempt to become an empowering teacher. My efforts at change were frustrated by conditions that were beyond my control. However, through the process of reflection and my attempts to interpret what happened, I found that I learned much that I had not seen before about the dynamics of change and its possibility. This knowledge I found ultimately empowering.

4

Preservice Teacher Supervision and Reflective Practice

Pat Schuyler & David Sitterley

This chapter describes a collaborative action research project by two teacher education associates (TEAs), traditionally called supervisors, in a teacher certification program (TCP) in a large research university. Our experience in our TEA role[1] influenced our decision to engage in an action research project focused on the way in which our supervisory practice encouraged reflection by our student teachers. We also were interested in the influence of the institutional context on our efforts to promote reflection.

The conception of teaching as the reflective practice of a profession has historical precedents extending at least as far back as John Dewey (Experience + Reflection = Growth) (Posner, 1989, p. 21). Although reflective practice can have a range of meanings, it provides a framework in which the underlying assumptions of schooling, the impinging social structures, and the goals of education, as well as the techniques for reaching those goals, can be examined. Rather than being viewed as technicians, teachers can be considered reflective practitioners or professionals who examine these broader issues, as well as the immediate practical concerns of classroom teaching. For example, teachers can question the goals, the effects, and the social context of schooling in a way that will allow them to make conscious their contribution to the agenda of schooling and the achievement of that agenda.

Unfortunately, our personal experiences indicate that teacher education often fails to prepare aspiring teachers to be reflective, or to respond–in ways that are consistent with their values–to the social, political, and educational contexts that circumscribe their work. Institutional factors are part of the problem. Some faculty in our teacher education program encourage students to examine the underlying assumptions, values, goals, and consequences of schooling rather than focus narrowly and exclusively on the most efficient means of reaching taken-for-granted ends. But there is relatively little dialogue within or across the several disciplines that contribute to teacher education, and many courses fail to grapple with such issues, fostering a conception of teaching as a technical occupation with a concentration on ways to present the required curriculum. We are concerned with this question as part of a larger interest in education and social change and because it grows out of our own work experience.

We begin this chapter with a description of the initial exploration of our situation. Then, using action research cycles (as described by Kemmis and McTaggart, 1988), we examine our efforts to foster reflective practice in the student teachers we supervised. The final section discusses what we learned from the action research process regarding our own practice and its relation to the institutional context in which our supervision took place.

INITIAL EXPLORATION OF OUR SITUATION: PERSONAL BACKGROUNDS AND SOME CURRENT CONDITIONS

While both of us had completed a teacher certification program and served as secondary school teachers in New York prior to becoming teacher education associates, neither of us felt that those experiences had prepared us adequately to be reflective or to respond to the social, political, and educational contexts of our work in schools. Pat began teaching at a high school on Long Island in September 1972 and quickly discovered that school was much more than classroom instruction. Racial and socioeconomic differences in the community led to tensions and misunderstandings in the school, but these were not discussed. Many teachers were concerned about issues such as racism and poverty, but they worked largely in isolation, with no opportunity to examine together why tensions existed or how the school might respond to them. On the contrary, the administration pushed teachers to deal with problems individually in their own classrooms.

Nothing in her university education had prepared Pat for that school and classroom reality. No course had ever discussed critically the relationship between education and racism or education and inequality. No course had examined the constraints that schools and communities place on teaching and learning. No course had ever helped her understand the history of teaching and the struggles (both successes and failures) of teachers. Her formal education simply had ignored a vital part of the working life she encountered in teaching.

Dave began teaching at a small, all-White school in rural western New York in September 1983 and slowly became aware of tensions, which, with the exception of racial differences, were similar to those discovered by Pat a decade earlier. Socioeconomic differences, the lack of an appropriate school response to social inequities, and teacher isolation were very evident. In a community as small as the one in which Dave taught, the entire socioeconomic range may be represented in a single classroom. While the diversity may have been less intense than in a racially mixed, inner-city school, students expressed and exacerbated social inequity through activities such as labeling and friendship-group selection.

School personnel legitimated social inequity by neglecting it. There was no observed attempt to resolve the inherent contradiction between the American ideology of equal opportunity and the reality of inequality and the resulting differential potential for achievement. In addition, teachers were isolated in their individual classrooms. There was no effort to bring them together to seek solutions to commonly faced difficulties. Rather, the administration encouraged teachers to solve problems—or at least cope with their continuance—individually.

Another decade later, we find evidence that similar problems still exist in teacher education. Colleagues and students have suggested that teacher education "covers" contextual issues in the social foundations courses. Preservice teachers, however, indicated varying interpretations of this "coverage." Many who were practice teaching did not feel prepared or empowered by their teacher education courses to engage in the real social-political world of teaching. Professors thought students were too oriented toward practical issues. Students thought professors were too theoretical or abstract. Many preservice teachers felt that the foundations courses were irrelevant to their future working lives.[2] We know that the connections exist, but the educational process in which the students are involved does not encourage them to analyze and theorize and make those connections (i.e., to engage in one kind of reflective practice). Teacher educators introduce issues such as race, class, and gender inequalities, and power relations in foundations courses. Students discuss them but are not encouraged to use their own knowledge and experience to connect ideas and concepts to real educational or school situations.

We found the same theory–practice gap in efforts to encourage reflective teaching among preservice teachers. The text used in field experience classes claims that reflective teachers:

> Actively, persistently, and carefully consider and reconsider beliefs and practices "in light of the grounds that support them and the further consequences to which they lead." (Grant & Zeichner, 1984, p. 4)

> Reflective thinking allows the teacher to examine critically the assumptions that schools make about what can count as acceptable goals and methods, problems and solutions. (Posner, 1989, p. 22)

However, there is no shared understanding of the meaning of reflective teaching beyond a dictionary-type definition of reflection. Each group with whom we have worked (preservice teachers, cooperating teachers, and teacher education associates) has asked for more information about reflective practice. Although most of us agree with the idea of reflective teaching, no one is clear about how we can enable preservice teachers to do it. At one meeting, a cooperating teacher said that the student teachers at her school did not know what reflective practice meant, other than to think about what they did in order to improve it. During initial discussions with us, preservice teachers expressed an individualized and technical conception of reflective teaching. As they began student teaching, they focused on survival in what they often perceived to be an overwhelming experience. Consequently, they questioned the importance of using our time together to examine issues such as the values underlying specific classroom choices or their views about teaching and learning and student–teacher relations. They wanted answers to questions about how to conduct tomorrow's class. Our initial exploration suggested, therefore, that an important part of facilitating reflective practice must be to understand better the needs and situation of preservice teachers.

Our action research project centered on how we could help new teachers to practice reflection as they enter the field. We began our project with the following questions in mind: How does our practice as teacher education associates facilitate the development of reflective practice among preservice teachers? To what extent does it meet needs felt by those preservice teachers? How can we improve our practice in both of these areas? How does the institutional context of the TCP affect our capacity, and that of the preservice teachers, to be reflective practitioners?

METHODOLOGY

We carried out the action components of our action research cycles individually, but collaborated in the planning, reflection, and reporting phases of our project. Dave's actions focused on postobservation conferences, while Pat's actions focused on class discussions and encouraging students to engage in journal-dialogues with her. We then reflected together on the implications of our individual actions with regard to our own practices and the institutional context of the TCP. It is important to note that there has been a constant tension in our project between our efforts to reflect on our own practice and the need to be attentive to how the institutional context affects that practice. We have tried, therefore, to allow both aspects to emerge in the description of our action research.

FIRST CYCLE: DAVE'S POSTOBSERVATION CONFERENCES

In planning the initial round of observations and conferences, Dave sought to gauge the extent of reflection occurring among preservice teachers with whom he worked. By posing a few well-focused questions, he also hoped to stimulate further reflection on teaching, the context in which it occurs, and the ends it serves. The responses, he hoped, would indicate the degree to which the preservice teachers thought about the issues he raised and encourage them to engage in self-evaluation.

Observing and Reflecting: While students willingly discussed the questions, Dave didn't feel the discussions had much significance for them. The preservice teachers had a very difficult time offering a rationale for a particular lesson beyond, "it's the next thing in the curriculum," or "they'll [the students] need it to pass the Regents," or to do well in next year's course, or to get into college. This may be due, in part, to the practice of many cooperating teachers of assigning the preservice teacher particular units to "cover." While sympathetic to preservice teachers' needs to explore a variety of approaches to teaching, cooperating teachers often feel (understandably) a much stronger need to ensure their students' success as measured by end-of-year examinations. Their first concern was to get their students through these exams. If, in addition to this, reflective practice could enable more creative, alternative approaches to teaching, well and good, but examination success would take priority. Consequently, Dave's next step would be to find a more appropriate way to stimulate reflection.

FIRST CYCLE: PAT'S CLASS DISCUSSIONS

Pat planned to make class discussions a key focus for her action research because of her experience in the program the previous year. During the practice teaching experience there had been no formal occasions for students to reflect together about their experience; in fact, there was no connection to the university at all except for TEA visits and two or three full-group (100 students) sessions planned by the TCP.[3] She believed that this separation of students from the university was not conducive to preservice teachers reflecting on their practice beyond the consideration of appropriate techniques for "covering" the material. Again this year, there were no required classes for preservice teachers during their full-time practice teaching. Pat decided to hold three classes during this 6-week period. She planned to find out the needs of student teachers, to try to respond to those needs, and at the same time to encourage collective and critical reflection on their work. During the first of these classes, Pat explained her action research project to the student teachers and asked if they would be willing to discuss: (1) their needs at this point in their preparation; (2) their expectations of her and of the program; and (3) the relationship of reflection to their work. Pat did not tape any of the classes since she felt it was important for the student teachers to be comfortable about being honest in their responses. Instead, her data come from field notes and therefore may not be exact quotes.

Observing and Reflecting: Two themes emerged from students' responses to Pat's questions. First, students said they felt inadequately prepared for the reality of their work in schools. Some argued that their methods classes prepared them to teach in ideal situations, and others that "ed psych and other theories" do not work in their schools. Others said that they do what they do "in spite of" what they learned; they act against their own nature; and they are not happy with themselves or their situations. Comments by two students illustrate this tension.

STUDENT A: Kids seem to want you to be the kind of authoritarian that you have learned not to be. When I'm nasty and crude and mean, students respond best. When I'm understanding, patient, and have a sense of humor, they don't. When I'm nasty, they like me. I go against all that I have been taught. I don't know any other way.

STUDENT B: My cooperating teacher says to punish students by taking 20 points off the test. We learned the opposite in ed psych class.

The students suggested that a more realistic orientation to the TCP could include meetings early in the fall with program and school people to explain the program and the actual conditions of schools, and to discuss and develop "informed" ways of working within the schools. Students said that school visits, required during Phase I of the TCP, painted a "rosy picture" or were a "sales job." They said they come from different backgrounds than most of the students in their classrooms (most preservice teachers with whom Pat worked came from suburban or rural schools and were assigned to city schools) and do not feel prepared to handle well the situations in which they find themselves. As one said:

The [program] could help us see a more realistic picture so we could discuss these issues ahead of time. Phase I paints a rosy picture. Methods class teaches us to teach in [a suburban school]. It's different there—where the majority of students have expectations of college—than where kids are running with gangs. How do you motivate someone who thinks he might be shot that night?

The second theme concerned a disjunction between the students' university preparation and their school experiences. Students reported that their cooperating teachers were not "open-minded" and acted in ways that "we are taught not to do"; or that they were resigned to accepting things as they are. One cooperating teacher's response to a student's request for a discussion about a problem was, "Oh well, what can you do?" Several students said they did not feel like reflecting on their lessons with their cooperating teachers. One student explained:

The advice I get from my cooperating teacher is not the same advice as we get from the program. He says he's open to innovations, but within his limitations: "Keep them busy and under control."

Most of these first discussions were taken up by the student teachers' concerns with these "working conditions" and with how to survive their practice teaching. In response to Pat's question about the relation of reflective teaching to their situations, students said: "Reflective practice is just another truth they are laying on us," and "The program is more concerned with effective reflection than effective teaching," and "Our courses teach us to fit into the existing [school] system" rather than to question it. When Pat explained her understanding of reflective teaching, that is, to question what is and how it got that way (including our own reasons for educational choices), to look for alternatives, to work together for change, one student responded: "No one has ever said those words to me before. Our education is not realistic or reflective."

Pat felt a bit overwhelmed by their responses. She had not expected them to be so negative and had not prepared for such a reaction. They apparently felt powerless to change their situations, and Pat was not able to respond in ways that they saw as useful. They were looking for solutions to very immediate problems and saw reflection as just another "theory" that had no relation to their work. Because their students' personal problems (e.g., outside work, pregnancy, motherhood) impinge on the teaching process, the student teachers lowered their expectations. Their experiences with their cooperating teachers reinforced Pat's initial concern about the strong influence of the cooperating teacher during the student teaching experience and raised the question: How could she (Pat) provide an opportunity for preservice teachers to see alternative choices of action in the classroom? As a first step, Pat wanted to find ways to encourage students to uncover their own values and beliefs in relating to such issues as teaching, learning, and control, and to think about where those values and beliefs come from (Liston & Zeichner, 1990).

SECOND CYCLE: DAVE'S POSTOBSERVATION CONFERENCES

In planning the second cycle, Dave approached his action from a framework in which teaching practice is examined at the instrumental or technical level (What do I do and how efficient is it?), the interpretative level (What does this mean in relation to the rest of the world? What norms/values am I reinforcing or challenging?), and the transformative level (What impact can my practice have on society?). Within each of these levels, reflective practice should be ethical (concerned with what is right as well as with what is efficient), collegial (as opposed to individualized and possibly tending to reinforce individual misperceptions), and multiply informed (open to information and suggestion from a variety of sources regarding each of the levels of reflection).[4]

To stimulate discussion in the second round of postobservation conferences, Dave developed a matrix of instrumental, interpretative, and transformative questions about what happened, as well as about assumptions, implications, and alternatives for improvement, intended to guide him through the conferences. He reasoned that the matrix also might help the students to make conscious their own goals in pursuing teaching and the relationship of a particular lesson to attaining those goals.

Observing and Reflecting: The matrix of questions proved to be too big to cover in a single postobservation conference. In no conference did the discussion adequately explore alternatives or ways to improve practice. Also, the matrix proved to be unwieldy to use. Dave had to hold the observed lesson in mind, fit the current conversation into the classification scheme, and make up questions to address the next "block" of the grid. Despite these difficulties, in one conference with two preservice math teachers, discussion centered around the interpretative issues of the selection, organization, and treatment of knowledge. One preservice teacher mentioned that a student she tutored in another school in the same district had quite different skills from students in the school in which she worked. The preservice teachers discerned a connection between the treatment of knowledge and skills emphasized (graphing versus word problem solution), and the perceived uses of knowledge (purely academic versus practical). Their responses, however, stressed their primary challenge—survival in the public schools—and also reflected their awareness that the TEA had some responsibility for evaluating their teaching. While humoring Dave's concern to practice reflection, they seemed to feel a greater need to positively impress the TEA than to engage freely in the reflection.

Although at the time Dave interpreted this feeling of being humored as a lack of commitment to reflection on the part of the students, there are alternative explanations. Students could have been so caught up in the intensity of student teaching activities that they had no energy available to practice reflection. Reflecting on the social and political implications of the math 12 or junior high French curriculum may have been perceived as unrelated to their daily survival.

Dave's strategy for posing questions and the issues he raised may have been inappropriate. One preservice teacher appeared to be personally inclined to activism, but by focusing on the question grid, Dave overlooked the opportunity to challenge her with the notion that teachers cannot be politically neutral, but must actively or passively support or challenge existing arrangements. Sticking too closely to an instrument that was intended to facilitate reflection, actually interfered with the practice of reflection by influencing the TEA to think about "the next question" rather than the issue at hand. "Reflection" became a technique.

If students did not see reflective practice as relevant to their daily work, this issue should have been addressed directly, rather than by encouraging them to reflect anyway and hoping they would see the value of the practice by being involved in it. In addition, Dave may not have made clear the kind of thinking and discussion he hoped to facilitate. Not until much later did Dave consider resolving possible differences of understandings of the meaning of reflection during the project. Dave might have been more successful if he had clarified to students what he meant when he talked about reflective practice.

SECOND CYCLE: PAT'S CLASS DISCUSSIONS

Pat decided to focus the next class session around a discussion of a Lisa Delpit article, "Skills and Other Dilemmas of a Progressive Black Educator" (1986). Delpit argues in the article that "many of the teachers of black children have roots in other communities and do not often have the opportunity to hear the full range of their students' voices" (p. 383). Although the preservice teachers in this class had not identified minority students as a focus of their concern, they did see themselves as coming from different (more middle class and suburban) backgrounds than their students, and minority students make up a large percentage of their schools' populations. Pat thought they might connect with Delpit's message about the need to hear other voices. With appropriate questions, Pat hoped to enable students to uncover some of their own beliefs and values, to discuss reasons for their classroom choices, and perhaps to identify some alternatives. The Delpit article would also allow some discussion of teacher expectations.

Pat began class by asking students to look at her typed notes from the previous class in order to verify the accuracy of her account of their comments. This focused the class on the same frustrations mentioned the week before, and it was difficult to pull them away. Most students had not read the Delpit article, so discussion about it was dominated by those who had read it. In response to some of the problems students raised, Pat asked questions about their values and beliefs about teaching and learning, about teacher–student relations, and about how their values related to their classroom choices. Some student teachers discussed the difficulty they have in working with "unmotivated" students. Their comments illustrate how they are tempted to conform to existing school practices and to lower their expectations.

STUDENT A: I have ideas that I want to try in the classroom—cooperation, giving students opportunities to discuss and analyze. But the resistance is awful. And I'm afraid that there are too many casualties.
PS: What do you mean, casualties?
STUDENT A: Students tune out, they don't want to participate. I'm afraid they won't get the information, they won't pass the test.
STUDENT B: I think our student teaching is being shaped by the cooperating teacher—who is a full-time overseer. We bend our methods according to them.

STUDENT C: Like, don't let discipline interrupt teaching. If someone is sleeping, or not doing an assignment, ignore them. If you try to encourage them to participate, you'll probably have a discipline problem.

STUDENT D: Or, if you want to have a class discussion, or small group discussion, the class will be more difficult to control. So you keep them busy.

Students talked again about their feelings about not being prepared for this experience, which led to some suggestions for alternatives.

STUDENT D: And on cafeteria duty today, I felt threatened. It was an emotional experience. I'm not prepared for this. If only I could have seen this kind of situation ahead of time, on video or something, I could have had some time to think about it.

STUDENT B: We could have had real situations to discuss.

STUDENT C: But there are people who have been teachers for 25 years, and they don't know—maybe there are no answers.

STUDENT A: But we could be more aware of situations before we go there. We could spend some time discussing alternatives.

STUDENT B: We could have a class with former student teachers.

STUDENT A: (to Pat) You say values and beliefs are involved, well emotions are involved too—I feel angry, threatened sometimes. We should have an opportunity to consider these things ahead of time, discuss what to do when you feel like that.

STUDENT E: We never talk about these things.

When Pat asked if maybe they should look beyond the classroom for some of the causes of their concerns, one student responded: "I feel frustrated when you ask all these questions and I don't see their connection to my problems."

Observing and Reflecting: Although some very important issues were discussed during this cycle, in general the discussion was unstructured, rambling, and difficult to focus. Perhaps Pat's attempt to orient the discussion to their concerns and her decision not to be directive, or offer solutions, were part of the problem. She had suggested, not assigned, the Delpit article, and the fact that most students did not read it limited the discussion. Her probe questions also may not have been appropriate for connecting the nonreaders' concerns to the issues addressed by Delpit. Students seemed to need to talk to each other about their experiences more than respond to the issues Pat had intended for discussion. Pat's efforts to steer discussion to the examination of their own values and beliefs about the educational issues they raised did not work and in fact seemed to frustrate them.

THIRD CYCLE: DAVE'S POSTOBSERVATION CONFERENCES

In the third round of postobservation conferences, Dave wanted to continue asking questions that had the potential to stimulate collaborative reflection both in the conference itself and afterward. However, he wanted to avoid using an instrument that might limit the discussion. He decided to use a simplified interview protocol, addressing the description, meaning, and history of, as well as alternatives to, practices to guide the conversation.[5]

Observing and Reflecting: In one postobservation conference, Dave and two student teachers began considering the uses of higher level high school mathematics beyond preparation for college and training in logical thinking. The students discussed and came to agreement on the position that mathematics could be used as a selection filter for advancement of those students who came from home backgrounds where academic achievement was highly valued and encouraged. But they did not perceive a significant connection between the race or social class from which students came, or their gender, and the likelihood of the student doing well in mathematics. Moreover, the analysis stopped at this level, extending no further than the connections between individual, experiential background, and academic success. Dave had hoped the discussion would include broader issues such as whether or not math 12, as it was currently taught, might serve the interests of particular groups in society at the expense of other groups, or the social and political reasons math 12 might be included in the high school curriculum. However, when Dave asked questions aimed at generating such a discussion, both preservice teachers looked slightly uncomfortable and did not respond. They may have misunderstood the questions, they may have simply needed more time to formulate a response, or they may have seen little reason to discuss the social/political ties between curriculum and power in society. While Dave felt the preservice teachers had made some progress toward understanding their practice in relation to the society that legitimated the knowledge they sought to teach, he didn't feel that his supervisory practice had very effectively facilitated their move in this direction. It had taken three rounds of observations and discussions before this movement was seen.

Similarly, foreign language and English preservice teachers did not respond to questions asking for consideration of the social context or the implications of their work beyond the classroom. They hoped to instill some humanitarian values in their students as a result of their teaching, but there was no consideration of whose knowledge was legitimated in the public school curriculum or why that particular knowledge was chosen. This is not to say that supervision failed. Each preservice teacher did, at one or another point, engage in consideration of the social forces impinging on the teaching and learning processes and on the effects of her or his teaching in the larger society. However, movement in this direction seemed slow and difficult.

Part of this last cycle included asking preservice teachers to respond to open-ended questionnaires about supervision. In their responses, they expressed the need to receive more supervision, including positive, practical feedback. Significantly, the preservice teachers praised the supervision for its practical usefulness, rather than for its reflective component.

THIRD CYCLE: PAT'S CLASSROOM DISCUSSIONS

Pat based her planning for the third class session on the fact that the questions that she asked previously did not receive much attention. She needed to find a common focus for their discussion that would include some new information that the student teachers would perceive as relevant to their needs. And she needed to prepare a way of sharing new information with those who did not read the assignment.

For the next class session, Pat decided to use a "Curriculum Dilemmas" excerpt from Berlak and Berlak's *Dilemmas of Schooling* (1981). Berlak and Berlak lay out the choices that teachers make (often implicitly) about the treatment of knowledge, the process of learning, and the role of the child, and they examine the beliefs and assumptions that underlie those choices. Pat believed that this might help students begin to discuss the reasons underlying their own choices and thus begin to think about their teaching with regard to broader issues. She decided to use small group discussions and prepared a page of abbreviated versions of the Berlak and Berlak curriculum dilemmas so that the class (including those who did not read the article) would have a common focus.

Observing and Reflecting: About half of the students had read the Berlak and Berlak excerpt on curriculum dilemmas. Pat gave out the abbreviated versions of the dilemmas and the class broke into small groups by subject area. Each group was asked to choose a dilemma (or dilemmas) to discuss, develop a plan for a lesson (or segment of a lesson) that illustrated a way they believed was appropriate to resolve the knowledge dilemma, and share their plan with the rest of the group.

One group discussed mathematics and included two dilemmas: "knowledge as content versus knowledge as process" and "intrinsic versus extrinsic motivation." One student talked about a math class "review book project." There are no exam review books for the class, so she and her cooperating teacher decided to have the students write one. This required the students to take on a new role as question writers, rather than question answerers. It gave the students a more active role in the class and more confidence in their ability to do the work. "If they can write the questions," she said, "they can certainly answer them." And when the review book was put together, the students' names were "published" next to their own questions, which was a source of motivation in itself. This discussion group pointed out that they believed the math project had been successful because two dilemmas had been thought about, one involving process and one involving motivation. The process of figuring out how to write a question related to a particular math concept enabled more understanding than had the explanation of the concept by the teacher. And the process of involving students in producing a valued component of the math class—a review book— had motivated them.

During the last part of the class Pat asked students to fill out an evaluation form. The first question asked: "Has your understanding of reflective practice changed during the semester? If yes, how has it changed? Why?" In addition to the evaluation form, Pat returned to students the statements they had written about reflective practice in the beginning of the semester. She asked them to respond to the evaluation question by looking at those initial statements and commenting on whether they would change them now and, if so, how. Their responses suggested modest changes in their understandings of reflective practice. Most indicated a move from seeing reflective practice as an individual activity to understanding it as collegial and/or collaborative. One student commented, "And now I think it is necessary to do it with other people. Reflecting by oneself just isn't enough."

The second evaluation question asked about the class sessions. Two responses capture the two main points raised by most students: the need to discuss their "survival" concerns in practice teaching and the value of sharing those concerns.

STUDENT A: We've brought up a lot of good points. At the beginning I felt that your discussions were a little too in-depth for us. But you adjusted to our needs and allowed us to talk about things we had on our minds.

STUDENT B: Class sessions have been most useful in providing a forum for venting frustrations, and in showing me that others are going through the same problems. They might be improved by having more of them, so that once the need for "griping" has passed, more structured activities (like today's session on dilemmas) could be focused on.

Three issues also stand out to Pat with regard to her effort to encourage reflective practice during these three class sessions. First, student teachers have other important needs. Encouraging reflective practice should not have been the priority until Pat became more attuned to these needs during the critical period of practice teaching. Second, the students engaged in reflection and examined assumptions about their choices when Pat provided materials that directly related to their classroom needs. Third, she noticed a tension between her desire to be nondirective and the need to challenge implicit and commonsense notions about teaching and learning, to introduce contextual issues and provide new perspectives. These goals require sufficient structure to enable understanding of the issues discussed. As one student noted:

> Although I understand the class sessions were open-ended, or meant to be whatever we as students chose to make of them, I would have liked a little more structure to keep our sessions "on task."

Although Pat would not define the "structure problem" in terms of keeping the class sessions "on task," this student's comment, and the very general responses of other students to the question about their conceptions of reflective practice, caused Pat to question the progress she had made toward her goals of better understanding their needs and enabling them to be more reflective. In thinking about this and other class sessions, Pat referred to her own understanding of reflection. Do these preservice teachers now reflect on the ends and purposes to which they are working? Sometimes. Do they question their own values and assumptions? Yes, when a specific question is asked or made part of a class discussion related to their needs—as in the discussion of the Berlak and Berlak dilemmas. Do they reflect on the educational, social, and political contexts in which their teaching is embedded? Yes, but they feel overwhelmed and disempowered by the structures they discover. Has Pat's practice enabled them to be reflective toward their work? The best she can say is . . . maybe . . . sometimes.

RETHINKING REFLECTION IN TEACHER EDUCATION

We set out to improve our practice as teacher education associates by using action research to examine our interactions with preservice teachers. We wanted to explore how our practice facilitated the development of reflective practice among preservice teachers and to what extent it met their perceived needs. In addition, we were concerned with the effect of the university context on our work.

We were only marginally successful at encouraging reflective practice for the preservice teachers with whom we worked. We lacked experience in reflective practice and, given the multiple pressures on students, they did not see it as a priority need. As the semester (and our projects) ended, we were just beginning to understand reflective practice ourselves. A related concern was our failure to question our concept of reflective practice and whether it was appropriate to our practice with preservice teachers. We simply accepted it as a "good thing" and thus opened a gap between the concept and its relevance for student teachers. We made a central mistake in not addressing directly our students' perception of reflective practice as irrelevant to their daily work experience in their schools.

Closing this theory–practice gap involves thinking about the situations that preservice teachers encounter in their practice teaching. They face conditions that often contradict the understandings they have taken from their university courses. As they plunge into practice teaching, they have little choice except to conform to the norms, teaching practices, and operating procedures of their schools. Discussing these school experiences with their peers is a high priority for student teachers, but there are few opportunities to do so. The concepts and theories of their teacher education program (including reflective practice) do not appear meaningful to their "survival," and we were insufficiently prepared to make reflective practice relevant to their needs. Any approach to reflective practice by student teachers must be grounded in their school experience. We stumbled when we attempted to push students into grappling with concepts of reflective practice gleaned from working, reading, and theorizing in the university. Pat's relative success in using the Berlak and Berlak dilemmas as an approach to reflective practice suggests that there are ways in which such concepts can help student teachers deal with the "survival" problems they face in their practice teaching. But TEAs' understanding of the concept and its appropriateness for student teachers involves an awareness of how the university setting affects their own practice.

THE UNIVERSITY SETTING

Kemmis and McTaggart (1988) imply that a natural component of action research is the broadening of focus from individual practice to institutional contexts.

> We look for changes in three different aspects of individual work and the culture of groups: changes in the use of language and discourses . . . , changes in activities and practices . . . and changes in social relationships and organization . . . the ways [people's] relationships are structured and organized to achieve consistency between the principles and practices of educational administration and teaching and learning. (pp. 15–16)

In retrospect, however, we are less certain that action research leads naturally toward a focus on contexts. We think it happened in our case because both of us were concerned with institutional context from the beginning. Even with this initial motivation, we sometimes slipped into forgetting it, blaming ourselves, blaming the students, or focusing on technical solutions to our own or the students' problems. Throughout our projects we felt a tension between the need to focus on our own practice and at the same time explore the contextual factors that affected our practice. We also have some concerns about the leap we are taking from the practice of two teacher education associates to more generalized considerations of the university and the teacher certification program in which we worked. We recognize, therefore, the fragility of our observations. [6]

Our action research project revealed the difficulty of encouraging reflective practice in a university setting that may not be conducive to such practice. In most universities teacher education rests on a multidisciplinary base, but course content is highly individualistic (Lanier & Little, 1986). University faculty, like their counterparts in the public schools, often work in isolation. Frequently, there is a lack of dialogue among teacher educators within departments, across disciplines, or with the schools. The absence of shared understanding about what reflective practice is and the gap between university theory and work in schools underline the need for structured opportunities to examine together priority concerns.

The situation of TEAs exemplifies the need for such opportunities. TEAs are graduate students who come from a variety of teaching backgrounds, and most stay with the TCP only a year or two. High rates of turnover among TEAs contribute to the lack of shared understandings of reflective practice; many of us have had little or no exposure to the concept. Yet there are no formal opportunities for TEAs and others involved in teacher education to come together to deepen their understanding of reflective practice or to discuss ways to develop reflective habits in their students. During the 1990–91 school year, for example, only one lunchtime meeting included a discussion of reflective practice.

Within the TCP a pilot study is underway to restructure teacher education and do related research. This involves TCP faculty working with a small group of cooperating teachers (clinical faculty) in an effort to bridge the gap between university and school. But reflective practice will not occur automatically from the restructuring process. It requires scheduled opportunities that provide time for university faculty, TEAs, student teachers, and cooperating teachers to discuss reflective practice and its relation to other school issues, both separately and together.

ACTION RESEARCH

Action research has helped us to become more reflective in our supervisory practice by giving us tools for reflection. These tools have included cycles of systematic engagement (in contrast to just thinking on the way home); journal writing to help us hang onto our thoughts long enough to analyze them systematically and translate them into appropriate actions; and our collaboration, which forced us to deal with context and examine our own assumptions. Thinking of ourselves as researchers changed our perception of the classroom processes in which we participated. Discussion with others has given us new perspectives and new questions. [7] Kemmis and McTaggart (1988) suggest that collaborative action research in education "is about helping people to become more conscious and critical of their agency in processes of historical change" (p. 44). In this aspect of our action research project we have been successful.

NOTES

1. The TCP has four phases of gradual immersion into the school setting. During Phases III and IV, the TEA role is similar to the more familiar-sounding role of student teacher supervisor. This includes filling out observation forms and ensuring that interim and final evaluations are completed. However, during various parts of the school year, TEAs also participate in selecting the next cohort of students to enter the TCP; teach the field experience course, which includes school visits and discussions; and generally assist in the day-to-day operation of the TCP.

2. These comments are informed by data from several sources: informal conversations with professors, students, teachers, and colleagues in our graduate work and study; comments made by preservice teachers during our 2 years with the TCP; and data from a pilot research study on knowledge and teacher education.

3. Topics have included multicultural and race relations, interviewing for a job, and a state-mandated seminar on recognizing and reporting child abuse.

4. C. Cornbleth (the TCP director) discusses reflective practice as occurring on a variety of levels and as being collegial, ethical/principled, and multiply informed. This implies a collaborative rather than an individualistic approach.

5. These questions were drawn from the work of J. Smyth (1989) as cited in Wellington (1991).

6. Our comments in this section and elsewhere in this chapter relate to the teacher certification program as we worked with it from 1989 to 1991. The program continues to evolve and some of the suggestions we make here have been implemented by faculty.

7. This action research project was completed in partial fulfillment of a graduate education course.

5

Teaching Action Research

A Case Study

Robert B. Stevenson, Susan E. Noffke,
Eduardo Flores, & Susan Granger

Courses in action research at universities have been increasing in current years. A part of those courses often involves students engaging in action research into their own educational practice. It seems only logical, if not also necessary, that teachers of action research engage in inquiring into their own practice as well. This chapter presents such a study of our teaching of a course in action research.

At least in some forms, action research assumes that neither the process of education nor that of educational research is neutral in its political stance. Rather, it reflects a concern with improving educational practices toward building a more just and caring society. Teachers of action research, therefore, should question whether their own practices reflect such a concern. This chapter begins with background information on the course and its participants, outlines our initial concern, and then describes our efforts to improve our practice in fostering what we came to call a "democratic classroom community," our understanding of that practice, and the situation in which our practice took place, through the cycles of action research. The next section examines both factors that contributed to building such a community as well as barriers that were encountered. The final section addresses issues that emerged from our study and have affected our subsequent practice in teaching action research. Particular attention is paid to the dilemmas of collaborative teaching of action research within a university-based structure.

BACKGROUND AND STRUCTURE OF THE COURSE

The course was conducted at the State University of New York at Buffalo in the spring semester of 1991. Both instructors (Bob and Susan) had experience working with action research, and a course had been offered once before with a small group of students (see Stevenson, 1991), but this occasion was the first time it had been team taught. Although planned from the beginning as one course, it was listed on the university's class schedule as two separate courses: one in the Department of Educational Organization, Administration, and Policy (EOAP) and the other in the Department of Learning and Instruction (LAI).

The dual listing resulted in the enrollment of a large (38) and diverse group of students. Those from EOAP tended to be older, experienced teachers and counselors, most of whom were aspiring to become school administrators. A few already were administrators, either principals or superintendents. In contrast, students from LAI were generally beginning or inexperienced teachers who were enrolled in a master's degree program (which in New York State must be completed within the first 5 years of teaching in order to satisfy permanent teacher certification requirements). Many of the students were familiar with one or the other of the instructors through previous coursework. A small number of the participants were full-time students, either completing their residency requirement or completing a degree while seeking employment. Two of these students, Eduardo (a doctoral student from EOAP) and Sue (a masters student from LAI) were invited to work with Bob and Susan in studying their teaching of action research.

The aim of the course was to engage participants in the practice of conducting action research as well as in the study of action research theory and scholarship. The first involved either the study of practitioner-students' own educational work or, in the case of full-time students, collaboration with a practitioner. The second involved reading and discussing various meanings and interpretations of action research and addressing specific epistemological and political issues in its practice. The intent also was also to study our own practice. As with many of the students, our exact focus emerged over time, yet was grounded in our own previous professional and personal experiences.

A major function of the class sessions, including time devoted to collaborative group work, was to share and critique our action research experiences. To this end, everyone was encouraged to work throughout the semester to seek ways of connecting the abstract concepts and principles examined in the literature to the actual conditions of classroom work. We also were concerned that the experiences and perspectives of each member be shared and accorded recognition. In other words, we sought to create the kind of atmosphere participants would want for their own classrooms and schools, where open and nurturing discussions could occur.

Participants were asked to keep a journal in which their experiences in studying and carrying out action research were recorded on a regular basis (i.e., at least weekly). The purpose of the journal was twofold. First, it provided a means for students to express their evolving thoughts about action research and the outcomes of reflecting on their educational practices, including the formulation of ideas for actions or changes in practice. Journal writings were shared in class in project groups and collected once in mid-semester for written feedback from the instructors, but were not graded. This was to encourage the expression of whatever thoughts came to mind unencumbered by concerns about evaluation. Journals were also to serve as a data source for the major assignment, an analysis of the student's action research project. This research project would be written up as a case study according to guidelines that were to be developed and negotiated in class.

LEGITIMATING THE STUDENT VOICE

In planning the course we decided to focus initially on the professional experiences of class members and on teachers' published reports of their action research. Our intent was to emphasize that action research is grounded in the study of educational practice and that practitioners' voices are a valued source of knowledge about practice. This was based on our feeling that courses in action research should focus on students' experiences in doing action research rather than solely on the study of action research as viewed by scholars. This framework for the course was influenced in part by Bob's previous experience in teaching the course when an initial concentration on studying scholarship on action research seemed to suggest to students that they must rely predominantly on traditional sources of knowledge on teaching and research, namely, the voice of external authorities (Stevenson, 1991). Another factor was Susan's comparative study of action research practices in the United States, United Kingdom, and Australia (Noffke, 1990). Rather than presenting the various "versions" of action research, with the tacit implication that the students should "buy into" one, we hoped to have their understandings of action research emerge from their practice of it.

The first half of the course focused on the process of doing action research, beginning with the identification of a thematic concern and an initial review of one's situation in relation to that concern, and then moving through planning for action and data collection, acting on those plans, observing, and reflecting on one's observations in relation to the initial concern. After a series of such cycles, a final report would be written.

It was not until the ninth week of class that we began to examine different conceptions of and issues in action research as represented in the writings of scholars (e.g., Kurt Lewin, Stephen Corey, Lawrence Stenhouse, John Elliott, Stephen Kemmis, Robin McTaggart, and Gaby Weiner). The precourse planning established a broad outline for the course and identified readings for each week. The pedagogical approaches to be employed, as well as the specific questions and issues to be addressed, were determined at weekly meetings, initially with the two instructors and soon after with all four authors.

While our initial curriculum planning attempted to legitimate the collective voice of practitioners, we also recognized that our pedagogical actions had to allow the individual voice of each member of the class to be heard. Upon learning that the class size was to be approximately 40, we realized that smaller group work would need to play a major part in the class. Consequently, in the first class session we discussed our desire for students to work extensively throughout the course in collaborative groups and handed out guidelines for working in a "collectively led" group, although no small group activities were structured for this first meeting. We also informed the class that we would be conducting action research on our own teaching of the course.

The first class session highlighted our concern with creating what we came to call a critical community of equal voices within such a large and diverse graduate student population. From the very beginning, there was an asymmetry of communication among the students, with the discourse being dominated by very experienced teachers who worked in staff development or resource/advisory positions and by school administrators. Yet the class was a microcosm of a school district, with first-year teachers, experienced and veteran teachers, counselors, staff developers, principals, and superintendents. We saw an opportunity to address a concern about equity that is often mirrored in schools and other institutions in society.

At the end of the first class, in reaction to our observation that the discussion was dominated by a small number of older and more experienced practitioners, we mentioned our concern about recognizing everyone's voice and asked that students pay particular attention to that concern, especially when meeting in groups. We began the second class by emphasizing small group discussions to allow for more voices to be heard. Students were invited in these groups to articulate the limitations of traditional research as perceived by practitioners and to identify criteria that they viewed as appropriate for desirable research. The intent was to legitimate student voices and not merely those of research "authorities." During the following class, we emphasized that everyone was free to construct their own conception of action research, provided an argument could be offered to justify that conception.

CREATING A CRITICAL COMMUNITY:
ARTICULATING RATIONALES

In addition to the keeping of an action research journal, participants in the course were asked, as advocated by some writers on action research (e.g., Kemmis & McTaggart, 1988), to develop a rationale for their action research project as one way to explore the topic. This was to be turned in as a short essay for instructor feedback during the fifth week of class. It seemed only logical, then, that one of our first tasks, too, should be to articulate to each other our thoughts about why (and if) work toward developing a critical community of equal voices would be appropriate. We each wrote essays and exchanged and compared them. It was readily apparent that as instructors and students we emphasized similar as well as differing justifications: an unsurprising realization given our varied investment in the topic at that time, in addition to our parallel and dissonant life experiences and ideological positions. We shared a view that the collective involved in a graduate course, or perhaps any course, begins for the most part as a loosely bonded group, although it is important to recognize that students and instructors belong to communities both within and outside of the university. The task of building community for us, however, is made problematic by the fact that course structures in which our practice takes place brings together many different people—in class, age, gender, race, ethnicities, as well as their resultant experiences with power and politics and their educational, personal, and cultural manifestations.

In this context Susan's focus of concern was: How do we work together across these differences? "Equal voice" to Susan meant being able to raise questions and express alternative perspectives and still feel a sense of acceptance and belonging. In addition to the ability to speak and be heard, she also felt that there is a responsibility on each of us to be receptive to hearing voices other than our own. Thus, for Susan an important justification for the "critical community of equal voices" was that it can allow for the development of understanding and informed actions in relation to our differences. This understanding is likely to emerge, Bob emphasized, only in a climate of openness and trust where each member's voice is accepted and valued as a contribution to that end.

At the same time, however, we all believed that members of a critical community should be willing to engage in mutual critique of contributed thoughts and ideas, but in a way that does not violate anyone's human dignity. Put simply, we sought a class where people engage in a constant process of re-examining taken-for-granted or "commonsense" assumptions. In Susan's words, the role of the educator is to create with others situations in which people can both support and critique, can mutually construct understandings, and can connect thoughts and actions.

Bob argued that if our educational goals include contributing toward greater equality and social justice in the larger society, then we must examine ways that our small actions at a local level can be congruent with that global goal. A critical community offers a structure in which the active pursuit of democratic and caring ideals can be explored, practiced, and critiqued. As Susan stated, by participating in such a forum where these ideals can be developed, we seek to make our global goals more possible.

Similar issues and concerns were discussed in Sue's rationale. However, since she has not had the experience in the classroom to explore her concerns regarding critical and democratic communities, her explanation tended to be based on her beliefs about the ways schools ought to be. But also, Sue's focus was on high school students rather than on graduate students. It is her belief that students' voices are not heard enough in the classroom and that educational institutions, particularly public ones, do not support or encourage the expression of students' voices. She considers that if these voices can be tapped and explored early enough, and a supportive atmosphere created in the classroom to share these voices, students will internalize a sense of trust in expressing their voices. For her, the importance of this research is in how she can develop her own strategies in building critical communities of secondary students.

As a full-time doctoral student interested in designing a dissertation study that would involve action research, Eduardo was interested in the topic from yet another focal point. While he agreed on the desirability of such a community, he noted its improbability given asymmetrical power relations, the lack of a minimal consensus on a shared purpose, and the uncertainty as to whether people possessed the required knowledge, skills, and dispositions to create it. Despite the fact that these could be changed and developed, the time required might make the task unattainable.

Eduardo's comments highlighted the formidable, even naive, nature of our concern. Some critics of the "emancipatory" form of action research (e.g., Winter, 1987) have drawn attention to the inadvisability of choosing an unattainable goal. We were aware, too, of Ellsworth's (1989) critique of forms of critical pedagogy that clearly matched our intent. These concerns notwithstanding, we decided to embark on a series of actions, loosely coupled into two cycles, designed to intervene in the obvious imbalance in the class and hopefully to improve our understanding of what was involved in such an idealistic goal. To do less seemed not only to deny any hope, but also to contradict the notion that knowledge could emerge from action by practitioners—in this case, us.

BEGINNING A CYCLE OF ACTIONS: A FOCUS ON SMALL GROUPS

As with many of the class participants, the cycles of our action research emerged over time as we met together to discuss issues and plan class sessions. This section describes a portion of the class meetings in which we tried various activities designed to both continue our attention to student voice, while at the same time building communities within our classroom. For example, when discussing data analysis (in the sixth week), we made another effort to highlight the voices of practitioner-students by advancing the notion that practitioners possess the potential for generating knowledge. Specifically, we emphasized the use of data to shape and articulate students' own theories as an acceptable alternative to using data only for testing someone else's theory. The purpose of this action was in part to demystify theory and help students recognize that practitioners, as well as academic researchers, can engage in theory building. As Lawrence Stenhouse noted:

> Good teachers are necessarily autonomous in professional judgment. They do not need to be told what to do. They are not professionally the dependents of research-ers or superintendents, of innovators or supervisors. This does not mean that they do not welcome access to ideas created by other people at other places or in other times. Nor do they reject advice, consultancy or support. But they do know that ideas and people are not of much real use until they are digested to the point where they are subject to the teacher's own judgment. In short, it is the task of all educationalists outside the classroom to serve the teachers; for only they are in the position to create good teaching. (Stenhouse, in Rudduck & Hopkins, 1985, pp. 104–105)

Data from the students' projects could serve as the basis for recognizing and articulating the theories embedded in their practices. As we will address later, this highly individualized notion of teacher knowledge and theory building actu-ally may have served to act in tension with the notion of community building.

After reflecting on the first three classes, we recognized that our own language was excluding the nonteachers in the class, and therefore we decided to change our language from discussing "teacher" research to referring to "prac-titioner" research. A conscious effort also was made to extend examples of action research to include school administrators and counselors.

Our observations of the second class had indicated that even in smaller groups, certain students, notably the most experienced practitioners and those in the highest status positions, were still dominating the discussion. This confirmed our initial concern, which we then announced in the third class meeting, explain-ing that the focus of our own action research project was how our teaching practices could promote the development of a democratic community of equal voices. Our intent was not only to model the development of an appropriate concern for an action research study, but also to fulfill an ethical obligation to keep the class informed of our research in which they were inevitably involved. Such announcements also served to maintain attention on the need for us to work together to create equal voices within the class community.

A process for forming project groups also was initiated during this third class by asking students to share their current interests or concerns in two groups, each led by one of the instructors, who recorded each student's stated concern. At our weekly planning meeting we created common interest groups from the two lists and formed small groups around them for the following class. We stressed, however, that the groups were only tentative and that students should feel free to change groups as they clarified their concerns and if they identified other groups whose interests were a more appropriate match.

In subsequent weeks, there were some changes; however, the membership of the groups appeared to become reasonably stable. To stimulate thinking about how students wanted their groups to function, they were asked to set their own agendas by addressing three questions.

1. What kinds of things do you wish to share in your groups?
2. How do you want to go about sharing? (Not only the procedural aspects, but how you want to function as a group)
3. What role would you like Susan and Bob to·play in your group efforts now, and after the course is over?

We suggested that they might want to revisit the handout on collectively led groups discussed during the first weeks of class. Written group responses to these three questions were collected and tabulated by Sue for our weekly planning session.

The responses to the first question indicated that most groups wished to emphasize the sharing of data collection and analysis techniques. Some groups identified a desire to share more general problems encountered in their action research endeavors, which one group described as a need to "share our struggles." As far as ways of sharing were concerned, there was less unanimity. Some groups mentioned in general terms a "loose" or "open" structure for sharing and providing suggestions or functioning as "a sounding board," while others discussed specific ideas such as dividing up the time allocated so that each member receives equal time. Finally, most groups expected feedback and guidance on the action research process from the two instructors, although one group did discuss the idea that Susan and Bob participate in their group only when invited. This group, the one in which Eduardo and Sue participated, included primarily full-time students who were working on projects that involved them as collaborators with people outside the class. The group also contained a disproportionate number of foreign students, several of whom worked on projects related to their assistantships or to their dissertation interests. Their primary worry seemed to be to provide a space where their concerns could be aired safely, given some of their dual roles as students and collaborators in someone else's practice.

The small group discussions also left hints of issues that would re-emerge later: concern with the "fuzziness" of action research, with being "guinea pigs" in the instructors' project, with being treated as "objects," and with course requirements. Overall, though, each group seemed to be developing comfortable parameters for their conversations and their ability to articulate concerns. Many expressed the need for class time to meet, as their schedules did not coincide well.

Time was provided each week for project groups to meet, during which each group could set its own agenda since decisions had now been made on what everyone wished to share. This in-class time was well received. Bob and Susan's role during these subsequent sessions was to move around the groups and provide feedback and guidance on their action research endeavors, as requested. Usually, however, rather than offer direct authoritative answers, they tried to ask questions to promote the students' own critical thinking about actions or data collection methods being planned, about data being analyzed, or about understandings of the action research process being examined and clarified.

Later in the course, in the context of discussing three assigned readings of action research case studies, students were asked to begin thinking and talking about in their small groups guidelines for writing their own project reports. The groups were asked to consider the format for reporting on projects and the criteria they thought should be applied to the evaluation of project reports. A whole class discussion followed to share initial ideas. Although each project (which in most cases meant each individual) was asked to hand in a statement outlining proposed reporting format and evaluation criteria, both of which were intended to be negotiated with the instructors, two groups elected to offer a common proposal that had been agreed on by group members.

A REFOCUS ON A WHOLE CLASS COMMUNITY

In our group reflections on our focus on small group work, we noted that our concern had became one of promoting multiple democratic communities rather than a single class community. Our response to this realization was first to recognize the need for some information on the extent to which students felt a sense of community in their small groups, and second to plan a pedagogical action that would refocus attention on developing a whole class community. In the first case, we sought, during the tenth week, voluntary assistance with some data collection for our project. Prior to that session, we had agreed to shift the discourse from "critical" to "democratic" communities, feeling in general that the term was closer to the ways that people in the class, as well as we, addressed the issues. Responses to the following three questions were requested:

1. What does your action research group mean to you at this point in the semester?
2. To what extent do you feel that the groups that have formed in this class are becoming democratic communities?
3. How does the action research group relate to other groups both in this class and in other settings (e.g., other classes, school, work, home, etc.)?

Responses to the questions were not extensive and generally emphasized a support group notion where interests and concerns could be shared in an atmosphere of safety and trust. The group was seen as a vehicle for helping "to articulate ideas," "solve technical problems," and generally "help see the project through." One group, however, described a motivating force "where there is pressure to perform."

In response to the second question, most responses conveyed a feeling that the groups were becoming democratic communities, with two students arguing that they experienced a democratic community from the start. Groups were most commonly perceived as democratic communities because of members' respect for each person and his or her views, the effort to give each project an equal share of time and attention, and the capacity for each member to be sincere without offending the others. Two individuals, however, indicated that they did not belong to democratic community groups, in both cases because they believed such communities cannot be created when people are assigned to groups.

Responses to the third question were quite diverse, with family and personal relationships being the most often mentioned groups to which students felt their action research group was related. On the other hand, a small majority of students suggested that their group did not relate to any other group. Sue discussed how our group afforded her the opportunity for heightened self-reflection and inquiry into concepts that have become meaningful to her both professionally and personally. She stated that without the group, this exploration would not have occurred. Regarding the extent of her group becoming a democratic community, Sue was one of the students who held that from the beginning the members operated from a democratic stance. With regard to how her group related to other groups in her life, Sue said that she was beginning to look at her relationships with others a little differently, paying particular attention to, and giving weight to, her own voice.

Despite these comments about the smaller groups, and perhaps because of a growing awareness, prompted by Eduardo's comments, of the highly individualistic nature of the course, we shared a continuing concern about the lack of a sense of community among the whole class. As a result of our group meeting, during which Sue and Eduardo played a much larger role in the class planning than before, we decided to use the film "Stand and Deliver" during the eleventh week to create a shared experience among everyone in the class, which would offer an alternative medium through which understandings could be explored. Our sense was that the visual images of teaching would provide a more broadly accessible entry into discussion than that of academic writings. A large circle was formed in class for discussion instead of the usual seating arrangement in rows or small circles. Although there were clearly still silences, particularly across race and national origin, 20 people contributed to the discussion, making a notable increase from the six to ten who usually participated actively.

As a result, the large circle arrangement was continued for the discussion of readings segment of the next class. Again more people talked than in prior whole class discussions in rows, but not as many as in the previous week when the film provided the stimulus for discussion. As students thought through the nature of action research in developing educational practice, questions posed by the readings were evident. Some were about the tension between democracy and social engineering in action research (see Noffke, 1989), first in the response to the role of university faculty involved in promoting action research with their students, and second in relation to the project groups in class.

In discussing the proposed presentation of project reports to be given during the last two class sessions, Susan and Bob reiterated concern for promoting a whole community in the class and enabling everyone to hear from people whose position and interests in education are different from their own. In groups, each project was asked to decide whether or not they wished to make an oral presentation, and if so, with whom (individual project, project group, or subgrouping of projects) and to whom (small group or whole class). In the final two class sessions, project reports were presented, beginning with three concurrent sessions of two small group presentations, followed by a break over shared refreshments, and then three whole class presentations. Interestingly, only one of the groups with multiple projects decided on a single collaborative presentation. That group was the group of collaborators to which Eduardo and Sue belonged.

As Sue noted, the decision to present a single collaborative effort did not come easily. The six people in the group were working on other people's research, and did not think it was going to be possible to work collectively on a presentation. Yet they wanted to. Rather than working individually or in pairs, they finally decided that a talk show format might work well, with some of the individuals supporting collaboration in action research and some rejecting it. Eduardo was the moderator. They all agreed that collaboration in other people's research was problematic and that it was their hope that they would project to the audience the dilemmas they experienced in exploring their roles as collaborators.

WHAT WE LEARNED ABOUT CREATING
DEMOCRATIC COMMUNITIES

How do *we* create a sense of critical or democratic community? Perhaps one of the most telling reflections on the whole of our process lies in the need either to transform our sense of "we" to include our own students more directly in the process or to narrow our focus to attend more carefully to the ways in which our actions actually constrain the students' own communities from emerging. One instance of this lies in our formation of groups around what we perceived to be common interests in the course. Most tellingly, this was an example of many instances in which "we," particularly Susan and Bob as instructors for the course, presumed that we knew what constituted a "critical community." Many students viewed this process as one of assignment to a group and felt uncomfortable in initiating any movement to another group. On questioning these students about this reluctance, they indicated a concern that their actions would be interpreted as a rejection of the group. Paradoxically, given our concern, the stronger the sense of community in a group, the more unlikely it became that a member would elect to transfer to another group even if his or her concern was closer to those being discussed in another group. On the other hand, we could argue that the stronger the sense of community, the more likely that an individual's need for support (and hopefully critique) was being met. Yet, students in their course evaluation did focus a great deal of attention on the various kinds of communities they experienced in the course. Several noted personal and academic sharing as benefits, while others noted that without prior commitment to a "critical perspective," groups actually functioned to reinforce what they felt to be oppressive conditions in schools.

Perhaps also paradoxically, some of the most salient issues in the development of our understanding of the process of working toward more critical or democratic communities came not from our analysis of the data from our students, although this was clearly important, but from our examination of the whole of the process as we experienced it. After we collated and analyzed information from course evaluations, we each wrote responses to questions related to our understanding of critical communities.

In some ways the differences that emerged mirror those present in our rationales, that is, as a group, we too were just beginning to find ways to express our understandings of the barriers of time, power, and ideology in the development of communities. Eduardo's comments seem appropriate here.

> In our group, either expressly or tacitly, we reached consensus on certain points throughout the semester, and I consider that we are still working at it. In other words, we have agreed on some points, or so it seems. I am understanding consensus as more than simply agreeing to meet and work on the project. It has been interesting to note that *we have not agreed on common definitions*. Although the issue has come up at times, we have agreed to avoid it. . . . We have agreed to engage in action research, but not on what action research is. We have agreed that creating a critical community of equal voices is valuable and desirable, but not on why this is so.

We had only one semester together, yet touched on many issues dear to each of us. We were each challenged, yet also very careful in the issues we raised. Power relations within our group, silences, and differences remain only partially addressed. Yet we agreed to and continued to work together across those, or at least seemed to. In Eduardo's words:

It seems that, as the group becomes smaller, the specific ways in which power relationships operate are more salient, thus making it easier to modify them (or to maintain them) by all parts concerned.

Because of our differing identities and locations in relation to power in society, we have brought out a lot of different perspectives on our topic. We began, at least at the end, to act together, if not to think together, which seems at least to be another beginning.

ISSUES AND DILEMMAS IN TEACHING ACTION RESEARCH

This course was taught within degree programs in a graduate school of education. As such, we operated within a set of assumptions already well critiqued within action research circles (Noffke & Brennan, 1991; Stevenson, 1991). Time constraints, well-entrenched patterns of teaching–learning relationships (including those framed by the large numbers of students whom teachers and other educational practitioners encounter daily), as well as the competitive grading structures affected our work. Some, however, were unique to university settings. These included the definition of teaching load, especially across departments, the concurrent roles of faculty in courses and on dissertation/thesis committees, publication versus teaching demands, as well as the framing of an incremental kind of learning within a semester course sequence.

In some ways, these issues, while significant, hide more powerful constraints on both the teaching of action research and our particular concern with doing so within our own pedagogical frameworks. Highly individualistic and unproblematized notions of liberal democracy, without attention to the failings across gender, class, and race that that model has tolerated, permeated our actions. These interacted particularly at points of our individualistic notions of teacher knowledge and theory building. Inadvertently, our concern with trying to legitimate student voices seemed to work against the creation of critical communities. First, by not initially addressing conceptions of action research in the literature, students were left in a confused state about what constituted action research. They had an insufficient basis on which to construct their own understanding. Second, our focus on individually formulated definitions of action research may have fragmented relationships among members of some groups and across groups. Instead of encouraging students to question and challenge each other's understanding, there was often a relativistic acceptance of other students' definitions. In other words, critiques of individual conceptions were silenced by the belief that everyone was entitled to construct their own understanding, irrespective of whether that understanding was logically flawed. An excerpt from Susan's journal reflects this concern.

Eduardo's insights are again helpful. We have, by focusing on having "them" develop their own definitions of action research, set up an individualistic framework for the course. "Choosing" one's own definitions of action research ignores the basis of choice. Can we get folks, including ourselves, to look at why *this* definitions over others—"values"/ideology, biography, structure, context, etc.?

Studying, teaching, and learning through action research do not occur within a vacuum. We live out, in our educational settings, the same structures that permeate other institutions in society. Yet, perhaps, by living action research, while we seek to teach others about it, we move closer toward living the same contradictions we ask others, through its practice, to address.

6

Confused on a Higher Level
About More Important Things!

Catherine Battaglia

For the past 5 years I have been employed as a staff developer for a large, inner-city school district in western New York. My work focuses on designing and conducting staff development programs to improve teaching and learning. To that end, my school district regularly has offered an Instructional Theory Into Practice Seminar (ITIP) for its tenured instructional staff that is designed to examine in-depth current research on teaching and learning practices. The intent of this seminar is to spark interest and encourage continued professional dialogue and growth among teachers. However, we also recognize that teachers need ongoing support in their classrooms. It was this need to develop a support component for our staff development program that led to my action research study.

When ITIP was first conceived, initial plans included the concept of support but did not specifically address what the support would look like or how it would be implemented in the district. More important, these plans did not discuss what the role of the staff developer would be in that process. I envisioned coaching as central to this follow-up support, but I knew that meant I would need to study myself in action as a coach.

This chapter describes the phases of my study and explains the ways in which action research served to help me understand my professional self. What initially began as a study of the coaching process and my role as a coach, emerged as more of a personal journey into the thinking, language, and even the dispositions I bring to my work. The most significant learning occurred when I shifted from being the practitioner to the student of practice.

BACKGROUND TO THE ITIP PROGRAM

At the time of this writing approximately 300 teachers (from a population of about 700) have taken part in the ITIP program over a 4-year period. Teachers and administrators are invited and may choose to take any one of three, 30-hour cycles of ITIP seminars that are offered during the school day and paid for through individual building plan funds. Although the program is based on research regarding effective teaching, my staff development colleague and I have endeavored to restructure the content in an effort to downplay the technical, positivistic interpretations of teacher practice. Our version of the ITIP material emphasizes teaching as a creative, decision-making activity rather than as a routinized, habitual act that can rely on field-tested recipes. The program emphasizes a constructivist approach in which teachers are seen as reflective decision makers who are involved in sense-making activities. Our ITIP program, like other courses we offer at the staff development center, adheres to the following tenets of teaching and learning:

1. Teachers create knowledge about their practice by reflecting on their physical and mental actions. Meaningful staff development, therefore, poses tasks that bring about conceptual reorganizations in teachers, helping them integrate new knowledge into their existing structures of knowledge.
2. Learning is a social process and teachers require an environment where they can engage in reflective discourse about their practice with members of their profession.
3. An important goal of teacher education is the emergence of empowered learners who question, investigate, and reason about their work and who find joy in learning.

When the program was first conceived by members of the district staff development advisory committee, it was hoped that staff development that took place during the regular workday would produce better results than that which is available after school. Since it is part of the workday, there is no monetary or course credit compensation for attendance. Participation is viewed by teachers as a reward in and of itself.

When I began my action research, administrators reported seeing the impact of ITIP in their schools. For example, they noted that teachers were talking more about *teaching* and less about *students*; that is, they were discussing things they did and thought about in regard to the teaching process instead of focusing on incidents involving individual students. Administrators also reported that teachers were speaking favorably about the ITIP course and encouraging colleagues to participate. In fact, teachers were so enthusiastic about their experiences that, when surveyed, they explained that they needed and would appreciate some kind of personal contact in their classrooms to support them in their attempts to enhance and improve their practice. They asserted that without such support, they would tend to fall back into old routines and patterns regardless of their good intentions to implement innovative practices.

COACHING SUPPORT

Anticipating this need for classroom support, my colleague, Terri Guerrucci, and I developed a coaching component as follow-up for the seminar. Our rationale for what would become known as the "Follow-up and Support Component of the ITIP Program" was as follows:

1. Without support, teachers transfer few ideas from workshop to workplace. With coaching, they are more likely to incorporate changes and innovations.

2. Teaching often is done in isolation. Teacher-to-teacher support, whether found in a teacher-coach or peer coaching relationship, can enhance collegiality among professionals.

3. A support component to the regular instructional program would cause a "ripple effect" and continue to activate a spirit of professional improvement throughout the district.

4. Many of the teachers in our district have been teaching a long time. Without continual coaching and support, many new programs, such as Whole Language, Cooperative Learning, and Tactics for Thinking, will have limited impact for teachers who have not had the opportunity to update their skills.

We had been studying several support models to find components that would fit our philosophy of staff development. We attended many conferences and learned to use several different coaching and supervision processes, but none of them seemed to capture the overall intention of our program, that is, the encouragement and development of reflective practice. Many clinical supervision models, for example, claim to view the teacher as a decision maker, but place much emphasis on the observer's ability to name and label instructional decisions and the behaviors that accompany them. Much of the literature and training implied that teachers draw from a somewhat similar and discrete body of knowledge and that they utilize a language derived from that knowledge. In other words, if one did not know how to, for example, "set the minds of the learners," "task analyze a learning," or "plan for active participation," one couldn't coach or be coached. In addition, these models assumed that there was only one way to view a lesson and that the coach would observe, script, and "play back" that version during the postconference period. I wrote about this concern in my journal.

> From what I have seen, many of the models seek to label and subsequently correct teaching behavior. . . . "I saw you do _____ and I called it _____. What you did had _____ effect on the learners." . . . etc. I am concerned that many approaches really stem from a deficit mentality, a "fix

'em up" perspective. I am concerned that they do not accomplish what they theoretically intend to do and risk leaving teachers with feelings of inadequacy in the process.

In an effort to understand these various coaching models and gain a sense of how each worked, Terri and I practiced coaching one another. We shared insights regarding both aspects of the process: how it felt to be *the coach* and how it felt to *be coached*. During this period of investigation, I continued to be uncomfortable with the models and self-conscious about the need to speak precisely about an inexact subject like teaching. I felt there had to be something better.

In December 1990, I had the opportunity to see Arthur Costa and Robert Garmston present their version of cognitive coaching at the National Staff Development Conference in Toronto, Canada. This model was different from the ones with which I had been working, for its intent was to coach teacher *thinking*, not *behavior*. Its major premise was that people construct their own meaning to make sense of the world around them; the coaching process is a vehicle to enhance, stimulate, and develop intellectual functions of professionals. They believe, as I do, that teaching cannot be reduced to a formula or a recipe. Costa, Garmston, & Lambert write:

> Teaching is thinking. Effective teaching involves the cognitive, perception, and decision-making strategies that teachers use as they plan, teach, analyze, evaluate (reflect), and apply improvements to their own teaching. (1988, p. 151)

I liked that. It recognized that a teacher's observable classroom performance is based on internal, invisible thought processes that drive the overt skills of teaching (Joyce & Showers, 1988). Philosophically, I felt more comfortable with the cognitive coaching concept, but I recognized that, before making it a part of our program, I needed to study myself in action.

THE MEANING OF "MY PRACTICE"

Action research involves improving an aspect of one's practice. Early in my journal I asked, "What exactly is my practice? What aspects combine to define what my practice is?" In other words, I needed to really understand the nature of my work before I began the process of trying to improve it. These became key questions for me because I was confused about how I would study myself without simultaneously studying other people or the effects my behavior had on other people. Later I also came to realize that even posing these questions was a way of improving practice since clarity of intent and purpose help to focus action.

I began looking closely at all facets of my work as a staff developer, involving teaching and coaching teachers. This helped me realize that interactions with others form the basis of my practice. I began to see that a study of my practice would include those interactions. I wrote in my journal:

> While I may need to observe and study the behavior of others in order to see what it is I may need to change or the results of changes already made, the intent of that study is to better understand myself. Improving my practice, therefore, does not mean improving other people; unless, of course, helping other people improve is the object of my practice.

The difficulty for me was in trying to maintain the focus on *my* actions and *my* decisions so that I could better understand *my* practice.

MY FIRST ACTION CYCLE

My first action involved working with Jaye, a highly motivated, experienced, competent math teacher. Previously, he had approached me with a concern that I documented in my journal.

> Jaye is really interested in cooperative learning and wants to experiment with ways to engage his students in the classroom so that he is not the "sage on the stage" but more of a "guide on the side." Jaye is concerned that he is the leader, expert, and star performer in his classroom. He feels that too much responsibility for student engagement rests on him and this has left many of his students unaccountable for staying focused. He knows a little about cooperative learning and thinking skill instruction, and is in favor of incorporating some of these in his repertoire, but he doesn't know how to begin or what to do to teach the skills of cooperative learning to his students.

While this presented me with an ideal context in which to study myself in action, it posed additional concerns for me as well. In many ways, this was a very uncomfortable place for me to begin because I do not feel particularly confident about my mathematical ability. I can recall worrying that I might find it difficult to sustain a prolonged coaching relationship with him because, before too long, he would see me as an impostor (someone who doesn't really know anything about math) and would seek out a more knowledgeable, legitimate mentor. I wrote:

> I am awed by Jaye's expertise! How will I step into this math world where I know so little? I am very aware that I need to work hard to earn his re-

spect and continued support of the process. But two things are happening right now that are really good: I am facilitating a need for Jaye, who really is motivated to make some changes in his practice, and, by the same token, I am in a wonderful position to use this partnership to study the process of cognitive coaching. While I work with Jaye and support him in his efforts to change the interactions in his class, I will be studying my behavior and the effect that it has on him and the way he approaches his teaching practice.

Planning the Coaching Project

I set up a meeting with Jaye and, together, we planned our coaching project. He needed to define for me what support and involvement he wanted. I remember being mindful of the fact that I was working for him; my role was to support and facilitate, not lead and manipulate. We talked openly about this distinction and I asked him to help me monitor my coaching moves to ensure that I remained consistent. Having aired the ground rules and discussed the process, we scheduled our first coaching session.

Our first interaction was very interesting. I literally rehearsed what I would say to Jaye. This rehearsal was more of an effort to practice what it was that I would avoid saying to him, since I was beginning to be aware of my language. The words of Thomas Greenfield (1982) were ever-present in my thoughts: "Language is Power. It literally makes reality appear and disappear. Those who control language control thought—and thereby themselves and others" (p. 8). I felt burdened by this responsibility. Even though I didn't yet know how a coaching session should look, I did have some sense of what a nonexample would be like. My experience told me that developing trust was an integral part of the process, and many years of teaching and working with teachers helped me learn how to bring this about.

To my surprise, Jaye was even more nervous than I was during this initial encounter. It was his planning period, and we had agreed to meet prior to his fourth-period class so that we could preconference about his lesson. I can recall that I arrived at his classroom a few minutes earlier than expected and saw him coming down the hall. His face looked pale and serious, like he really did not want me there or regretted that he'd asked me to come. I was uncomfortable knowing that I was precipitating his discomfort, but I knew, intuitively, that I would have to learn how to work through this with him. At that moment, I remember thinking, "Forget about coaching . . . just be a human being and you'll get through this!" That's what I did; I relied on my "people skills"—friendliness, empathy, humor—to get me past that initial discomfort. I tried to be conscious of my body language (I wanted to look confident, yet relaxed and friendly), my communication (I consciously worked to paraphrase his thinking in order to be sure that we were understanding one another), and my trust (I openly shared my anxieties with him in order to help him see that I, too, felt awkward with this first step).

Reflection

Several sessions later, when we came to know and trust one another more, Jaye and I talked at length about that first session, and he helped me understand some of the dynamics of what took place. As he perused his own reflective thoughts and writings, he told me that, at the time, he was uncomfortable at that first session because he was concerned that his nervous reaction would cause me to feel uneasy about our working together. Through his journal and written feedback, I came to see how important it is that a coaching relationship begin with establishing a safe, comfortable climate with the teacher.

In addition, Jaye brought an interesting idea to my attention. He wrote that I had invaded his "bubble of expertise." He explained that this meant that I had entered his "math world," and he now felt a heightened sense of awareness and accountability. He told me that he was very protective of that "bubble" during our first session. He remembered talking more about math teaching than teaching in general. Interestingly enough, I was working to do just the opposite. I knew that Jaye had a high degree of regard for me and that was precisely the reason why I did not want to play the role of "the expert." I guess, in a way, I was hoping that he would pierce that "bubble" and let me inside. Eventually, that happened.

In fact, later on in the semester when Jaye became more of a collaborator in this project, he articulated how our working together broke down several "barriers." He said:

> Historically, math teachers know it all—there's an aura to math, you know—I know it and you [don't]—I think for the mentor system to work, you need to break down the barriers. This has been the best stewardship of my life because of the barriers being eliminated. You are a female, a non-math person, and younger than me—just look at all the barriers that breaks down! This really breaks the stereotype of what happens in math. And the humor is helpful, too. Your letters show me that you care and that we have an understanding—that takes time to write and I appreciate it. I think friendship is a plus for a good mentorship.

I continue to find it interesting that Jaye regarded our relationship as a mentorship, even though we spoke of and used the language of coaching. I was careful to defer to his judgment about how to integrate some of the cooperative strategies we were trying to implement, and my transcripts reveal that I repeatedly used phrases such as: "What do you think about . . . " and "In what ways might we . . . " and "In your experience, how would this work?" Despite these attempts, Jaye always solicited my opinion. He explained it this way: "Cathy, if I could figure out how to do this all by myself, then I wouldn't need you here, would I?"

I began thinking about many other questions as a result of that early session. In fact, as my journal and notes indicate, I started to bounce around from one idea to another, because I was overwhelmed with the research possibilities that could be studied through coaching. Further reflection at the time of this writing has me thinking that being inundated with wonderful ideas and ambiguous possibilities is a dissonant yet necessary part of the action research process. It really is a matter of making sense of a messy situation. My background in creative problem solving helped me be patient with this. I will comment further about this insight at the end of this chapter.

As I read my journal entry of February 6, I can see how language-related issues kept recycling through my thoughts, for I asked: "How do teachers come to create an epistemology for their practice?" and "How might I become more aware of the suppositions embedded in my dialoguing about teaching practice?" I continued:

> What kind of dialogue about teaching is of the most worth? What is it we hope to accomplish when we engage teachers in discussions related to their teaching practice? What does it mean to coach teacher thinking as opposed to teacher behavior? What kind of thinking? What does a coaching session look like and how does it sound? How will I learn to use the language of reflection?

I studied these questions carefully in order to understand what it was that I was asking. I saw that the first question regarding how teachers produce knowledge and form a language about their practice was "other-related," meaning that it focused more on *other* teachers and less on me and *my* actions. The second group of questions was very different. Here I seemed to be thinking about *my* language interactions; the words, patterns, concepts I send to others. In addition, I think I was struggling to create a sense of what a "good" conference would "sound like"; by "sound like," I think I was searching for a definition or a model I could create to help guide my actions. At this point, I began to study my language interactions with Jaye.

A SECOND ACTION CYCLE

I spent a considerable amount of time thinking about how to initiate a discussion with Jaye during both the preconference and postconference phases of our sessions. I remembered Art Costa's admonishments about presuppositions in language: the implicit messages embedded in our conversation. I knew I needed to be careful about making value judgments or focusing him on my version of reality. I wanted us to engage in reflective discourse; I didn't want to sound like I was checking up on him. There was an expectation that we would discuss his teaching, so the question for me was how to bring that about.

Planning

Looking back over my notes from those early planning stages, I can see the intense thinking I generated regarding this issue. I must have brainstormed about two dozen questions in an attempt to find some that matched the intent of what it was I was aiming to do. This was not an easy process, but I was adamant about not usurping Jaye's control or decision making in his class; I wanted to be a helpful partner.

Some of the ideas included in those early notes were:

1. Tell me what you're going to do today.
2. What's this lesson going to be about?
3. As you thought about the lesson for today, what was it you were thinking about?
4. When you picture yourself teaching this lesson, what concerns come to mind?
5. How does this lesson connect with your overall goals for this class?
6. What role would you like me to play today?
7. Is there anything specific you would like me to look for or do?
8. Where would you like me to sit?
9. Should I take notes?

These last questions were intended to let Jaye know that he was the one who was going to define my role in this session. In other words, I was working for him; he was not working for me. I later found out that he really appreciated this "invitational approach." In one of his final correspondences to me he indicated that this effort did not go unnoticed.

Questions 3, 4, and 5, were the kind of questions I ultimately used at the next session. I decided that they were more engaging and different from 1 or 2, both of which had a kind of demanding ring to them . . . *"tell me. . . ."* I knew that Jaye's time was valuable to him (he was already sacrificing much of his valued planning period in order to meet before and after his class), so it was important for us to use the time we had efficiently, avoiding too much extraneous conversation.

A Second Action

I approached our next two sessions with an informal script that had some of the questions I had generated as guides. I explained to Jaye why I was doing this, and he commented that he appreciated my diligence; he later admitted that he was relieved to find that I wasn't "real slick" and polished at first, for this made him feel that we were truly struggling to learn about coaching together. I was happy about that, because I wanted to be seen as an authentic student.

The first of these two sessions went well. We used our time compactly and Jaye really did the majority of the talking and reflecting, as I had hoped. As I play back that taped conversation, I can see that he was thinking about his thinking and decision making and was not just focusing on his actions. In other words, his comments helped me to see that he was thinking about *why* he did what he did; he was less preoccupied with the "doing." For example, he used phrases such as: "It's really important for me that the kids . . . ," "Whenever I do this I find myself . . . ," "You need to understand that this is why," . . . and so forth. He made a strong effort to explain his practice to me, which, in turn, seemed to facilitate his own reflection. What I realize is that it was important for him to articulate the beliefs and principles that serve as the foundation for his practice. It was as though he was saying, "This is who I am, what I believe, and what I feel is important."

However, at our following session a week later, something unexpected occurred. Jaye was very anxious about his teaching. We were working together to integrate some complicated cooperative strategies with his students and, as a result, he was experiencing some problems (i.e., moving students in and out of base groups, cueing students, approximating wait time, etc.). I documented this event in my journal.

> I worked with Jaye again and something he said really troubled me. We have just begun working on rather sophisticated procedures (Jigsawing, Heads Together, Expert Groups, etc.) and I have tried to make him feel that it is OK for him to not be achieving a smooth transition at the moment. He is really doing so much and has come along so far from the way he used to work with those kids (this is his perception as told to me – not my evaluation of his "progress"). Today, when I left our coaching session he said he was "sorry" that the lesson did not go as well as he would have liked and that he wanted to apologize for "wasting my time." I was very concerned about why he perceived the lesson to be a total failure, and I worked with him to reflect back on the significant highlights of it. He is such a perfectionist that it is difficult for him to accept affirmation about what he felt went right, unless it is in the absence of error. My concerns are: What happened in our conversation that might have triggered this emo-

tion in Jaye, and how could I (1) avoid this language, and (2) try to refocus the discourse in the event that we begin getting into this again?

After much thinking and "reliving" the experience with my colleague and collaborator, Terri, I realized that this session went poorly because I became a little too cavalier in my approach and, inadvertently, asked Jaye a question that immediately triggered him to evaluate his teaching rather than just talk about some of the things that were central to his thinking. "Is this such a bad thing to do?" I questioned. "Shouldn't he evaluate his teaching? Isn't that part of the process?" I decided that while self-assessment may be a result of reflection, it should not color one's thinking entirely, nor should it be the starting point for a coaching session. I realized that I usually begin all our sessions with questions such as these:

1. Talk a little about what happened for you as you were teaching today?
2. What felt good?
3. Why did it feel good?
4. What did you do to bring that about?
5. What would you want to do again if you were to teach this lesson at another time?
6. What does this affirm for you?

I came to understand that my mistake was in opening with the question, "So, how do you think it went today?" which immediately triggered a very emotional, evaluative response that shaped the remainder of the conversation. I wrote:

> Jaye is so careful about what he does with those kids, and quick to assess the downside of his action, neglecting to see the more positive aspects of his moves. Once fixated on these thoughts, he was reluctant to accept that there had been any redeeming features in that lesson and was more resistant than usual to talk about what had transpired. Next time, I think I might want to try saying something different, like, "Let's look at your purpose for teaching this lesson. Talk a little bit about some of the decisions you made that helped you achieve your purpose."

I think that this was a good "mistake," because it afforded me the opportunity to extrapolate some important principles about coaching teacher thinking. For one thing, it reinforced the need for me to be very focused about the kind of language I use. It is easy to become sloppy in this respect, and I had now experienced the concomitant problems that could emerge. In addition, I learned that it was better to go from the specific to the general in terms of reflection. It was better, for example, to look at specific incidents, actions, and decisions and then summarize the whole in a reflective way, rather than begin the discussion with a general view that would become the lens through which the entire teaching scenario would be perceived.

When I studied the notes from our meeting more carefully, I realized that there were some themes that were repeated through many of our discussions. I could see some categories and patterns that I did not initially realize. I documented these insights in my journal and wrote: "I am beginning to see that we often talk about Jaye's concern about keeping the attention of his students, now that he has them working in more cooperative arrangements. He is afraid they may be 'checking out,' to use his words. . . . He wants them 'on' and 'on' all the time. Also, he questions whether the cooperative grouping will weaken individual responsibility."

Later, I reread this journal entry:

> Cooperative learning has surfaced the need to hold students collectively and individually accountable for the learning, and this fits in nicely with much of the research on teacher expectations and student achievement. The challenge for me is: How might I use this language in my coaching sessions? In what ways might it help me develop the kinds of questions that facilitate teacher reflection? Terri and I have had many conversations about the need for a language, but I have never really been certain how to bring this about. I am beginning to see!

A NEW PLAN

It seemed appropriate to use my experiences with Jaye to develop another reconnaissance from which I could draw a new direction and plan of action. I was eager to see if the ideas I had "discovered" would indeed be helpful or even applicable to another teaching situation. So, I decided to coach Marie, a veteran elementary teacher who had invited me to work with her. I made this choice because she differed from Jaye in a number of ways: (1) She was an elementary teacher who taught all subjects, not just math; (2) she was less confident than Jaye about her teaching; and (3) she had a very different teaching style than Jaye (he was very sequentially oriented, while she was more randomly inclined). It seemed like a good idea to work in a different context and with another person in order to study some of the insights I was beginning to have.

This time, I developed a different script of questions, one that would direct attention to the concepts of *focus*, *engagement*, and *accountability*. In studying my field notes and journal entries of my coaching work and discussions with Jaye, these three concepts emerged as general categories that might be used to develop the kind of reflective dialogue I was striving to achieve. For example, we had not talked merely about teaching to an objective, but about the importance of focusing the learners on the learning and of the teacher maintaining focus on the goals of the lesson. Therefore, I came to understand that *focus* questions might be important to include in my coaching sessions. *Engagement* surfaced as another generic category as Jaye repeatedly discussed keeping the students "on" and actively involved. He also wanted to be certain that he maintained engagement with all students, including those who want to "check out." *Accountability* issues were a third area of discussion. We discussed the need for the teacher to promote a feeling of student responsibility not just for participating in learning, but for emerging with knowledge and understanding.[1]

Focusing students on the learning, keeping them actively engaged, and maintaining a level of accountability where they feel responsible and committed to the learning are not matters of style, but can be better defined as duties of the teacher. How the teacher chooses to respond to those duties is, in my view, where style-related issues emerge. It is the coach's role, therefore, to engage the teacher in discourse relative to these duties. Through reflection the teacher then may come to see and understand his or her specific actions and decisions.

Using this newly acquired language, I practiced with Terri the skills of active listening (paraphrasing, "playing back," etc.), and I was prepared to try using some statements such as: "Let me see if I understand what you're saying. . . . " and, "So, I hear you saying. . . . " For this next coaching session, I was even more intent on observing myself and my language patterns because I had already begun to see that the art of coaching is really the art of using language. I prepared a set of questions to encourage reflection about these concepts (see Table 6.1).

My final set of questions was modeled after ones that I had learned from Arthur Costa. The intent of these questions was to help the teachers summarize the teaching and coaching experience: What patterns, principles, or generalizations have emerged for you as a result of your teaching this lesson? What does this affirm for you? Is there another way to say that? What has this conference caused you to think about? What are you taking away from this conference? Where will you go from here? What role would you like me to play?

Using this script brought focus to the conference. I continued to add, delete, and refine questions until I had internalized this new language of cognitive coaching. In fact, it became a whole new way for me to converse with people, both in and outside of my practice. It kept me focused on the general areas related to instruction and helped me generate fluid, reflective discussions with those whom I coached.

Table 6.1. Questions to Encourage Reflection

Teacher Focus Questions
- What are your goals for this lesson?
- Where did they come from?
- What is a reasonable expectation for this lesson?
- How does this fit in with past/future learnings?
- As you were preparing to teach this lesson, what concerns came to mind?
- What decisions did you make in regard to those concerns?
- Help me understand . . .

Student Focus Questions
- What did you do to focus the learners on the learning?
- What indicators did you use to tell that they were focused?
- What did you observe your students doing?
- At any point in the lesson, were you concerned about their focus?
- What prompted your concern?
- What decisions did you make in regard to that concern?
- What does this tell you?
- How do you explain that?
- Would you do that again?

Student Engagement Questions
- What indicators helped you monitor student engagement?
- What does that tell you?
- As you think back about the level of engagement, what stands out for you?
- Why is that the case?
- Tell me more . . . .

Student Accountability Questions
- In what ways were you holding the learners accountable for what they were learning?
- What indicators did you use to monitor that accountability?
- At any point in the lesson, were you concerned about their accountability?
- What were you thinking when . . . ?
- Do you think the students felt accountable for their learning?
- What causes you to think so?

More Reflection

It dawned on me that these three generic themes of focus, engagement, and accountability, could actually be applied to me in my coaching role. I began to see that my job was to focus the teacher on the thinking he or she did in regard to the teaching done. By so doing, I could avoid having the discussion take into account only teacher actions and behavior. And, was it not my job to keep the teacher engaged in reflective discourse about her or his practice? So much of the energy I expended during a coaching session was in an attempt to do this very thing. Finally, there are accountability issues involved in coaching (however, at the time I was less clear about what they were). What I did know was that all educators, teachers and coaches alike, are accountable for decisions they make in regard to the teaching and coaching they do. The concept of accountability was never meant to imply blame, but rather professional responsibility that is essential to practice.

With a new set of eyes and ears, I returned to my earliest journal entries and notes to review some of my first attempts at coaching both Marie and Jaye. I was now more alert to the language of control that I initially used in my journal: "I *want to put* her at ease . . . ," "In what ways can *I have him* do . . . ," "It would be good if *I allow her* to . . . ," or, "How can *I make her see* . . . ?" The words jumped right out at me.

Why did I use such language in my journal? Was that language indicative of how I really thought about my role as a coach? I now see that I was so excited about what it was that I was learning that I was not paying attention to what now seem very strong messages about "who's in control." Although not immediately apparent, those messages were there; it was through the processes of action, reflection, and collaboration that they became visible to me. Once they were visible, I had something to study.

What I have recognized since then is that journal language is often a language of *practicing*, not practice. When we engage in journal writing, we rehearse ideas and tentatively entertain thoughts that do not always accurately convey what we mean or intend. At least, that's how it functioned for me. The conversations I had with both Jaye and Marie were sometimes different from how I portrayed them in my writing. Intuitively, I must have realized this, for in the preface to my journal, I apologize by saying:

> I now invite you into my thinking, reminding you that I know more than I can describe and can speak about things that I do not yet fully understand. Tacit knowledge plays a great role in all kinds of thinking and, particularly, in the action research process. I fear that many of my most fragile thoughts will not survive the test of explanation. What follows is a sometimes awkward search for meaning, the kind that can only be found when we have the courage to face ourselves.

At this point I felt that I had become a student of practice who, in the words of Sergiovanni and Starratt (1993), was more interested in "truth-making" than "truth-seeking." I developed a set of questions and a pattern for a coaching dialogue that I continue to use and refine today. And while I learned a great deal about my practice and about myself, I learned even more about the art of studying myself in action.

CONCLUSION

Reflections on the Action Research Process

I now believe that action research is as much a process of asking questions about one's practice as it is deciding what to do about solutions. Action research enables you to live your questions; in a way, they become the focal point of your thinking. My questions took on an almost mantra-like quality; they seemed to seep into my thinking and conversation, creep into my reading and writing when I'd least expect. They also kept me focused. I appreciate how professionally healthy it might be to adopt an "action research mentality" whereby one is always thinking about or attempting to polish another facet of the work one does. Perhaps, then, action research is an attitude or becomes an attitude that is brought to one's practice.

My enthusiasm for action research has led me to share my understanding of the process with other teachers and staff developers by using the skills and dispositions associated with the creative problem-solving process (CPS; Parnes, 1976). My research has led me to experiment with ways of helping teachers use action research on their own practice. The work of Roger van Oech, author of *A Kick in the Seat of the Pants* (1986) and *A Whack on the Side of the Head* (1983), provided strategies for helping me accept the challenge of looking at myself and my practice in new and different ways. My experiences in conducting action research, coupled with the knowledge of CPS strategies, suggest the following set of "guidelines" for those planning to initiate their own study:

Map Out Your Plans. Now that I understand the whole concept of cycles of planning, acting, observing, and reflecting, I will be more diligent about mapping out my plans to have a better sense of where I have been and where I am going. It's easy to "lose yourself in the action research process"; in fact, there were times when I became so inundated with ideas and questions I could barely see the things I needed to study.

Listen to Your Hunches. We are often taught to appeal to "those who know better"—the experts, the research, the authorities. This process taught me to trust my thinking and my ideas more . . . not in an arrogant way, but in a professional way. Journal writing and audiotaping my thoughts were powerful sources of data; the simplest ideas had a way of growing in importance once I reflected on them later. I emerged seeing the journal as a "greenhouse for ideas to be stored," until I could later use the "energy of reflection in order to help them germinate and grow." One could never be too diligent about recording all aspects of the research process, for, over time, the seemingly insignificant becomes relevant.

Solve the Right Problem . . . Whatever That Is! Problem formation is a vital part of the action research process. Just when I thought I knew what question I was asking, several more presented themselves and I grew confused over which ones should receive attention. I now say, "Attend to them all!" You never know which question is the most important.

Change Questions. The questions that I ask regarding my practice keep changing. Action research involves refining questions until you feel you have landed upon the right ones. I now see that the way you frame questions will, inevitably, determine the methodology you plan to study them. Differentiated solutions and subsequent understandings will be generated by the way questions are posed. Playing with your language in an effort to refine your thinking is vital.

Reverse Your Viewpoint. Action research is so much a matter of "seeing," that it is a good idea, I found, to develop a little intellectual schizophrenia. Be your own arbiter. Wear another hat, use a different lens, and try to unpack your thinking in a different way. The truly talented action researcher, I envision, has a "toolbox" of strategies to use to enhance the process.

Find a Second Right Answer. In CPS we were taught that nothing is more dangerous than an idea when it is the only one that you have! I have learned to not fall in love with ideas and have gained the courage to "kiss them good-bye"— especially old metaphors, which can, literally, strangle my thinking.

Afterthoughts

About midway through this project, I wrote a journal entry where I described action research as being "confused, but on a higher level and about more important things!" As I document the events and the thinking of this project in preparation for publication, I realize that there is much truth to that statement. As I write, I find that my attempt to distill experience into words is frustrating, difficult, trying, and agonizing. One fails more than one succeeds. The words that come and offer themselves as expressions never quite seem to capture my experiences. The experiences always seem just beyond the reach of words. And yet, words are the tools we use as the primary means of expressing experience. It is a challenge, and one that I know is never completely met. My words are, therefore, always provisional, incomplete, partial.

What is written here I understand for the moment, maybe for tomorrow, but maybe not. What is true is that I emerge knowing one more thing than I knew before and, although confused, I am definitely thinking at a higher level and about more important things.

Acknowledgments. I wish to thank Jaye Sturtevant and Terri Guerruccci for their thoughtful collaboration and for the enthusiasm and commitment they contributed to this project.

NOTE

1. Since this study I have added a fourth category of *dignity*. A duty of the teacher should be to keep students feeling capable and "smart." In the absence of this element, students may lose focus, become disengaged from learning, and have little or no personal commitment for trying to do well.

Part II

ACTION RESEARCH IN SCHOOLS

7

Putting the "P" into a Participation in Government Course

Gregory Bronson

I discovered action research as a means by which to examine and improve the Participation in Government (PIG) class that I teach at a western New York high school (LHS). My conception of action research was critical to my use of this methodology within my social studies classroom. I view the action research process as rooted in the desire to critically examine the practices one employs in an effort to improve those practices and the understanding of those practices. Furthermore, the process of critical self-reflection should not only focus on classroom behavior, but also extend to the social contexts in which these actions occur.

The following account, which is a condensed version of the research I conducted during the second semester of the 1990–91 academic year, focuses on a number of action research cycles that occurred when I was changing the PIG course for a particular group of students. The central issues involved methods of expanding student participation both within and beyond the classroom. In particular, the traditional roles of students and teacher were changed by allowing students to negotiate the curriculum for the course. This experience with democratic participation in the classroom was intended to serve as a model of effective participation in the wider context of society.

My general concern was how to make the course more participatory. I wanted to move beyond the established curriculum of the course and the boundaries of the traditional classroom in order to have students learn about government and citizenship education through active participation. The effort to keep focused on the course objectives, while incorporating student ideas of how to pursue these objectives, constituted a major part of the research. Another key concern was how classroom role changes created by curriculum negotiation influenced student development of the skills, knowledge, and attitudes essential to effective democratic citizenship. Documenting these changes and their effects on the students, teacher, and classroom environment was the first step in improving the course.

THE PARTICIPATION IN GOVERNMENT COURSE

The PIG course is a state-mandated, twelfth-year social studies course that focuses not on an examination of how government functions in the United States, but on the roles played by individuals as they participate in the creation and implementation of public policy (NYSED, 1985). The curriculum utilized at my school is based on the Office of the Citizen model described in the New York State syllabus (NYSED, 1985), with the text and materials from *Participation in Government: Making a Difference* (Ketcham, Meiklejohn, Julian, Fetsko, Zalewski, & Julian, 1988) providing the structure for the course. These materials are supplemented with other activities designed to increase opportunities for student involvement beyond the classroom. These activities include required participatory activities (attending government meetings, volunteer experiences, community education, etc.), local government day activities, and familiarizaton with community resources (voter registration, local politicians and community agency personnel as guest speakers, etc.).

This curriculum functions well within the traditional context for which it was designed. However, the group that I teach is composed of students from several area school districts who are members of a Cooperative Educational Program. Students spend alternating periods of 1 or 2 weeks at the Harrison Division of General Motors Corporation in a work cycle, and at LHS in a school cycle. The co-op program is designed to provide internship-type experiences to high school students who are interested in pursuing a career in engineering or business. During the work cycle students are paired with a wide variety of salaried employee supervisors (engineers, computer programers, marketing personnel, etc.), and work at tasks ranging from administration (typing, filing, etc.) to assisting their supervisors in the technical and business projects for which they are responsible, such as time/motion studies, quality control procedures, laboratory testing, and computer-aided design projects.

The experiences and background of these particular students made me desire an alternative to the approach to teaching PIG that is employed for more traditional students at LHS. I wanted a PIG course that would acknowledge and employ the skills, knowledge, and attitudes acquired as a result of these students' 2 years of interaction with adults in the corporate environment.

The objectives of the PIG course were to develop skills, knowledge, and attitudes requisite for effective democratic citizenship. At the heart of effective citizenship education and participation is a focus on the public good rather than private self-interest. The notion of participation extends beyond voting to more active involvement in public policy creation, such as attendance at government meetings and membership in citizenship advocacy groups. Through such participation individuals should develop the ability to take action on public issues. This ability could be developed, I believed, by providing students with an expanded role in creating their own methods of citizenship education. I felt that allowing students to negotiate the curriculum by increasing their role in planning, creating, and evaluating the course would make the classroom a microcosm of democratic government and serve as a basis for increased participation beyond the classroom in the wider contexts of school, community, and government policy.

This notion of student participation also would require a change in the role of the teacher from expert in control of learning to facilitator and partner in the educational process. The role of facilitator would require me to become more familiar with school and community resources that would assist student efforts, and to utilize teaching methods that would promote more student involvement, such as cooperative learning and group presentations.

I decided to use action research as the vehicle to create this new version of PIG because this methodology stresses the involvement of all members of the educational community in the creation and formative evaluation of a course. The goals of the PIG course could be examined by the class, methods of accomplishing these objectives could be devised collectively, and critical examination and evaluation of the process could more actively involve students in their own citizenship education.

However, I recognized that our effort also would affect, and be affected by, the context in which citizenship education took place. The structure of the co-op program and the students involved in it, along with the dynamics of education within the school, would influence the methods of participation and learning available to us. The constraints of the school environment and the degree to which school and community could interact also needed to be recognized and addressed. Hopefully, the result would be a more constructive relationship where the boundaries of school and community would blur as students tried to influence the course of events and the creation of policy in the community.

Action research seemed particularly well suited to my research questions and my desire to create cooperatively a more participatory course in citizenship education. The cyclical nature of the action research process would allow the class the opportunity to identify our concerns and objectives for various parts of the course, devise activities to accomplish these objectives, evaluate the success of our efforts, and move forward to new concerns and issues. The data collection vehicles that seemed most fitting to capture the development occurring within this research were student and teacher journals, class notes and recordings, and documents of student and teacher work related to the various aspects of the course.

Student and teacher journals were invaluable in documenting the social, personal, and intellectual development of the students and instructor. The personal nature of these sources served to illuminate areas of development that were not evident in class documents such as homework, essays, or tests. This was particularly true in regard to student attitude toward participation in the course activities. More traditional course documents, such as tests and homework, were useful in assessing students' intellectual development and grasp of the content-oriented knowledge base related to the course. Taped recordings of class discussions provided a permanent record of events as they unfolded in the classroom. These were used to examine the collaboration process and as a method of triangulation to confirm the perceptions of different parties to the events. Other sources of data such as student presentations were utilized as they applied to the particular stages of the research.

FIRST CYCLE: BEGINNING CURRICULUM NEGOTIATION

Our experiment in revising the PIG course began with a journal assignment to solicit student opinions on the purposes and methods of the second unit of instruction on the judicial decision-making process. I intended to give students a greater role in planning and evaluating Unit II activities in order to assess the effects of this participation on their development and my own practice. This negotiation began during a series of class discussions focusing on the journal assignment. We discussed the concepts of Unit I (definitions of citizen and the distinction between the public good and private self-interest) and how we could incorporate and expand upon these in Unit II. I wrote notes on the board to focus on two major objectives from the units: the decision-making process and ways to evaluate public issues. The students' confusion became apparent. The text approach included a question about the rights of students in regard to search and seizure in school, which eventually was decided by an appeal to the United States Supreme Court. A case study model of decision making was employed to illustrate how two responsible persons or groups (the majority and minority of Supreme Court Justices) viewing the same situation could formulate different assessments, opinions, and resolutions. The students' journal entries and class discussion revealed that a quarter of the students had focused on the issue of civil rights employed to illustrate the decision-making process rather than the process itself. Therefore, we reached a consensus that our efforts to create an alternative Unit II would focus on the decision-making process rather than the area of student rights in school.

It was interesting to note that most students regarded the text's method of realizing the objectives as "boring," "long-winded," and "confusing." While students agreed that the text could be effective, virtually all of them suggested alternative approaches to our study of decision making. This situation was the beginning of our struggles with the notion of negotiating the curriculum. One student acknowledged the importance of the course and our approach to it, but also expressed concern that the opportunity for student participation in planning course activities could be used by students as a means of supporting any alternative that required minimal effort and exertion. These comments illustrated how the course objective of public good versus private self-interest was a real concern within the classroom environment as well as in the arena of public policy creation. Although I hoped that increased feelings of ownership over their education would increase students' responsibility and motivation, I also realized that this might not be the case for all students. This dilemma would have long-term consequences for the class, which will be apparent later in the chapter.

Many alternative approaches to Unit II suggested by students, such as holding a mock trial, reading other Supreme Court cases, and observing an actual trial, seemed to reflect a concern with the legal process rather than general decision-making skills. Other suggestions centered on the desire to examine public issues not so intricately tied to the legal process. Students suggested that debate over a public issue of interest to the class could serve as a means of investigating the issue and the decision-making process as we tried to create public policy to address the issue. The benefits of learning by doing, rather than reading about someone else's decisions, were utilized as an argument in favor of this approach. My desire to keep focused on the course objective of decision-making skills and processes led me to suggest the use of a National Issues Forum (NIF) curriculum package that would utilize the case study model emphasized in Units I and II of the textbook.

SECOND CYCLE: TWO APPROACHES TO DECISION MAKING

Our negotiations resulted in the formulation of two distinct approaches to instruction. One group of students wanted to examine the issue of changing the legal drinking age, while another wanted to use the NIF package on freedom of expression. Although I favored the more structured NIF approach, believing that it emphasized process over content, I also wanted to allow the negotiation process to involve students in the issues and methods that they had chosen, so as to maximize their involvement, motivation, and responsibility. Should I allow my own desire to pursue a particular objective to overpower the potential gains in citizenship education to be made through adherence to a more democratic method of classroom interaction? Further reflection convinced me that my concern in this matter was tied to my own previous experiences as a teacher. I realized that allowing two groups to progress toward similar goals through different means would require me to relinquish control over student actions. I would not be able to monitor and control all aspects of the learning process. While this loss of control concerned me, I realized that it would foster the exact type of student responsibility for their own citizenship education that the course was designed to develop.

Each group was to use the case study model of decision making to guide their work. The freedom of expression group had the materials of the NIF package to structure their investigation, but the drinking age group needed to collect information and structure their work differently. As I wanted to provide a focus for that group that would emphasize the decision-making process, I had the group members identify questions of legalities, rights, ethics, practicality, and public policy associated with a change in the drinking age. I hoped that these questions would help them identify and compare different viewpoints regarding a change in the drinking age. Each student could then examine his or her own perspective on the issue by using these questions to address the desirability, feasibility, and consequences of such a change in public policy.

The drinking age group utilized these questions to structure their examination of the issue and develop three distinct perspectives or policy options, which were to lower the drinking age to 18 years, eliminate the drinking age altogether, or keep the drinking age at the present level of 21 years. Debate related to the focusing questions allowed students to compare the reasoning behind the different perspectives. Other means of investigation utilized by the group included library research to discover reasons behind the current legal age and to obtain comparative information from European countries with no legal age, and invitations to guest speakers who favored the different perspectives on the issue.

The freedom of expression group used the text booklet and videotape of the NIF package, which provided three perspectives on that issue, as follows:

- Some forms of expression are so harmful that public access to them should be limited.
- Some forms of expression place children at risk since they do not possess the maturity to differentiate between the ideas they encounter and participate in. Therefore, children's access to such ideas should be limited.
- The benefits of free expression are so important and the consequences of censorship so potentially dangerous that no restriction of expression can be justified.

To stimulate discussion and encourage consideration of each perspective by each group member, I supplemented the curriculum package materials with examples of situations in which the three perspectives would be at odds. Issues such as flagburning, obscene art displays, and censorship of news reports from the Persian Gulf War were examined from each of the three perspectives.

The investigations continued for a week, and I checked with each group as I or they felt necessary. I continually monitored the drinking age group to ensure that their own preferences for a lower legal age would not stifle the process of examining the reasoning behind the current law. I felt that the structure offered by the NIF package was somehow missing from the drinking age group, so I suggested that they use a public opinion survey to uncover views that their discussions might have overlooked.

THIRD CYCLE: EVALUATING OUR EFFORTS

My own observations, as well as those of the students, made me realize that we had been conducting much discussion and activity without a clear notion of how this related to our original objectives concerning decision making. We decided that we could connect our work to our objectives and evaluate our efforts by holding a public forum on the two issues under consideration. Members of each group would present their perspective on the issue along with the reasoning behind the perspective. Each student's contribution to the presentation and previous investigation would serve as one means of evaluating the effort. A second evaluation tool would be an individual essay in which each student would relate his or her initial and final position on the issue and the activities that helped shape that position. The final evaluation would consist of a journal entry in which students reflected on the objectives, methods, and outcomes of the unit. This would be used as a means of individual reflection to structure our group discussion and also as a springboard to the next cycle of research.

My own observations of the class project caused me to think about such questions as: evaluating student work, deciding how to collectively reflect on our efforts, and determining the course of further action. How did students view the degree of participation by the teacher as a factor in helping or hindering their activities? Did students perceive the difference in amount of structure across the groups as I did? How did the public opinion survey fit into each group's investigation?

The degree of teacher guidance in each group was tied to the degree of structure in a unique fashion. The highly structured approach of the NIF package made me feel that I had provided a great amount of guidance to the freedom of expression group. The lack of such materials in the drinking age group caused me to perceive a lack of structure and served as the impetus to using the public opinion survey to uncover the reasons for people holding differing viewpoints regarding drinking age changes. I also hoped the survey would lead the students to discover the reasons behind the current legal age, since no member of the group supported this perspective.

The groups' preparation for the public forum also reflected my concern about formal structure within the investigation. Contrary to my perceptions, it was the NIF group that had more difficulty preparing for the forum and using the public opinion survey, even though the survey was a part of that package and I had seen their efforts as being highly structured. This group wanted to use the opinion survey results to support their own view on the issue as being more correct or better than the other perspectives, even though the intended purpose of the survey was to elicit reasons for people's support of the various viewpoints. Did the structure of the NIF package inhibit the students' ability to perceive the decision-making process being modeled and to use this process in formulating their own decision?

The drinking age group utilized the survey in a manner more consistent with its intended purpose. An exchange student from Germany talked to the group on the day before the forum and explained the differences in drinking age and cultural attitudes toward the use of alcohol. This discussion helped to flush out some reasons why our current legal age was necessary and desirable. My concern that the lack of structure and personal preferences of this group would cause them to lose focus on the decision-making process and neglect an important perspective on the issue now appeared to be unfounded.

At the public forum presentation each group split into three smaller groups, each of which presented a particular perspective on the issue under consideration. The groups were well organized and comfortable with the format. Each perspective was thoroughly explained, and survey results were utilized to add support to claims or to inform the audience of the reasons behind the different opinions. Perhaps the best judgment of the success of the forum was provided by the co-op program coordinator who sat in on class that day. During the course of the presentations, he made a number of comments regarding the information he found to be interesting or new to him, which I took as an indication that he was considering the information as he formulated his own perspective on the issues. The number of questions asked by the other students suggested that they too were evaluating the various perspectives in their own effort to reach a conclusion. These two incidents suggested that the forum had been successful in modeling the case study approach to decision making.

The evaluation of our effort continued with a journal assignment, followed by a class discussion that attempted to arrive at a common assessment of the relevance, successes, and shortcomings of our efforts. Student journal entries cited the group activities in class and public forum presentations as having been influential in identifying important issues and different conceptions of the public good, balancing private and public interests, and arriving at and defending an informed decision. Most students identified the small amount of formal group structure from the instructor as having been effective in promoting student responsibility for learning. Common assessments were that I provided "directions without being overbearing" and that activities centered around "our participation" not the teacher's.

A recurring incident within the freedom of expression group illustrated how redefinition of classroom roles could foster student responsibility. Virtually all members of that group expressed displeasure that the group's discussion often centered around a personal debate between two individuals with diametrically opposed viewpoints. I often reminded them to "criticize ideas, not people" as their discussion ventured into thinly veiled personal attacks. While these two students and the other group members expressed a desire for me to control these episodes, I had deliberately withdrawn in the hope that those two students, or others in the group, would take it upon themselves to regulate the situation. Initially, I regarded the continued outbursts as a failure of the students to develop a regulatory function within the group, but continued reflection caused me to re-evaluate the situation. Perhaps their inexperience with group dynamics, especially when confronting emotionally sensitive issues, left them ill prepared to address this problem, and more experience with group relations would have been a helpful precursor to our activities.

The collective reflection session mirrored many feelings previously expressed in journal entries, and reinforced the concept of collaborative decision making central to democratic citizenship. Student perceptions of the effectiveness of the forum differed. Many students felt they learned more about the particular issue they addressed than about the decision-making process in general because they were required to make personal decisions about the issues rather than create a public policy that all could accept. This shortcoming of our effort was frustrating to some students who wished to focus on group policies and create real alternatives for addressing the issue.

The idea of public policy creation led to a discussion of how this actually occurred in society. Students' observation at a county legislature that most votes were strictly partisan made them aware that political considerations could render ineffective the benefits of reasonable compromise and promote self-interest at the expense of the public good. The recognition of the antithetical philosophies at work in the classroom, as opposed to the community, left the students disillusioned, but cognizant of the need for effective citizenship education to extend beyond the schoolhouse walls.

At this time, an interesting difference of perception emerged between myself and the students regarding the dichotomy of structure across the two groups. Whereas I had seen the NIF materials as providing a highly structured format for the freedom of expression group, students expressed the feeling that activities were relatively unstructured as they utilized materials as they saw fit, regardless of whether their uses were consistent with my intentions. My perceived misuse of the public opinion survey by this group was due to the fact that they had failed to see its relevance and consequently downplayed its importance to their efforts.

The drinking age group shared the feeling that their approach was loosely structured and my role was that of a gadfly in refocusing their efforts on aspects of the issue they had downplayed. They listed the formal research, public opinion survey, focusing questions, and guest speaker as aspects of the investigation critical to development of decision-making skills and knowledge. The effectiveness of these activities was underscored by the fact that two students who initially desired to change the legal age to 18 years eventually favored the current age due to the information they had encountered.

Overall, my intentional withdrawal from the role of classroom leader and the responsibility afforded students through their role in negotiating the curriculum were beneficial. Students emphasized how their choice of groups, issues, and activities was influential in creating motivation and responsibility for the outcome. Most agreed that they did more work than they had anticipated at the outset, but were satisfied with the gains they had made.

FOURTH CYCLE: FROM DECISIONS TO ACTIONS

The plan for the next cycle of research emerged from a combination of the concerns identified from reflecting on the first cycle and the course objectives I wished to pursue. My desire was to provide experience in the formulation and implementation of public policy (by starting a school recycling program), and also to continue the idea of negotiating the curriculum that was established in the previous cycle. During class discussion of how to proceed, we recalled the objectives of the previous units and I offered policy implementation as the next step. I was concerned, however, that my preconceived notions about the next unit would inhibit the potential gains to be made from allowing true negotiation of the curriculum by the students. I wondered if advancing my own ideas rather than allowing for more student decision making would affect their motivation and attitude.

I decided that imposing a focus on policy implementation would not necessarily deprive students of a role in determining the specific methods or issues to be utilized and would help them recognize the contextual constraints applying in any policy decision. The two alternatives offered by the students included an issues discussion forum and a recycling program, although neither of these seemed to motivate students to any great degree. The failure of our public forum from Unit II to yield any real decision or finalization influenced students to choose the recycling program as the issue for Unit III. The recycling option offered opportunities for actual participation in policy formulation and implementation that were clearly evident to students.

FIFTH CYCLE: STARTING A RECYCLING PROGRAM

Our planning addressed the question of researching areas of investigation necessary to begin a recycling program. Through class discussion we identified the important areas as community education, types of wastes appropriate for recycling, collection logistics, and the school's current policy of waste disposal. Since we had no idea of any present recycling effort at LHS, we assumed that we would formulate the policy from the ground up and we assigned groups of students to research these areas over spring break. Groups were assigned to contact school administration and maintenance personnel to identify current waste disposal procedures, other schools to gather information about their programs, two waste disposal companies to investigate recycling procedures and seek advice, and the local legislature and an environmental protection group to solicit other pertinent information.

During the spring break I realized we needed to receive permission for the project from the school principal. He informed me that an assistant principal was working on just such a program with the district's budget director. I contacted the assistant principal and learned that LHS was one of four district schools where pilot programs were being established. Since we had hoped to have students plan and implement the program from start to finish, I asked him to visit the class and address the idea of how we could get involved. My concern that the work already done would deprive the students of the opportunity to fully participate in planning and implementation served as another example of the situational constraints of policy work and citizenship education in the school environment.

The assistant principal informed us that the school's current plan consisted of saving xerographic paper boxes until there were enough to start a paper recycling program on one floor of the school. He suggested that we could help by orienting students and teachers to the program and expanding the pilot program to include aluminum cans and newspapers. Student questions and comments about the proposed program included expansion to include nonreturnable juice cans from the cafeteria, the type of papers that were recyclable, the companies involved with collection of the waste, and the possibility of using the Student Council in the orientation process. Following this meeting, the students expressed disbelief that a project under the guidance of an administrator could be in such a state of apparent disarray and questioned the administration's desire to actually see a program get started before the end of the school year. The idea of having to work within the constraints of the school and district's directions frustrated some students who had visions of a more ambitious project that would be more comprehensive and possibly profitable to the school.

Suggestions on how to proceed within the already established framework included collecting enough boxes at Harrison to expand the paper collection to the entire school rather than just one floor, and using Student Council homeroom representatives in the orientation phase of the project. Student frustration emerged as students viewed this type of participation as being used as lackeys in completing the tasks already planned by the administration. The comment of one student that a class of "our status" should be planning such a program rather than merely collecting boxes, alerted me to the perception of the co-op students that they were somehow superior to the other students in the school. They felt that they should be the organizers and thinkers, not the workers. This incipient elitism was contrary to the goals of a course that stressed the importance of participation by every individual in whatever manner possible. I was sure that their participation in corporate projects as co-workers was responsible for these feelings, but I emphasized the need for our class to do whatever was necessary at the present time to get this project underway, despite the apparent bureaucratic inertia of the administration.

The following day a group of students drove to Harrison to collect boxes, while another group planned the orientation pamphlet and discussed expanding the project beyond paper recycling. With the exception of one student, the planning group's efforts were lethargic and unmotivated. I realized that with any group, especially a group of seniors late in the second semester, there would be differential levels of participation and I decided to allow this to continue as long as the students allowed it to happen. Despite the disillusionment of those students who did work, I hoped that student realization of this situation would serve as an impetus to more determined efforts in future endeavors.

The last class of the school cycle saw one group of students separate boxes for colored and white paper, another group talk to the assistant principal about the orientation program, and a third group review material for inclusion in the orientation pamphlet. Assignments for the upcoming work cycle included creating a prototype pamphlet for review by the administration, contacting the budget director about expanding the scope of the program, and reflecting on our effort in a journal assignment. We set a tentative timetable for the start of the project and discussed the journal assignment. The assignment consisted of the following questions:

- What are your feelings about participating in a school recycling program?
- How does this project fit into the PIG curriculum?
- How should we evaluate this unit?
- What should we address as the final component of the PIG course?

Student comments about these questions focused on evaluation and continuation of the course. Students wanted everyone to receive a grade of 100 for the project, but, reminding them of the different levels of participation and motivation, I asked if this system of grading would be fair. Another attempt to receive maximum results from minimal effort was apparent in the students' feeling that the recycling should be the final unit of the course even though there were 10 class periods left after the projected starting date of the recycling program. I informed them of my responsibility to teach them the course for an entire semester and my expectation that they would assist me in fulfilling this responsibility, just as I had taken their perspective into account in planning for the activities in the course.

My reflections during the work cycle centered on the notion of receiving recognition for the recycling program. A district memo about the recycling efforts was sent to me by the principal since he considered our class to be in charge of the program. This indicated to me that our role was acknowledged and our efforts were having an effect on policy within the district. The students viewed recognition differently. They wanted to know if they would receive the assistant principal's pay since they were doing his work. They also were planning to identify themselves—the Harrison Co-op Class of 1991—in the pamphlet as the originators of the program. I was concerned that this indication of pursuing their own self-interest rather than the public good was contrary to an important attitudinal objective of the course.

When the students returned to school from their work cycle their assigments were incomplete except for the journals. I made my disappointment clear and proceeded to engage them in a discussion of those tasks necessary to start the program. This discussion degenerated into a gripe session where students vented their frustrations with the project, the course, and the instructor. Central issues included the students' perception that the course lacked a planned curriculum, their questioning of the appropriateness of a recycling project within the PIG course, and their reluctance to start another unit at what they believed to be the end of the school year. There was tension between the students and me, and among the students themselves. Their frustration with me concerned the intended generality of the course and my continual fading into the background whenever conflict and decision-making opportunities occurred. They wanted more specific guidelines while I wanted them to take these opportunities to make important decisions on their own. I did not perceive the development of responsibility I had hoped to create through curriculum negotiation. Although I had expected to deal with "senioritis," the extent of this phenomenon was becoming unbearable for everyone.

Their frustrations with one another stemmed from the different degrees of participation by various students, even though they expected the grades for all to be consistent and high. This suggested that they failed to internalize the idea of personal responsibility within a group context. Tension also pervaded the inability of some students to see the pertinence of a recycling project in a PIG course.

Some students addressed their classmates' concerns that our efforts were indeed appropriate and having an effect. When the course goals of student decision making and implementation of action consistent with the public interest were made explicit, students were able to see the recycling program as appropriate since it involved school policy, a specific area of public policy. Student concern that, because of the perceived lack of administrative support, the program would die at the end of the school year was addressed by discussing the current state laws regarding recycling. Students knew that recycling was mandated by state law beginning in 1992 and they suggested that our efforts would make compliance easier for the district. They believed that the effort and interest of other students would increase as the program started and new habits formed. This student action to refocus our efforts showed increased initiative and leadership, and allowed me to observe the personal and social development that was occurring.

I asked the students to answer the question, "What is Mr. Bronson doing?" Their responses included: I was not solving problems for them, I was letting them make their own decisions, and I was showing them what it would be like in college and the real world. One student's comment, empathizing with my frustration in finding an effective way to teach the course, also reassured me that the goal of accepting other people's perspectives was being advanced.

The next day, the very same students who had expressed concern about the various aspects of the project took the initiative in addressing these concerns. The student who was concerned that the program would die when this class graduated, volunteered to lead the orientation session for homeroom representatives and wrote an introductory address stressing the importance of all students' participation. The student who had been upset at the apparent lack of administrative support led a delegation of students to meet with the assistant principal to set a timetable for implementation.

The next 2 days were spent preparing for the start of the recycling program the following week. Student motivation and enthusiasm were greatly enhanced as a result of the reflection session that preceded these efforts. On the first day of the next week we finalized our preparations by conducting the orientation of homeroom representatives, distributing pamphlets to homerooms, and placing the collection boxes in the appropriate rooms. These tasks all proceeded smoothly due to the organizational and implementation skills the students had gained in the corporate environment. The recycling program began the following day with distribution of the pamphlets to all students during an extended homeroom period during which homeroom representatives explained the program to the students. Two members of the co-op program spoke over the public address system to officially start the program.

SIXTH CYCLE: ASSESSING OUR PROJECT
AND EVALUATING THE PIG COURSE

Assessment of the project and our success in achieving the course objectives was addressed through individual and collective reflection, including a final journal assignment. We began the collective reflection session by discussing how to evaluate our efforts. Some students appreciated the chance to participate in determining the evaluation, while others just wanted me to give them a grade. The students who had not participated to any appreciable degree in the recycling project also were silent in the discussion of evaluation. They seemed tired of making decisions and appeared not to be concerned about the grade they received or how it was formulated. Nevertheless, we developed some criteria for consideration, one of which was participation in tasks/activities.

Most students felt that their participation had helped them to develop skills necessary for democratic citizenship, such as organization and planning, cooperation, communication, and presentation skills. A new conception of participation was cited as the most common content acquisition from the course. This conception included a broader variety of ways in which individuals can influence public policy creation. Students said they came to realize that more formal avenues of participation, such as voting and jury duty, were not as frequently engaged in, or as important to influencing policy, as more informal means like interest group membership and attendance at public meetings. The recycling project helped to broaden this conception of participation and also to enlighten students about the variety of contexts (school, community, state, etc.) available to them.

Students also mentioned learning that individuals participate in a group context to differing degrees. A considerable amount of frustration stemmed from this uneven degree of participation. For example, one student, who was not active in many aspects of the project, expressed concern that the class was fragmenting when frustration occurred due to the differential participation by individual students.[1] My desire for all to participate eventually gave way to the hope that the lack of involvement of some students would serve as a reminder that everyone isn't motivated by the same issues and that successful participation in the process of change requires individual involvement and responsibility. It is probably significant that most of the approximately one-third of the students who were only marginally involved in the planning and implementation of the program indicated that they had not developed any skills during the project that they had not already used in other contexts, such as at Harrison.

In discussing how my role as instructor influenced progress and participation, some students indicated that my withdrawal from leadership and the laissez-faire approach I took toward instruction had resulted in a sense of ownership of the project, the chance to make mistakes and work through problems, and the opportunity to learn independently of the teacher. These students enjoyed the opportunity that collective reflection offered for student dialogue beyond the individual journal entries, and appreciated the chance to really participate in creating the curriculum as we planned our next activities collectively. There were a number of students, however, who were concerned that the time lost in their "floundering" could have been used more efficiently by learning more about participation. They felt that the entire course included too much time discussing and evaluating what we had done and were going to do next, instead of actually participating in activities.

This loss of time was an unfortunate consequence, but one that I was willing to incur in order to develop more democratic decision making and individual responsibility. I suggested that this loss of time was necessary for us to learn about the importance of individual initiative when planning projects in public policy. The periodic apathy and disorganization we experienced were influential in the realization that the times when the class moved slowly were also the times when no individual or group took the initiative to address the activities that needed to be completed.

I also suggested that our familiarity with traditional student and teacher roles within the classroom inhibited students' ability to exercise effective leadership in planning, implementing, and evaluating the recycling program and unit of instruction within the course. Their expectation that the teacher was solely responsible for specific guidance and final evaluation kept them from participating fully at all times. This feeling was also evident in the comments that some students really felt as if they had no choice in determining the issue for the unit. Even though they knew that we had negotiated the topic of inquiry, the lack of variety of alternatives compelled them to choose recycling. I reminded them how their expectation that I would provide all the alternatives may have been influential in this perception.

Some students suggested that the lack of experience working in a decentralized, democratic classroom environment had been at least partially responsible for our inefficient use of time during reflection, planning, and evaluation. Expecting increased leadership and responsibility from seniors who are used to playing a more passive role in the classroom is an enormous challenge for both students and teacher. More familiarity with new classroom roles prior to the senior year might help make this type of class environment more productive. Therefore, I offered the possibility of more preliminary work in group relations and cooperative learning to improve the ability of students to lead and monitor their own progress. The greater use of cooperative learning techniques would presumably create more focus on group dynamics, which would be transferable to contexts beyond the classroom as well as allowing for more efficient use of time in the classroom. The ability to recognize and address group malfunctions, distribute tasks more equitably, and cooperate in realizing a common objective are all possible benefits of increased proficiency in group dynamics.

Other suggestions for future semesters included creating a more formal structure in the curriculum, forcing all students to participate, allowing students to choose their own topics for investigation and action, as well as extending the context of participation to their own local communities. Imposing more formal structure on the curriculum could lead to better use of limited time, but could also deprive students of real opportunities to learn about participation in expanded contexts by focusing on participation in planning and executing the course. The degree of differential participation and support for relatively easy activities inherent in negotiating the curriculum with students needs to be balanced with the benefits to be gained. Continued negotiation within an atmosphere of more specific objectives for units and timetables for completion of activities may help to meet those goals. The democratization of the classroom, increased motivation stemming from student ownership of curriculum and activities, and participatory experience gained from learning of democratic government in the micrososm of a democratic classroom are all reasons for continued efforts in negotiation.

My withdrawal from classroom leadership during negotiation of the curriculum fostered independence, but also created uncertainty among students unfamiliar with filling this void. I now see my role throughout the course as having been one of laissez-faire leadership, in which I virtually withdrew from any direct control over classroom activity. I purposefully allowed students to flounder in the hope that they would develop the initiative to lead and accomplish the goals we had set. This style of leadership resulted in wasted time and frustration for the students and myself. This experience has led me to favor a more democratic style of leadership for curriculum negotiation rather than a laissez-faire approach. Democratic leadership differs from a laissez-faire style in that the instructor plays a more active role in delineating acceptable alternatives from which the students can choose. This style of leadership would allow for more efficient use of time and a more structured environment, while preserving the democratic element of student participation necessary to develop positive attitudes about participation in general. Using cooperative learning and democratic leadership in the co-op students' junior year will help to prepare them and me for the expectations of this approach to PIG.

The final area of professional development relates to the impact that my teaching practices can have on the school environment. The opportunity to work with the administration on a project of benefit to the entire school provided me with a new perspective on my role within the school organization. The willingness of the administration to allow me to do this research and the recycling project illustrates the potential that exists for teachers to utilize new techniques and participate in formulating school policies. My teaching not only affected the students in my classroom, but extended to the entire school community.

In essence, my actions in the course created an impetus for increased democratization between teachers and administrators that parallels the changes within a district brought about by shared decision making. The recognition that practitioners have valuable insight into the methods best suited to producing desired outcomes is a requisite component of democratization within educational institutions and bureaucracies. Action research offers a methodology to systematically conduct research that contributes to these goals.

COURSE CHANGES INSPIRED BY THIS PROJECT

These reflections on student and teacher outcomes have influenced the way in which I have taught the course over the past 2 years. A number of changes have been made to address the areas that fell short of our original desires, and many aspects have remained due to their appropriateness and past success. The general progression of course units from introductory readings in the text, to decision making, and finally to action and implementation of public policy has remained consistent, as has the negotiation of the curriculum.

A major change has been to incorporate activities related to group dynamics into the first and second units of the course so as to better prepare students for the leadership and cooperation I expect them to demonstrate when creating and implementing public policy in the latter stages of the course. A variety of activities, including role playing, communication and cooperation skills, and group regulatory roles, are done in cooperative groups and serve as the basis of the action/implementation phase of the course.

The action/implementation phase of the course also has been modified to meet the opportunities available. In the spring of 1992, a group of students involved themselves in the policy process regarding the issue of teacher contracts. Teachers had been without a contract since June of the previous year, and the actions of the union and press coverage of the situation prompted action within our class. Students researched teacher contracts and negotiations in their home districts in an attempt to assess the situation in Lockport and suggest a reasonable resolution. Their contacts with administrators, teachers, parents, and students in a variety of districts provided them with valuable insights about school policy and their role in it. The students' actions in this issue caused concern among the administrators of the co-op program, and the superintendent of BOCES (Board of Cooperative Educational Services) addressed the class to express his concern that they were involved in such an issue. This concern suggested that the students were learning about the various interests involved in such an issue and were gaining valuable experience in public policy creation. This cross-community approach to this unit of instruction allowed contact with a large variety of individuals involved with the policy process and gave students an excellent basis for future action in similar contexts.

Another major change change occurred in the fall of 1992 when I moved the PIG course for the co-op students from the spring to the fall semester. My past 2 years of experience in the course informed me that meaningful participation was more likely to occur in the seniors' first semester, prior to the distractions of college interviews, proms, and graduation. I also linked the independent participatory activities project more closely to class activities. The entire class now attends the same government meeting in the first weeks of the course to create a practical basis for comparison of our efforts in the classroom to the arena of local politics and policy creation. The other two participatory activities are done in conjunction with the action/implementation phase of the course to better link the activities to our needs within that part of the course.

CONCLUSION

The final issue of this account is the effect that action research has had on the efforts to improve democratic citizenship education in my PIG course. The student, teacher, and contextual outcomes have been discussed in detail. The appropriateness of action research to citizenship education is unparalleled. The cyclical nature of the action research process is highly consistent with the trial and error approach I have used to improve the PIG course. As new concerns are identified, classroom action is formulated by teacher and students to address concerns, activities are completed, reflection and assessment occur, and the cycle begins anew. The whole PIG class has, in essence, turned into a continual action research project. Our efforts are recorded in journal assignments, collectively discussed, and evaluated as I constantly try to provide students with the most effective preparation for participatory citizenship that I possibly can. The skills, knowledge, and attitudes developed through this approach can be transferred from the democratic classroom to the areas of school policy, and into the community on a local, state, and national level. The leadership the students experience as they negotiate the curriculum, address important issues, formulate public policy, and deal with the consequences of their actions should serve as a sound basis for their future efforts to promote the public good through participatory citizenship.

The collaboration among students, teachers, administrators, and the community that is characteristic of the efforts in this class over the past 3 years serves as a foundation for improving the ways in which education, community involvement, and public policy creation are carried out. As students experience policy making within the school and community, whether these experiences are successful or even disappointing and frustrating, they will develop a perspective of participation rooted in individual responsibility for public matters, motivated by the principles of equity, justice, and democracy.

My use of action research in this project was designed to accommodate my desire to learn more about my practice and the context in which it occurs in order to improve my performance as a teacher of citizenship education. It was also intended to develop members of our citizenry who can be responsible and effective in promoting the public good. This effort has not proven anything about the best way to approach this important task. It has, however, served its purpose in informing me and others of important aspects of citizenship education. Current situations in regard to financing of education, decision making within the public school system, and the inadequacies of high school graduates for job and citizenship requirements, are all plagued by complaints of individuals; such complaints are often heard without plans to participate in addressing these issues. This continuing research effort and its reliance on action research represent my personal way of addressing these challenges.

NOTE

1. Interestingly, without the journal entries I would not have been aware of the degree to which this student was cognizant of events, but reluctant to discuss her observations.

8

The Principal as Action Researcher

A Study of Disciplinary Practice

Elizabeth Soffer

An important part of my role as an elementary principal is my responsibility for discipline. In a general sense, this involves promoting and maintaining a school climate that fosters positive relationships among children and between children and adults. However, on a daily basis, the focus is on incidents of misbehavior, dealing with those children who cannot get along with others and who break school rules. In my school, a suburban K–6 elementary school of 425 students from predominantly middle to upper middle class homes, both the number and seriousness of incidents has tended to be small during my 5-year tenure as principal, owing no doubt to the highly competent and very experienced staff. Most of the teachers have more than 15 years experience and yet retain a high level of enthusiasm for and commitment to teaching and a willingness to address issues of concern. However, in spite of the relatively minor role of discipline problems, discipline has still been a primary area of concern both for me and for the staff. What has disturbed us is that in spite of our efforts, the number of incidents has not decreased and certain students continue to have problems during all of their elementary school years.

In the fall of 1990, our level of concern escalated as the number and seriousness of behavioral incidents increased, particularly among the fifth-grade students. These students showed little respect or caring for each other; they made fun of each other, even harassed and threatened each other, got into numerous fights, and were rude and disruptive both in class with their teachers and on the playground with the teacher aides.

I began to wonder if this increase was a local sign of the national trend so widely reported in educational journals and in the general media. Writers on discipline (Curwin & Mendler, 1988; Nelsen, 1987; Saphier & Gower, 1987) suggest that many of the factors causing this trend lie outside the school, including increased violence in our society, more reporting and portrayal of violence in the media, greater instability in family life, and a culture of self-centeredness. However, they also locate some causes within the school, such as policies and procedures that lead to student powerlessness, lack of challenging activities and appropriate outlets for feelings that result in student boredom and frustration, and staff attitudes and actions that convey unclear limits on student behavior. Whether the primary causes are outside or inside of the school, the school must work to identify causes and develop approaches that will maintain a positive climate in the school and help individuals to both grow and function in the school community.

As I began to search for causes and for solutions, I focused on what our school could do and what action I could take. I realized that because most problems had been minor, I had taken a rather narrow view of discipline as maintaining order through the punishment of misbehavior. This obedience approach had worked in the past in that incidents had not increased and most students were not habitual problems. Now, however, it was no longer working. Every day brought another case of rule-breaking, malicious teasing and classroom disruption, with an abnormally high proportion (sometimes up to one-third) of the fifth-grade students involved. The whole atmosphere in the school was deteriorating.

I needed to take action and involved our school counselor in devising a plan. We decided on a three-pronged approach. First, we would seek to involve the parents of the fifth-grade students; second, the counselor would work with the fifth graders in groups; and, finally, I would focus on actual incidents and the individuals involved. It is my involvement in this last approach that is the focus of this chapter.

While I was considering changes in my own interactions with individual and groups of misbehaving students, I became aware of action research. With its emphasis on a systematic approach to taking and critically reflecting on planned actions, action research seemed to offer an appropriate approach to addressing my concern. In this chapter I first describe the reconnaissance phase and the initial cycles of my project. I then share my reflections on the project and on action research as a way of studying and improving my disciplinary practice.

BEGINNING THE ACTION RESEARCH PROJECT: THE RECONNAISSANCE

In order to plan my first action cycle, I examined three areas related to my disciplinary practice: the way others see me, how I see myself, and alternative practices and models of discipline.

The Way Others See Me

I adopted two approaches to get a sense of how teachers and other staff members viewed my disciplinary practice. First, I reviewed the written staff evaluations of my performance as principal from the past several years. My general awareness that discipline was not an area of strength was reinforced by a close examination of both ratings and comments. Although in other areas (such as support of innovation, openness to suggestions, management of building funds, and support of instruction) I received mostly 5's (the highest rating), in the discipline area, there were many more 2's and 3's. This was consistent over the 3 years I surveyed, in spite of my efforts to address discipline issues in cooperation with the staff. Typical among teacher comments were such things as "a need for more strictness with upper grades," "more evenness with application of rules," "need for more follow-through with discipline," and "need for more consistency."

Second, I did informal interviews with four or five staff members, including the nurse/teacher and the counselor, with whom I work closely, and heard the same concerns. One said that while she knew that I got tired and was sometimes overwhelmed, she felt that I tended to avoid taking action in tough cases. Another mentioned my lack of consistency, noting that I could come down hard one day and let something go the next.

How I See Myself

When I examined my day-to-day practice, I found that I was in basic agreement with these concerns. I realized that when my job got hectic, what often suffered was consistency, both in application of rules and in follow-through with students and parents in the area of discipline. I also became aware that I did avoid some difficult cases, partly because I was unsure of what action to take. Often my inaction resulted in dissatisfaction among teachers and parents and additional incidents involving the same student. Thus, inaction led to larger problems.

Alternative Models

In order to get some perspective on disciplinary practice, I reviewed a number of articles and books on discipline and found several that seemed both promising and relevant. Particularly relevant to my own practice was the chapter on discipline in Saphier and Gower's *The Skillful Teacher* (1987). Like other writers on discipline, they emphasize the importance of clarity of expectations and the need for consistent and persistent application of these expectations. Saphier and Gower (p. 88) suggest that those involved in discipline need to ask themselves the question: "Do I deliver consequences in a way that is tenacious, consistent, prompt, matter-of-fact, and indicates student choice?"

A general approach that seemed promising was the responsibility model described by Curwin & Mendler (1988). The goal of this approach is to teach children how to make responsible choices. The central notion is an internal locus of control, a person's belief that he or she has control over certain outcomes in his or her life. The opposite, external locus of control, suggests that things happen to a person because of actions by powerful people or external forces. To be able to take responsibility, a person must know what he or she can and cannot control. I reasoned that if we can help students be aware of what they can control, then they might be better able to acknowledge their mistakes, to learn from these mistakes, and to plan so that similar mistakes or poor choices can be avoided in the future. I hoped that this understanding would reduce incidents and at the same time improve the students' school experience.

Another useful notion, pointed out by Dreikurs (1968), is a recognition of the difference between punishment and logical consequences. Dreikurs believes that punishment tends to breed resentment while logical consequences that are tied directly to the behavior tend to teach students social responsibility. I thought this might be worth pursuing.

Finally, in Saphier and Gower, I found a different approach to dealing with problem students. They suggest that for very difficult students, no one model of discipline will work. Instead, the model of discipline must be matched to the characteristics and behaviors of the student. They assume that people behave in certain ways for reasons and that patterns of student misbehavior may be manifestations of underlying psychological needs. The disciplinarian must attempt to identify those needs and then choose an appropriate model. For example, if a student has needs related to self-esteem, the best choice might be Glaser's reality therapy, which emphasizes the development of responsibility and self-worth. On the other hand, a student whose need is affection might be helped by self-awareness training, which enables students to become aware of their feelings and develop coping strategies. This individualized focus seemed to be worth exploring, but as each of the six models is complex, I realized that I would need extensive training before I would feel confident in using this specific approach. What I could do was to be more aware of the differences among the causes of behavior problems in individual students.

FIRST CYCLE: KEEPING RECORDS OF MY DISCIPLINARY ACTIONS

Planning and Action

Based on my reconnaissance, I decided that the first change in my practice must focus on consistency and persistency. While I had always kept notes and records of disciplinary conferences and actions with students, I was not using a standard form, nor did I keep the kind of records that would allow me to identify trends. I decided to implement two forms: first, a form for each incident listing the students involved, a description of the incident, the action taken, and comments. These forms would be filed alphabetically by student so that patterns with individual students could be followed. The second form was a type of spread-sheet, to be filled out weekly, listing problems by type and by grade of student. I hoped this information would allow me to see what kinds of behavior prob-lems—such as inappropriate interactions with other students, inappropriate inter-actions with adults, fighting, swearing—were occurring most often and which age groups were having the most problems. Once a pattern emerged, I could refer to the individual incident forms that detailed my actions to examine and gain a better understanding of my practice.

I designed the forms and used them every time a student was referred to me, whether the incident was major or minor. When I was absent from the building, I had my replacement use the forms so that my records would be complete. I tallied these individual forms onto the spreadsheet at the end of each week.

Observation and Reflection

The first thing I noticed was that I had difficulty making myself use these forms consistently. The forms were more time-consuming than my former notes, and I had to consciously retrain myself to get out the form as soon as a student came into my office. This was not surprising given my distaste for repetitive administrative tasks involving paperwork, but even at the end of the first week, I began to appreciate the potential of these forms to provide revealing information. I became aware of certain patterns in behavior both among individuals and age groups. I noticed, for example, that during the first 3 weeks 85% of the incidents involved the fifth-grade class and that only a small number of students were involved more than once or twice. I also noted that certain types of behavior problems were prevalent, primarily those involving disrespect for persons, both adults and students. For example, a group of fifth-grade boys, when asked to stop playing tackle football, became rude to the playground aides, then refused to line up, and a confrontation ensued. In addition, one boy was referred a number of times for calling names and making fun of other students, incidents that had escalated into fights on several occasions. These fifth-grade students also had been referred by the music teacher on a regular basis for being disruptive in class.

I also learned from reviewing my descriptions of actions I had taken that after I investigated an incident, I simply assigned the consequence I thought fair and appropriate. Words like, "I reminded Jeff that this kind of behavior was inappropriate," or "I told Ann . . . ," or "I warned Bob . . ." appeared again and again. There was little evidence of my working with students to help them gain a sense of their own responsibility. Students tended to accept this type of action, but I did not feel that they were learning anything from their mistakes—they were simply being punished.

SECOND CYCLE: INTRODUCING A
RESPONSIBILITY MODEL OF DISCIPLINE

Planning and Action

This last thought led me to ask: How can I change the way I conduct disciplinary conferences in order to make them learning experiences for the students so that the incidents are less likely to be repeated. I went back to the work of Mendler and Curwin and focused on trying to replace a punishment model with a responsibility model.

To move toward this model, I decided to change the character of my interviews with children regarding discipline problems. I would continue to ask each child involved to present his or her description of the incident and would attempt to reach a shared account of what happened. However, instead of simply assigning consequences and asking for better behavior in the future, I would ask each student to attempt to describe what his or her responsibility was for what had happened. Then, I would ask, "If you found yourself in a similar situation, what could you do differently to prevent this problem?"

Observation and Reflection

As soon as I began to ask these kinds of questions, I noticed a difference in the tenor of many of my disciplinary conferences. In the past, after describing the incident, the students had been given a passive role. With this new approach, the students assumed an active role. As I noted both in my journal and on the discipline forms, when I would ask them about their own responsibility, they would pause, think, and say things like: "I didn't stop to ask if Jane bumped into me on purpose; I just pushed her back," or "I thought I was joking, but I guess calling Joe a jerk bothered him." Furthermore, when I asked them for a plan to avoid similar problems in the future, they came up with all kinds of suggestions, both useful and not. Often a first response might be, "I'd run away," or "I'll never talk to her or play with her any more," but with some prompting, students would offer more constructive suggestions, such as: "I could ask if she pushed me on purpose," or "I could talk to one of the aides." I would write down their suggestions, discuss which might be most useful, and try to get them to agree on future action. Children who had regarded each other as enemies just moments before often began planning together.

By changing my approach, I had hoped to stimulate children to think more about their individual behavior, but a side result was a deeper resolution of the conflict and at least a verbal acceptance of future responsibility for their actions. I realized that as I became less directive and involved the students more in the resolution process, the students became more responsive and active in solving their own problems.

Two other observations were that the majority of incidents occurred when students were supervised by aides and not their teachers, and that this change in my practice did not have much of an effect on the really difficult students. When the most difficult students described incidents, they would continue to deny any misbehavior even though it had been witnessed by adults. Even if they admitted their involvement, when asked what they might do differently, they would sit silently, offering no ideas. However, on several occasions, the second or third time I used this technique on particular students, they would suddenly enter into the process.

These observations led me to several new questions: First, what might I do to reduce the number of these incidents during the times the students were supervised by aides? Second, what could I do with the more difficult children who wanted neither to accept responsibility nor to work to improve their behavior? I decided to pursue both questions in a parallel fashion, but to think of them as two separate cycles.

THIRD CYCLE: REDUCING INCIDENTS WITH THE AIDES

Planning and Action

As most of the incidents occurred during recreation on the playground under the supervision of the aides, I decided to see if my presence would affect student behavior. I chose to be outside on the playground for an hour 3 days a week—Monday, Wednesday, and Friday—during fifth- and sixth-grade recreation.

Observation and Reflection

When I was on the playground there were very few incidents. In fact, I did not have to do anything except stand there most of the time. My presence alone was enough. I followed this procedure for a month. On the days that I was not outside, there were three times as many incidents noted on the discipline spreadsheets. Similarly, after I stopped going outside for 2 weeks, the number of incidents rose again.

This made me wonder what I could do to invest the aides with more authority in the eyes of the students, which I noted as an issue to discuss with the aides and the teachers. I also wondered, however, whether there was anything in the way that the aides dealt with the students that fostered misbehavior or disrespect—another area for study in a future cycle. Finally, I realized that I would not be satisfied if students treated each other well only when supervised by me or by other adults. I wanted to investigate ways to encourage positive interactions that were not the result of direct supervision.

FOURTH CYCLE: SEPARATING THE MOST DIFFICULT STUDENTS

Planning and Action

The changes in my practice had not affected three fifth-grade boys who continued to cause trouble both on the playground and in their classrooms on an almost daily basis. I had used almost every approach I knew, such as discussions, parent conferences, and serious consequences, including suspension. These interventions had had little effect and the boys were ruining the climate of their classroom. I wondered if a more dramatic action on my part might have an impact.

I decided to move two of the three boys to different classrooms for the last 10 weeks of the year. I had resisted this action as it might encourage other parents to demand classroom placement changes. I also expected phone calls from the parents of students in their new classrooms and worried about the teachers' reactions as well. However, after consultations with the teachers and with the parents, I received reluctant agreement to proceed.

Observation and Reflection

I chose not to move the boy whom I saw as both the most negative and the most powerful. According to his teacher, he stopped being a major problem once he no longer had his friends to follow his lead in making noises and rude remarks. However, the other two continued to misbehave and be sent out of class. Interestingly, they seemed to miss the "powerful" boy terribly. They would run to meet him as classes changed, share their latest exploits, and make sure they sat next to him at lunch.

What I learned was that situations can sometimes become clearer when elements are seen separately. Instead of viewing the three boys as a triumvirate with the same problems, I was able to see them as individuals with different problems, perhaps needing different interventions. I decided to plan further actions involving the two boys who were still having difficulties.

FIFTH CYCLE: INVOLVING THE PARENTS
OF THE MOST DIFFICULT STUDENTS

Planning and Action

In order to deal with each case individually, I decided to schedule conferences with each boy and his parents to determine further actions. The parents, the boys, and I agreed to draw up very strict individual behavioral contracts that specified consequences, beginning with removal from class and making up time after school, and ending with suspension for certain specified acts. The contracts were specific to the behavioral problems of each boy.

Observation and Reflection

This action did seem to reduce their negative behavior once the boys realized that the contracts were consistently applied. Furthermore, as they had agreed to the contracts, I could use their agreement as a frame within which to discuss their behavior. For example, the behavioral contracts included rewards and consequences related to the boys' individual needs and interests. In one case where academic frustration was part of the problem, we arranged a full psychological and academic evaluation and were able to develop classroom strategies based on the boy's learning strengths and weaknesses.

This use of different techniques brought me back to Saphier and Gower's notion of different disciplinary models for different students, and I decided that I should learn more about the theory and application of this approach. I also thought more about developing logical consequences fitted to the misbehavior because my limited repertoire was so soon exhausted. I found it difficult to come up with logical consequences for many of the misbehaviors and determined that this was an area for continued exploration.

EPILOGUE

As the school year ended, I realized that none of my cycles had been completed. Although some cycles raised questions that led to other cycles, the actions in each cycle suggested further follow-up actions. Because the practice of discipline is such a broad area and demands different techniques for different students, I found that I needed to keep several cycles going at the same time.

During the following school year, I continued to work on each of the cycles. For example, I further developed the record keeping cycle and was able at the end of the year to analyze a full year's data. I learned that of 441 referrals in a year, 26 students (or 6%) had five or more referrals and were responsible for 54% of the total referrals. Of these, 32% involved sixth graders (the group that had been problematic the previous year) and 19% came from fifth graders. The remainder of the referrals were primarily one- or two-time offenders. Thus, the majority of our discipline problems were located in our upper grades. I also noticed that 2 weeks before each major vacation, there was a significant increase in the number of referrals. I was able to share this information with staff and plan appropriate interventions, including discussions with students about these problem times. I also identified students who had a number of early referrals and began to work individually with them. Analysis of yearly and year-to-year trends has continued to yield opportunities for action and questions for further research.

I also pursued the question of the authority of the aides, begun in the third cycle. Here, I expanded my study to include the aides. We met to analyze our past actions and planned changes in our joint practice. For example, we agreed to hold grade level meetings the first day of school, at which I introduced the aides and reinforced their authority and explicitly went over the school rules and the consequences for violating them. We also informed students that the referral forms would be sent home to parents. The result of this action was that during the first 2 weeks, there were 20 to 25 referrals. Then, as students learned the system, referrals dropped to 5 to 10 a week, except before vacations and on the occasion of the first snow. The clarity and persistence of this approach had a positive effect. The aides and I also agreed that any student showing them disrespect would be immediately referred to me and that they would avoid confrontations with students. This reinforced our opening message to students that the aides were not to be treated differently from their teachers or me.

I also continued to work on my interviews with students, begun in the second cycle. I added a focus on perspective-taking, helping students see their actions from the point of view of others. For example, if a student denied that she had done anything, I asked her to pretend to be the other student and tell me what she saw. I was surprised that often the student would describe herself from a third person point of view as doing things she had previously denied doing. I remember one student saying that "Julie hit Jeff on the arm" and then looking at me in a shocked manner. I also have used this technique to help students become aware of how the other person felt when called names or otherwise mistreated. This perspective-taking, I believe, is a promising approach, one that I will continue to use and study.

In general, I believe my project has benefited both me and the school. Not only did my disciplinary practice improve, but the overall disciplinary climate improved. In their evaluations of my performance, teachers noted improvement but still marked discipline as an area of concern. I still have to work to be consistent and to find methods to deal with the more difficult students, including investigating with teachers the effects of their own classroom actions.

REACTIONS TO ACTION RESEARCH

In reflecting on the process of action research itself, some of the problems and questions I encountered are worthy of comment because they highlight basic differences between action research and traditional research. An initial issue with which I struggled arose from the fact that action research focuses on the actions and intentions of the researcher, while traditional research centers on the behaviors of subjects. The action researcher makes changes in practice and studies the effects of those actions. I first thought that, although the intent was to make changes in my own practice, once the action was taken, the focus would shift to the effect on the actions of others and to the improvement of their situation. I came to realize that the focus had to remain on my actions as the intent is to understand and improve my practice. However, since the only way to assess any improvements in practice is to examine their effect, there is a constant tension between the actions of the researcher and the effects on others. I had to maintain a continuous effort to keep the focus on my practice.

In addition, I became aware both that the achievement of certain effects was not necessarily an improvement and that improvement of my disciplinary practice alone was of limited value. Although I could, through changes in my practice, get more compliance from students, I realized that improved compliance alone was not a significant improvement. What I really wanted was to orient my actions toward fostering an environment conducive to positive behavior. In order to change the environment, teachers and other staff also would need to change their practice. I could, for example, encourage others to use the responsibility model, but I would then risk manipulating them for my ends.

I asked myself: If I believe that I know which actions will create a positive environment, do I then have a right to "engineer" those changes for the good of all? I decided that I did not. A more democratic action would be to involve others in researching the same problem. I would still be in danger of manipulating the collaborators as, in my role as principal, it is often possible to influence teachers to "buy in" to my suggestions. However, this danger cannot be eliminated. The tension is inherent in action research and as such must be addressed openly within the group.

The use of a journal for data collection is a feature of action research that I found especially useful for keeping records of procedures, discoveries, problems, and questions. My journal was the vehicle that made it possible for my research to be reflective and flexible. My journal captured those fleeting but important ideas not reflected in more formal data collection. It provided the subject matter for reflection throughout my project and facilitated the ongoing evolution of my research. In a future project, I would make my journal records more extensive as it was these thoughts that pointed to new questions and new directions and to an altered understanding of the problem.

On the other hand, there is also the problem of time. It has been difficult for me to keep up my journal and data collection (and to find time to do the necessary planning and reflection). However, I believe that if the problem is significant enough and action research is seen as practically valuable, administrators will find the time, although it will not be easy.

Although my project, and action research in general, seeks to help the practitioner/researcher view her practice as problematic and to improve that practice, action research also should increase knowledge about education and educational practice. I have found it difficult to move beyond understanding my research as an approach to issues and problems in my own practice to an understanding of my research as a potential contribution to the knowledge base of education. I, like most other administrators, tend to view myself as a receiver of knowledge rather than a producer of knowledge. Perhaps one of the benefits of action research will be to help administrators involved in action research to value their practical experience and to see themselves as able to contribute to improved educational practice. Additionally, I think it is important to share what one learns with staff and other educators. The problem is often finding a suitable vehicle to share this knowledge without sounding like an "expert" attempting to tell others what they ought to do. In describing what I have learned to my school staff I have invited them to participate in the process, and hopefully through this case study I will stimulate others to improve their practice and their knowledge of practice.

Not only have I been stimulated by being involved in research, but I also have gained a different perspective on my own practice. Even when I am not involved in a systematic project, I continually ask myself questions about my own practice and the limitations of my individual actions. By reflecting on the impact of my actions, I now see my practice as problematic.

9

Embedding Action Research in Professional Practice

Allan Feldman & J. Myron Atkin

Part II of this book highlights action research by teachers and education administrators in the field. The focus of this particular chapter is on the need for such research to become part of the regular and continuing activities of a large number of teachers in a significant number of schools. There are formidable obstacles in the way of the teaching profession taking such a turn. Nevertheless, we believe such a transformation is necessary if action research is to become a major force for educational improvement.

Right now, action research, in those places where it happens, is often impressive, energizing, and inspiring. It is attractive and appealing for many reasons, but one of the most important is that it garners warm endorsements from participating teachers. Action research also comports with a strong, emerging belief that increased teacher autonomy will be a major and necessary element in educational improvement.

However, the present scale of action research on the total education scene is tiny. Furthermore, it faces imposing barriers in a period like the present when standards, assessment, and accountability—along with trying to cope with unprecedented budget pressures—are the most prominent features of policy debates in education. At the risk of sounding discordant in the pages of a volume that is largely celebratory, we believe that unless action research becomes part of the natural and regularized activities of the school, it will become a historical curiosity—a phenomenon that seems to claim avid and affectionate attention every few decades, but then fades as quickly and as puzzlingly as it surfaced. In short, we believe that action research must be self-sustaining to have broad impact. But is it possible? What are the prospects and challenges?

OUR STYLE OF ACTION RESEARCH

As with many expanding movements, action research is beginning to take a variety of forms as people adapt the basic concept of inquiry by teachers to their own views of desirable educational research or approaches to teacher education.

It is best for us to try to be clear about our own orientation to the subject and how we characterize it.

First, it is collaborative. This collaboration is primarily among teachers, not between teachers and an outside researcher. Although we ourselves have been outsiders in the groups with which we have worked, we have tried to play a role that was peripheral to the group's own sense of itself. For example, we have not tried to influence the focus for the research. We have commented about research methods, but usually to point out that teachers need not use techniques that dominate educational research; the methods can be more personal since they are engaged in teaching, and the teachers can use reporting styles that tell that personal story.

Our reasons for getting involved center, in part, on an ideological commitment to promote research by teachers on issues they consider salient, because we believe they have special wisdom about such matters. We want, also, to do what we can to lead the research community to place higher value on the knowledge possessed by teachers. Unique knowledge is generated by teachers in their own practice-based inquiries; we want to understand more about it.

Thus, within the groups with which we have worked, we have tended to view ourselves as facilitators. A more apt characterization might be fans, or even cheerleaders. We are impressed with the wisdom of many teachers and irritated by the fact that it is so little understood and appreciated in attempts to "reform" the schools. So we try to make it easier for teachers to engage in research they themselves consider to be important. It follows, then, that the collaboration we advocate is basically among teachers.

A second characteristic of the approach to action research that we favor is that the teachers focus on their own practice, not on the practice of others. The teachers can be thought of as being the "subjects" of their own research. The self-reflective nature of this process leads to the third characteristic: It is self-developmental. The expectation is that the teachers will improve their practice and come to a better understanding of their educational situations by doing so.

Finally, our expectation of improved practice suggests the fourth characteristic: There is a significant moral component to the process. Since teachers determine how children will spend much of their time, decisions by the teacher regularly and unavoidably involve questions of worth and morality. A great deal of teacher conversation reflects moral dilemmas they face—how this student or that one should be treated. Since action research focuses on teacher-identified issues, it must be amenable to the consideration of moral questions.

THE RELATIONSHIP BETWEEN UNIVERSITY RESEARCHERS AND SCHOOL TEACHERS

A major concern that we have, as university researchers involved in action research, is the nature of this relationship with teachers and the ways that it influences teachers' research. This concern is salient because much of the action research being done by teachers at the present time is stimulated and supported by outsiders; little of it is undertaken on the teachers' own initiative. To compound the matter, the research in which teachers engage often reflects a circumstance in which they are under obligation to someone outside their own school. The most common pattern is for teachers, either pre- or inservice, to be required to engage in action research as part of coursework for a credential or degree. In other instances, payment of some sort is offered, typically from the university (which, in turn, has secured the funds through a special one-time grant). Action research also is being seen increasingly as a tool for reform efforts in schooling. In these initiatives, teachers are often put in the position of doing action research as a means to implement changes in practice conceived by outsiders, such as state and national education officers and other policy makers.

At a more indirect level, teachers, a generally isolated group, sometimes engage in action research because of their responsiveness, even gratitude, to those who seem to want to help. Some teachers act out of a sense of obligation when people of relatively high status, like professors, offer to work with them.

So what? As long as teachers engage in action research, one might ask, why is it important that the impetus does not come from the teacher herself? There is more than ample evidence that many teachers see their preservice education as a rite-of-passage or set of ritual hurdles they must clear on their way to a credential, a requirement having little to do with the realities of schools. If action research is included as a required part of a credential-oriented program, then it might be viewed in the same way. When the stimulus for research comes from sources that are not part of the teacher's ongoing professional life, there is often little motivation to continue when the course is over or when the outsiders leave.

Furthermore, in much action research associated directly or indirectly with universities, the teacher operates within an intellectual framework established not by herself but by a professor. The university researchers may be interested in concept formation in children, and the teachers try to learn how such concepts develop in the classroom, thus enhancing the research program. Or the professor has a theory about "authentic" assessment, and the teacher works with the research team to devise suitable exercises. In an important sense, the relationship can be collegial; both parties value each other's ideas. The basic, intellectual framework for the inquiry, however, comes from the academy.

In such efforts, there is seldom the inspiration to continue the research when the professors leave (as inevitably they do). The collaborative research enterprise between university researchers and school teachers may have provided the teacher with a valuable perspective, but it is unlikely to have provided her with the desire and confidence to identify issues that remain to be investigated or, consequently, the disposition to continue research independently. She did not, after all, play a major role in selecting the topic of research with the professor.

Relationships in collaborative work involving teachers and professors usually mirror a status division that places the teacher in the position of trusted assistant or, worse, star pupil. Teachers have learned in many of these projects that the major source of ideas that are deemed worthy of investigation is the university. The teacher is there to help with the implementation. Often (if unintentionally), the collaborative work with outside researchers serves to heighten feelings of intellectual dependency (Feldman, 1994). Even if this is not the case, the ways of the university are dominant in educational research and tend to frame the norms by which educational research, even by teachers, is judged.

SOME FUNDAMENTALS: RESEARCH TO EXPAND A "KNOWLEDGE BASE" OR TO BECOME WISER?

What are some of the underlying characteristics of action research that may enhance the chances of its becoming self-sustaining in the lives of teachers and less dependent on outsiders? In particular, what purposes might teachers see in action research that enhance their own feelings of accomplishment and satisfaction, and therefore motivate them to make action research part of their ongoing activities?

For 5 years, we have been working with preservice and inservice teachers engaged in collaborative action research with one another. For the most part, the teachers have been working in small groups on a range of practical issues and dilemmas, trying to get smarter about and better at what they do. In the process, as is evident also in many of the other descriptions of action research in this volume, they have been wrestling with complex sets of political, moral, and practical problems as they have generated and shared knowledge with one another.

We engage in this activity with teachers for several reasons—but none of them involves asking teachers to conduct research because we think the topic is important. Our primary motivation is a set of convictions about the nature of teachers' professional knowledge. First, we believe that action research is consequential in developing a deeper wisdom about the educational enterprise than is usually sought by researchers. In stating this opinion in such a manner, we make a distinction between expanding the "knowledge base" for teaching, which is the usual aim of well-established modes of educational inquiry, and becoming wiser about education practice, which we see as the goal of action research.

The notion of a knowledge base, which has gained currency in recent years (Shulman, 1987), is drawn mostly from an interpretation of the nature of professional work in fields other than education. Physicians, to use the quintessential and commonly cited case, are assumed to possess information about the biochemical effects of certain medications in combating disease, for example.

They have a knowledge base derived from their study of chemistry and biology, augmented by information generated from clinical trials that have been conducted by medical researchers. Their knowledge is acquired through their own university education, through journals, and through pharmaceutical salespeople. Producing and disseminating such knowledge is a primary ingredient in the improvement of health care. With knowledge of the patient, the physician tailors the therapy prudently to the case at hand.

Putting aside the question of the accuracy or thoroughness of this characterization of the physician's professional knowledge and its use (and the sketch here is admittedly incomplete), the medical model is a powerful image for many of those engaged in educational research. Produce knowledge (the job of the researcher), convey it to the teacher (the job of the professor), then apply it in the classroom (the job of the teacher). Such a model clearly specifies the role (and priority) of research.

To be sure, the model, when applied to education, incorporates the fact that the teacher must understand research findings to make practical use of them. But we believe that much of the wisdom associated with the intelligent use of practical information lies in a particularized understanding of the circumstances in a specific classroom (and, indeed, of the particular teacher). It is that site-based and person-specific understanding that often is poorly grasped and undervalued as the medical research model is usually applied in educational research.

Knowledge bases are treated by educational researchers as remote from context. But professional wisdom is all about particular events, people, and conditions. It is in the pursuit of professional wisdom that one realizes the singular potential of action research. Research by teachers is unlikely to become a significant element in their lives unless they see it as improving their own school-centered circumstances in ways they identify as salient.

Second, we believe that teachers' engaging in action research will have a positive effect on the future of teaching in general by changing the perception that people have about the teacher's role. By participating in this process, teachers begin to see themselves—and can be seen by others—as more than implementors of policy, curriculum, and pedagogy devised by those who usually are considered authorities. Instead, teachers are recognized as the experts that they are in domains of their own experience. It is possible that such activity by teachers will lead to a redefinition of teaching that recognizes how teachers have the capability of taking the lead in obtaining the insights necessary to improve their own practice. Such recognition begins to create a climate of encouragement wherein teachers become initiators of educational change, not solely implementors of the ideas of others. It encourages them to continue to probe, to do research.

Third, when teachers engage in action research, they often illuminate aspects of teaching and learning that have not been of previous interest to educational researchers. Since research programs tend to be initiated by professors, the topics that are chosen reflect interests in the university. These topics do not necessarily correspond with the responsibilities and concerns of teachers or other education professionals. Professors gravitate toward generation of and contribution to theory. They want to identify general principles that explain human activity. Scholarly contributions in this domain bring the greatest academic rewards and the highest status.

The theories professors concentrate on, in turn, tend to be those associated with the academic disciplines in the social and behavioral sciences: psychology, sociology, economics, political science, anthropology, and linguistics, for example. These disciplines often offer a window on practical and concrete matters, but their primary aim is to understand and articulate various regularities of human activity, not necessarily to do anything about them. Professors are usually pleased when their work seems to have practical payoff, but they do not have the responsibility for acting on the basis of their understanding in a way that affects other human beings (other than their researcher-peers). A teacher's life, on the other hand, is almost completely action-oriented and directed toward events in the present. The issues identified by teachers tend to be those associated with taking defensible action that has a direct and usually immediate impact on children.

Action research, research by teachers on topics they identify as important in better meeting their professional responsibilities, therefore adds essential topics to educational research—topics usually defined not by the disciplines but by the proximate and unavoidable demands of serving children. Teachers are encouraged to continue their inquiries when they note the saliency, even the uniqueness, of their own perspective on the problems and challenges of teaching.

A fourth reason for encouraging collaborative action research relates to the benefits that teachers derive from meeting on a regular basis in a professional community. It has been clear in our experiences working with groups of teachers that the support they receive from one another in self-identified communities of mentor teachers, novice science teachers, and experienced physics teachers has been a primary reason for their continuing to gather on a regular basis. The teachers who constitute these small communities have taken the time to learn about one another. They have noted their shared values, and they have decided to work together to maximize them in their collaborative research. To reach this stage, they have had opportunities to develop shared meanings.

For example, most science teachers assert that they value laboratory work. When they describe what they have in mind, however, it is not always apparent that one teacher's view of the ideal laboratory easily matches another's. One may emphasize original investigation by students, another a particular sequence of problem-solving steps, and a third the creation of a certain kind of laboratory log.

Particularly in the discussions that precede collaborative action research, teachers in a coalescing group probe each other's goals and meanings. In the process, they may modify some of their ideas, but they always center on what they share. This type of community, wherein people are professionally (and, in many respects, personally) compatible in fundamental ways, seems to us essential in carrying out collaborative action research. In such a community, the group moves toward a common goal, but, because they have a great deal in common, deep analysis and criticism are acceptable. The group itself fosters commitment— and therefore its own perpetuation.

SUSTAINING ACTION RESEARCH

Teachers change what they do for many reasons. A new approach seems merito-rious on its face and thus worth trying. The school district, the legislature, or the state education agency mandates a change, so teachers must comply. Sometimes a particular innovation receives popular attention and acclaim in the media; teachers feel pressured by parents and administrators to implement it. It is some-times prestigious to try something new that is advocated. Teachers also may change their practice because they appreciate the association (and sometimes the attention) of a dedicated educational innovator who advocates the change and also provides support; that person might be a professor from a nearby college or university the teacher has become acquainted with. Occasionally, teachers will try something new in response to incentives like released time or extra pay.

Each of these kinds of motivation to do things differently, however, tends to subside as the pressure or stimulus disappears. None of them is teacher-generated. For teachers to take possession of action research, for action research to be self-sustaining, several questions and challenges require concerted attention.

1. What basic conditions are necessary for action research to be embedded in teachers' practice?
2. How does action research begin to have the same sort of temporal and spatial flow as other aspects of teaching and professional life?
3. How is the methodology of action research tuned to the ongoing lives and work of teachers?
4. How does the focus of action research best match the actual concerns of teachers (as contrasted with the interests of outsiders)?
5. How does action research become intrinsic to a teacher's need to under-stand her own practices, to her own development as a professional?
6. How does action research continue to be collaborative among teachers so that they can profit from not only their own initiatives but also those of others?

None of these questions is trivial or easy. We will examine each of them in turn in an attempt to outline the issues and suggest some possible approaches.

First, with respect to embedding action research in regular practice, the obstacles are particularly formidable. Teachers are busy people. In California, it is not unusual for secondary school teachers to meet with more than 150 students each day. The task of grading papers in itself can fill several hours a day. Additionally, teachers are continually devising their curriculum or modifying existing ones. They often are involved in professional activities outside of the classroom, like coaching, advising student groups, and serving on restructuring committees. Many of them are active in professional societies and teachers' associations.

Some teachers also hold second jobs, are pursuing additional degrees, and are, of course, family members and parts of their communities. Action research can be and has been displaced by all of this. If action research can exist only as an addition to what teachers are already doing, ways must be found to release them from some of their other duties or to provide them with adequate compensation. The issue of identifying time is fundamental.

With respect to action research coming to match the temporal and spatial flow of teaching, our second point, the obstacles are also serious and complex. To clarify what we mean by this, we would like to suggest a distinction between the idea of context in the sense in which it is commonly used in educational research and what we prefer to call a teacher's "educational situation." The context for a teacher is the setting in which she teaches—the conditions that shape her actions. To speak of the teaching context conjures up an image of teachers as malleable and reactive entities, separable from and not always aware of their surroundings, but shaped by those other entities that make up the context. Those entities include their students, other faculty, the school administration, and the organization of the school and school district.

These influences are profound, to be sure. But teachers bring much that is personal to the classroom, also. They find themselves propelled into an educational situation constituted by all that has occurred in the past and from which they project themselves into the future. In their acts of being a teacher, they are immersed in the totality of their educational situation, which is made up of all the elements that constitute their context, plus the past and possible future actions of other people (Heidegger, 1962).

For action research to match the temporal and spatial flow, teachers need to be engaged in that activity within the educational situations of their classrooms. When research takes on the methodology and other characteristics of traditional forms of research, it ceases to be timely. This can be seen most clearly in the requirement that traditional experimental research be reproducible. For example, students typically reproduce historical experiments in physics. There is the expectation that a replication of Michelson's experiment would not find that the speed of light is different for different observers, or that a repetition of Galileo's experiment would find that objects do not accelerate uniformly under gravity.

The results of these experiments are identical whether they are done in the seventeenth, nineteenth, or twentieth century. That is, the reproducibility of the research depends on its being nontemporal, its aspiring to timelessness. In most research, the object under study is the same at all times. The investigator can set up the experiment at any time and expect similar, if not identical, results.

On the other hand, the object of teachers' self-developmental research is both temporal and spatial. As the teacher engages in the research process and modifies activities in the classroom, she comes to a different understanding of her educational situation. The new insights often result instantly in her deciding to act in different ways. The educational situation that she was investigating no longer exists. She has modified it irreversibly.

This reorientation might at first appear to be no different from what occurs in any sort of naturalistic inquiry. The community that the ethnographer studies changes with time as people interact with one another. Geological processes continue and affect the understanding of the earth scientist. Ecosystems are always in a state of flux. But in each of those instances, the object of the research is outside of the professional situation of the researcher. The phenomena themselves are unaffected.

Not so for the teacher. The impetus for the research, some discrepancy or dilemma of practice, might still be there (Altrichter, Posch, & Somekh, 1993), but the events that illuminated it for the teacher are in the past. By reflecting on those events and taking action, the teacher has gained insight, a new perspective, a different understanding of her educational situation. She knows more about teaching, as well as how and what she wants to teach. She has become wiser about her practice.

The outsider-researcher returns to the events of interest by examining documents and interviewing informants for different perspectives. By doing so, the researcher comes to an understanding that transcends the particular events under study. At least, that type of understanding is usually the goal. The researcher asks, "What is this a case of? To what theory can I generalize this case?" The purpose of action research for the teacher, on the other hand, is to come to a better understanding of her educational situation, so that she can improve her practice. She wants to be wiser, and wisdom lies in action. Modification of practice has occurred during the course of the inquiry. New events, which upon reflection can further illuminate her educational situation, continue to happen. Her knowledge and understanding grow through reflections on those events and circumstances.

To do the sort of research that the ethnographer does is to focus on what has happened and not on what is happening. There is a trade-off of reflection on practice for reflection in practice (Schön, 1983). The result could be a net loss for the teacher in terms of the immediacy and efficacy of her practice.

Our first two questions lead to the third, about the methodology of research. Because action research must be embedded in what teachers are already doing and must match the temporal and spatial flow of teaching, it cannot rely on the methods of the natural or the social sciences. These methods, whether those of the physicist, sociologist, or ethnographer, require teachers to step out of their function as teachers and to enter those other roles. At that point, the research is no longer embedded. The temporal flow stops. Of course, this is just what is expected when teachers are encouraged to be reflective practitioners. They step out of their roles so that they can reflect on action instead of doing the "monitor and adjust," or reflection in action, that is an ordinary part of good practice.

Our concern is that if the methods of action research do not allow for it to occur without the teacher stepping out of her everyday, professional role, it will not be self-sustaining. As soon as external support is removed, the teachers will return to their traditional roles and cease to be reflective practitioners. At this time in the history of educational action research, we are not proffering a view of the nature of this different approach to research, although many descriptions of action research, including some in this volume, comport well with what we have in mind. We feel that the form of self-sustaining action research toward which we are trying to progress is something that will emerge as more teachers begin to engage in the activity apart from coursework and externally inspired research projects.

Our final questions are intimately connected to the first three, and expand upon them. They are specifically related to ways in which teachers can see the fruits of action research as intrinsically desirable and not extrinsically inspired and utilized. First, and clearly related to the previous point, is that the action research agenda must be that of the teachers. If action research is to be a self-sustaining enterprise, teachers must know that their independently generated concerns are legitimate targets for research. As long as the agenda for teachers' research is established by outsiders, or if teachers consider only outsider research agendas as legitimate, the identification of topics of priority for teachers is unlikely, perhaps impossible. But unless the research agendas are the teachers' own, they have little reason to follow through.

In addition, the research must be self-developmental. An important intrinsic reward for engaging in this process is that the teachers get better at what they want to do, that it helps them move toward goals they value. This point highlights a fundamental issue. The chances of a teacher-based activity like action research becoming self-sustaining in the face of all the other demands on a teacher's time seem slim—unless teachers see a particular kind of potential for improving their own practice. That special promise centers on the teacher's perception that any change might move the teacher toward goals that she herself identifies as worthy.

Teachers will continue to modify their work with children without external pressure or unusual rewards if the change in practice brings the teacher closer to her own conception of desirable teaching—if the change enhances a sense of personal and professional fulfillment. In essence, a requisite for continual self-improvement to be embedded in ongoing practice is that it be seen by the teacher as helping to make her more like the kind of professional she herself wants to become. The motivation is internal and the situation her own.

Finally, there must be mechanisms built into the process that allow teachers to find out about the process itself, results of other teachers' research, and criticism and praise of their own work. We see much opportunity for necessary feedback stimulated and facilitated by the collaborative aspect of the type of action research that we espouse. In addition, however, there is a need to include a wider community of teachers. This outreach probably would not take place through publication in the usual academic journals, presentations at professional gatherings of academic researchers, or books like this. Instead, consonant with our earlier points, we see this sharing and exchange of information and insights occurring through the avenues that teachers already employ: meetings of subject-based professional societies and other teachers' associations, district and school inservice programs, and the small number of newsletters and journals that are beginning to publish teachers' stories.

The professional satisfactions derived from association with an identifiable, active, inquiring, and supportive community add significantly to the self-sustaining potential of the kind of teacher-based inquiry we envision. This sense of belonging to a like-minded and respected group, when added to the self-developmental features of action research (and to the other benefits we have outlined), begins to provide the kinds of conditions we believe necessary for action research to become part of the ongoing professional lives of teachers.

Part III

SUPPORTING ACTION RESEARCH

10

Developing Discourses and Structures to Support Action Research for Educational Reform

Working Both Ends

David Hursh

Two worlds. The university and the schools. The ivory tower and the trenches. Theory and practice. As an elementary and middle school teacher and administrator in the first half of my career and as a teacher educator in the second half, I have been concerned with the work of connecting both ends of education: the preparation and development of teachers, and the improvement in our understanding of educational theory and teaching practices. My current efforts focus on the development of a teacher education program in which preservice and inservice teachers use action research as a way to further their theory and practice.

By connecting theory and practice I desire to accomplish several goals. First, I am aiming for teachers and those learning to teach to see teaching as not merely the implementation of existing practices, even those practices that intuitively strike us as positive, but as the development of practices within the context of questions such as: What and whose knowledge should be in the classroom? What should be the relationship between teacher and student? How should we assess learning and what is the relationship between assessment and learning?

These are theoretical questions in that they are not only questions of how we apply research on teaching to our own practices and what we need to know of our subject, but also questions that require us to examine our own understanding of the nature of society, knowledge, and schools. They are, at heart, social and political questions of how schools as social institutions can either alleviate, produce, or reproduce both particular ways of acting in and making sense of the world, and race, gender, and class inequalities. For example, later I will detail how the practice of tracking came about because of particular historical circumstances that led to particular ways of thinking and talking about the purposes and practices of schooling. I will contend that educators need to be able to evaluate school organization, curriculum, and teaching practices in light of their origins and their implications for how we decide what and how students learn. My goal is to develop reflective teachers who realize that schools as

> social institutions, help reproduce a society based on unjust class, race, and gender relations and that teachers have a moral obligation to reflect on and change their own practices and school structures when these perpetuate such arrangements. (Valli, 1990a, p. 46)

Second, I want my work with pre- and inservice teachers to emphasize theory and practice as mutually constitutive. That is, theory or how we conceptualize schooling, teaching, and learning, influences and is influenced by practice. For example, the desire to implement a whole language approach to literacy learning might be based on ethical and political goals of respecting students and their own literacy, even when their literacy deviates from standard English. As such an approach is put into practice, educators might rethink and refine their theoretical understanding of how children become literate and the role literacy plays in children's lives, and, in an ongoing dialectical or spiraling fashion, rethink and refine their teaching practices. How far we advance in our own thinking or practice is linked to our advancement in each area.

Third, connecting theory and practice requires that we reduce the school–university split. If we are to examine and improve theory and practice, we need schools and teacher education programs where questions can be raised and practices changed. Therefore, teacher educators, teachers, and preservice teachers need to be mutually engaged in examining their own understanding and changing their practices. Action research provides a systematic method of undertaking such an examination.

In this chapter I first contend that the goal of collaboration should be not only to improve the teaching practices of those in schools and universities, but also to change how schools and universities are organized and the ways in which we talk about education. Then I turn to describing current efforts to working both ends at the University of Rochester and local school districts (Hursh, 1993). This includes a description of how pre- and inservice teachers have attempted to question dominant teaching practices and to develop alternative teaching practices, organizational structures, and educational discourses. Finally, I show how these efforts are situated in an ongoing attempt to rethink educational theory.

CONNECTING THEORY AND PRACTICE: SITUATING PRACTICES WITHIN DISCURSIVE AND ORGANIZATIONAL STRUCTURES

One way to examine the relationship between theory and practice and to situate that relationship within its social context is to examine the connections among educational practices, educational discourses, and organizational forms. Stephen Kemmis and Robin McTaggart (1988) succinctly summarize the relationships among practices, discourses, and organizational forms as follows:

> The institutionalization of educational activities in more or less well-formed and characteristic *practices* depends upon the availability of *discourses* which can justify and/or legitimate the practices as educationally worthwhile, and upon the existence of stable *organizational forms*. (p. 42; emphasis in original)

The necessity for situating our practices within such a context can be understood both by historically analyzing education and by examining the everyday situations teachers face.

The particular educational practices, discourses, and organizational structures that become institutionalized are neither inevitable nor natural but are outcomes of ongoing political, ethical, and philosophical struggles over schooling. For example, tracking, or the practice of sorting students into homogeneous groups, became the accepted response to the increasingly heterogeneous school population in the early part of this century. The change in school population resulted from increasing immigration from Eastern and Southern Europe and the more rigorous enforcement of compulsory attendance laws imposed by a modern industrial society. Tracking became an accepted organizational response for a variety of reasons, including assumptions regarding the neutrality of science and scientific management. The rise of the psychological discourse of behaviorism and the political discourse of meritocracy legitimated the assumption that individuals were born with predetermined abilities that could be assessed through intelligence tests. Furthermore, the political discourse of meritocracy legitimized the belief that an individual's ultimate social standing resulted from a combination of ability and effort. Hence, sorting students into ability groups and consequently narrowing their opportunities for changing social status were perceived as scientific and fair (Hursh, 1994).

Part of becoming a reflective teacher is realizing that educational goals, school and classroom organization, and curriculum content have been and continue to be struggled over (Kliebard, 1986). Tracking, for example, was only one possible response to the increasing diversity of student populations; other outcomes were, and are, conceivable. Now, as in the past, some educators have opposed tracking, arguing that the standardized tests used for placing students in tracks are culturally biased and that tracking unfairly diminishes the life chances of those in the middle and lower tracks. Alternatives to tracking can be envisioned, such as developing heterogeneous classrooms with less competitive, more cooperative learning and a greater emphasis on individual goals and authentic assessment. However, such approaches would require that we change not only our teaching practices but also how we organize schools and conceive of and talk about educational goals.

Reflective teaching means understanding education as a contested terrain in which different outcomes are possible. Becoming a reflective teacher means that teachers must not only analyze and change their own practice, but also change educational discourse and the structure of educational environments. Without the power to change the structure of educational organizations, teachers have limited control over their own classrooms and will have difficulty developing a learning community that does more than reproduce the status quo.

TEACHER EDUCATION AND ACTION RESEARCH

Student teachers, because they are customarily limited to teaching curricular units within the narrow confines of school and district requirements, rarely have the opportunity to examine the complex relationships among practice, discourse, and organizational structures. Therefore, they are not encouraged to become reflective practitioners within a community of learners. For example, in my earlier research, I observed and interviewed a student teacher who desired to implement whole language and authentic assessment in her classroom, relatively new approaches at the time of the research. Even though her cooperating teacher supported her, the principal intervened to require basal readers and traditional assessment. Because she and her cooperating teacher had limited influence regarding the policies affecting their classroom, she was frustrated in her efforts (Hursh, 1988). Therefore, in working with schools, our teacher education faculty are interested in creating environments where discussion and practice are focused not only on rethinking and reforming teaching practices and teacher preparation, but also on reconceptualizing the aims of education and the organization of schools. For these purposes, action research can be especially helpful as a way to negotiate and make sense of what can be for student teachers an overwhelming and chaotic experience.

The experience of the student teacher described above suggests that efforts to engage student teachers in action research cannot be carried out separately from a larger analysis and action within the school. Action research, when undertaken as an individual activity, is easily overwhelmed by the culture of the school. What a teacher attempts to do is easily stymied by the dominant and accepted practices, such as standardized testing, 45-minute periods, and required textbooks (Hursh, 1994). Therefore, action research within teacher education needs to be situated within a supportive structure that links analyses of discourse, practice, and organization of schools to change.

Over the past several years, I, along with my colleagues in the teacher education program, have been attempting to situate learning to teach within a theoretical context by both raising questions of what and how to teach and requiring students to implement action research projects. The teacher education program in the Warner Graduate School of Education and Human Development is an intense 15-month program that leads to a master's degree with certification in either secondary or elementary education. In aiming to connect theory and practice, we have developed a program with several unique characteristics.

During the past 5 years the secondary subject methods courses have been co-taught by a school of education faculty member and a teacher from the Rochester City School District. Similarly, half of the elementary education methods classes have been taught by practicing teachers who are also doctoral students in the program. At both the secondary and elementary levels we have been attempting to develop collaborative relations with schools, as part of either a Ford Foundation grant (1988–90), an American Federation of Teachers (AFT) grant (1990–93), or the current model, which is supported by additional funding from the school of education. Examples cited below come from my own work with either secondary student teachers and teachers in the AFT project or elementary student teachers recently enrolled in our program.

In our program we have explicitly informed student teachers of our aim to develop reflective teachers who are aware that education is a contested terrain in which they are engaged in not only changing practices but educational discourse and organizational structures. That students become aware of and engaged in such struggles is reflected in interviews of student teachers in the elementary program. The interviews also reveal the degree to which we have not yet developed programmatic structures that promote dialogue over the theory and practice of teaching.

Pauline (a pseudonym), a student in the elementary education program during 1992–93, described herself, in the spring of 1993, as having a theoretical and practical perspective about teaching that is based on particular ethical and political assumptions. She stated that her preference for a whole language approach to literacy learning is based on a conception of literacy and schooling that differs from that of the school in which she student taught. "Reading," she related, "is more . . . than just reading words and we [she co-taught with a second student teacher] wanted [the students] to enjoy it and see that there are a lot of great novels and [that] books are interesting." This approach, she noted, contrasted with the school's emphasis on basals and worksheets.

Her preferences were based on not simply differences in teaching styles or personal preferences but, she explained, "different views of what schools are about and what should be taught." Like most of the other students in the program, she realized that she conceptualized the theory and practice of teaching differently from the teachers in the school where she student taught. "What we wanted to do was put [a particular] theory into practice and [when we arrived at the school] we saw the opposite theories in practice." The student teachers realized that school practices, discourse, and organization reflected certain theoretical assumptions.

The student teachers also felt that their cooperating teachers assumed that student teachers, as novices, had nothing new to offer experienced teachers. Even if they did, the numerous, often disconnected reform efforts occurring in the school so escalated teachers' work as to permit only short, atheoretical conversations. As another student, Kathy, stated, referring to her interest in examining the uses and assessment of reading:

> I didn't feel the schools were set up to allow those kinds of questions. . . .
> The university wanted me to do that but the teachers at the school were so
> harried that they don't have time to answer questions of why they [under-
> take particular practices]. . . . Raising questions is not something they en-
> courage. (Spring 1993)

The students' comments indicate their awareness that real differences exist over what and how to teach and that such differences need to be examined not only in university classes but during student teaching. As Kathy stated:

> One of the things that is missing [in student teaching] is the kind of conver-
> sation we have with you [the author]. . . . Even though I am in a class-
> room that will allow me to do some things, it's really not supporting me be-
> cause we [she and the cooperating teacher] have talked together about
> what I'm trying to do but it's not really the same because she hasn't been in
> on other parts of the conversation and in our abbreviated conversations
> you don't get the same kind of meaning. (Spring 1993)

She adds that she and her cooperating teacher are "not trying to figure out answers together. I am trying to figure out answers. She probably has answers herself but that's not trying to figure out answers together."

Kathy is proposing, I would contend, that we change the structure of teacher education programs so that student teachers, teachers, and university faculty engage in ongoing conversations about particular issues and continually examine and reform our practices and organizational structure. Placing such conversations within the context of asking and answering questions also suggests undertaking action research.

DEVELOPING COLLABORATIVE STRUCTURES TO TRANSFORM SCHOOLS AND TEACHER EDUCATION

In the previous section I discussed how the student teachers expressed a desire to collaborate with teachers in an ongoing examination of educational practices, discourses, and structures. Over the past 4 years we have undertaken, with varying success, efforts to develop such collaboration. One project was set up at an urban high school under a proposal funded for 3 years by the AFT. While the project was unsuccessful in that it ended and our university is not currently placing student teachers at the school, the project confirmed the potential benefits of teachers formulating questions and undertaking action research. The project also highlights the need for universities and schools to reform their organizational structures to make collaborative action research possible.

Initial Efforts Toward Collaboration

In 1990 I began working with a team of seven high school teachers in an inner-city comprehensive high school where the majority of the students are African American or other minorities, poor, and at risk of dropping out. In the 1991–92 school year, the seven teachers decided to combine their classrooms by subject areas, thereby developing "blended classrooms" in which they team taught a group of special and regular education students. Teaching teams were organized for science, social studies, and English, while math was individually taught until a team was formed in 1992–93. Among the 150 or so students each team taught, the teachers were assigned a cohort of ninth-grade students who would take the four core subjects only from them.

Besides forming blended classrooms and teaching teams, the teachers met to develop specific goals. Their goals included developing an integrated, multicultural curriculum around major concepts such as diversity and empowerment, building on their students' knowledge and experience, and developing authentic methods of assessment. In addition to working in their own classrooms, the teachers as a group met weekly to collaborate on the changes. Each teacher also met with and supervised a student teacher who was placed in his or her subject area. As a teacher educator I was to conduct a weekly seminar for the seven student teachers, discuss with the cooperating teachers changes in their curriculum and pedagogical practices, and help them document their efforts. I also looked forward to conversing with the teachers about their problems, observing their classrooms, and learning about teaching minority high school students in an urban environment.

While our goals for the year were ambitious and we worked diligently at achieving them, our efforts were, in the end, undermined by a lack of support from the school and inadequate structural reforms in our teacher education program. The school administrators undermined the project by assigning the teaching teams 45 students to a class, assigning them the most difficult students in the school, and continually threatening to take away the teachers' common planning time.

Finally, my own efforts to work collaboratively with teachers and students were undercut by the organizational structure of the professional practice site and the university teacher education program. Because the student teachers were not supervised by me but by a university faculty member with whom they also took a seminar, they received no credit for participating in my seminar. The potential for serious dialogue and collaboration was undermined by teachers and student teachers meeting separately and by student teachers receiving no credit for the meetings.

Learning from Experience: New Plans, New Tensions

We began the 1992–93 school year having made a few adjustments. First, student teachers were to receive credit for their in-school seminar and were to use action research as a method for investigating a concern. Second, while the teachers were not able to change the structural conditions within which they worked, they desired to change what was within their control. Therefore, the teachers rededicated themselves to focusing on classroom practices and so began the fall term by proposing to use action research to address the following goals:

1. To first share and thereby clarify and strengthen their different conceptions of multicultural education, to be followed by developing and trying out new teaching strategies, and later documenting and assessing the changes.
2. To develop a better method for assessing students' learning.
3. To figure out how to incorporate students' own experiences into the curriculum (a project we called "kids 'n the hood").
4. To develop more explicit connections between theory and practice.

The action research process as outlined by Kemmis and McTaggart (1988) provided a structure for acting on these goals. According to our plan, each two subject-area teachers would begin by researching and discussing the issue they chose to explore, such as incorporating students' experience into their teaching, then develop and carry out a plan while documenting and evaluating the process. As a team they would share what they were doing and learning. Furthermore, the student teachers, who are placed in the school in the spring semester, would, unlike the previous year, receive course credit for undertaking action research and meeting in the school in a seminar.

Unfortunately, in-school events once again undermined the best intentions. During the fall of 1992 tensions increased among the students and between students and teachers. The already tense relations between African American and White students were exacerbated when most of the untenured minority teachers were laid off because of school budget reductions. Student altercations included several incidents with weapons, including a serious but nonfatal shooting. Groups of students customarily walked out of class. Tensions were further aggravated by the school administration confiscating an unauthorized student-published newspaper and suspending the students involved. Ironically, the student journalists included some of the most academically successful students in the school, who were using the paper to raise questions about teacher–student relations and relations between minority and majority students. Teachers and administrators disagreed over how to respond to the problems, with some African American teachers resigning from the school-based planning team, charging that some of the administrators and teachers were racist. By spring break the school superintendent had temporarily replaced the principal, who then took a leave of absence for the remainder of the year and was permanently replaced over the summer. In such an atmosphere, the teachers with whom I worked found it impossible to focus on the less crisis-driven questions of teaching. They also began to plan for the subsequent reorganization of the school into four smaller magnet schools and for activities after the expiration of the grant in the summer of 1993.

Given the school's problems, it was not surprising that in January 1993 only three students (two in social studies and one in math) chose the school for their student teaching. Two of the three student teachers decided to focus on the same issue: giving students freedom and responsibility in the classroom. In addition, I was approached by Brandon, a master's degree student majoring in "visual and cultural studies," who wanted to gain experience teaching urban secondary students. The four students did carry out abbreviated forms of action research.

When Brandon, who was not in our teacher education program, approached me regarding working with students in an urban high school, it seemed natural to approach the two English teachers I was working with at the high school. The English teachers saw this as an opportunity to have someone work with some of the more difficult students in their class and invited Brandon to work with at first four and later six students. After some reflection, Brandon decided to engage the students in a video project.

Student Teachers' Action Research Projects

In preparing a written summary of this project, Brandon provided his pedagogical justifications for the project. Brandon has thoroughly studied the development and aims of cultural studies programs both in and outside the United States, such as the Binghamton (U.K.) Center for Cultural Studies and the Education Video Center in New York City. He was drawn to cultural studies programs because of their aim to use ethnographic studies to explore "the ways in which youth sub-cultures negotiated with bourgeois hegemony" and to make it possible "for academicians to study/and become involved in the process of meaning-creation among sub-cultural groups" (Block, 1993, p. 3). Video educators, he notes, have undertaken a critical approach to pedagogy, encouraging students "to use the classroom as an opportunity [to examine] the social, political, and cultural complexities of the world. Critical pedagogy also emphasizes the importance [of] letting students empower themselves in the classroom and through the projects they pursue in the classroom" (Block, 1993, p. 3).

Teaching by having students make videos requires reconceptualizing pedagogical relationships. Block (1993) describes the use of video this way:

> Video projects can provide an opportunity for students and teachers to challenge traditional roles and participate in collaborative learning as they negotiate the shape, form, and content of the video they are producing. The aesthetic, political, and philosophical differences which emerge as the project goes forward can challenge students and teachers to become cognizant of each other's realities and discover spaces of common ground as well as irreconcilable difference. (p. 4)

Brandon, therefore, developed a project in which his students would gain knowledge, skills, and a greater sense of control over their education and learning, at the same time as he would learn about teaching and students.

In summarizing the project, Brandon describes how he, along with a second student, engaged the students in making a video about a topic of the students' choice. Numerous options were presented to the students, including sports, music, and social issues, but the students immediately pressed for making a video about violence. While they weren't at all clear what they wanted to say about violence, they were sure, because one student's brother had been killed and the others had both seen and been the subject of violence, it was the issue of central importance to their lives. Brandon describes his struggles over how much control he should have over writing, filming, and producing the work and in enticing students to stay with it.

But in the end as the finished video, titled "Fight the Violence," was shown in the school and copies were made available to friends and educators, Brandon notes that the students responded to the evaluation by writing moving essays describing their enthusiasm for the project. One student wrote that when he began the project he had "just gotten out of prison and was not an angel, but that this project showed him that he could work hard and accomplish something which he could be proud of" (Block, 1993, p. 26).

The other student teachers took on similarly worthwhile activities. Stacy, who student taught in several law education classes, examined when and how a teacher should give her or his opinion regarding a particular issue. She decided to use different methods and explore different contexts in which to express her opinion, observe student reactions, and, whenever possible, observe how students responded when other teachers expressed opinions. This was an especially appropriate topic in light of several events that occurred during the semester: intense debate among teachers and students in reaction to the distribution and administrative confiscation of an unauthorized student newspaper, as noted earlier; the publication of the results from an assessment of the school by a superintendent's fact finding committee, which led to the replacement of the principal; and racial divisions between students, between faculty, and between students and faculty.

A third student, Mark, taught social studies classes that had both regular and learning disabled students. One of his concerns was developing critical thinking and responsibility in his students. Consequently, he developed projects in which students would use resources in developing their analytical skills. For example, he had students develop a report on an African country, and as a group they analyzed television commercials for their intended audience and selling strategies. In his paper summarizing the project Mark questioned whether the New York State Regents final exam given to his students was appropriate given the variety of activities his students used to learn the material.

Finally, Nicolle, who student taught in math, worked on developing responsibility by giving the students more freedom. She often sought the students' input on lessons, let them make choices, and had them work in groups. She wanted them to experience freedom and responsibility so that they could see mathematics not as doing math problems but as problem solving. In her classroom Nicolle attempted to establish a "community of learners" where the students would see problem solving as a process to be learned from rather than as simply finding the answer to a problem.

While the student teachers' efforts demonstrated their ability to carry out projects that significantly affected students' learning and produced new knowledge about educational theory and practice, their work was, for the most part, separate from the cooperating teachers. What we have not yet been able to achieve is student teachers and teachers collaborating over issues of what and how to teach and what practices should be used.

Implications for Collaborative Efforts in Teacher Education

The high school experience under the AFT grant taught us several fundamental lessons. The teacher education program must be set up to support students' efforts in the school. A school's collaboration with a university must be agreed on more broadly than just by the teachers; administrators must also be interested in the success of the project and support it with time and ideas. Therefore, the faculty in the teaching and curriculum program are proposing a redesigned program that will promote stronger connections with schools and cooperating teachers. Rather than placing student teachers with individual cooperating teachers in schools, we are setting up relationships with numerous schools in which student teachers, teachers, and university faculty will share the responsibility for the education of students and student teachers. For example, secondary teacher education faculty will be placing six student teachers in a middle school with a team of 6 sixth-grade teachers who are responsible for developing a new sixth-grade curriculum. The teachers and student teachers will be team teaching an integrated curriculum that will include students' interests and will be authentically assessed.

This arrangement has several structural differences from the earlier projects, differences, we feel, that support changes in school discourse, organization, and teaching practices. First, the dean of the school of education and I approached the principal and the school-based planning team with a proposal to develop a collaborative relationship in which the university and school faculty have shared responsibility for the learning of students and student teachers. The school-based planning team approached the sixth-grade teachers because of the teachers' commitment to examining and reforming the organization, content, and assessment of the sixth-grade curriculum. Consequently, unlike in the past, the teachers, student teachers, and university faculty have the crucial support of the school and university administrators, and the teachers have the flexibility to change the organization of the school day.

Given what we, the teacher education faculty, have learned from previous experiences, we also have reorganized the teacher education program to increase the amount of time and collaboration between students and cooperating teachers. Student teachers are in the schools two semesters rather than one. Both semesters are restructured so that student teachers spend time not only teaching but collaborating with teachers in raising questions about curriculum content, teaching processes, and assessment. Student teachers are undertaking research projects and using the process of action research to implement and evaluate the changes.

Another lesson from the AFT project was that time needs to be set aside at school and that student teachers and teachers need an incentive beyond their own good will to engage in collaboration. Consequently, student teachers and teachers will meet for an hour every other week in a two-semester, three-credit course titled "Reflective Teaching" to make plans for action research and share and evaluate what they are learning.

Furthermore, the teacher education faculty and the school of education have shown a commitment to making a difference in the schools. The "Reflective Teaching" course is also part of the university faculty's teaching load, thereby supporting faculty to work with the teachers. Other school of education faculty are also committed to learning from the teachers' expertise and sharing their expertise with the teachers.

Similar professional development school relationships are being developed with other elementary and secondary schools. At each site it is expected that teachers, student teachers, and university faculty will use action research as a method of responding to their concerns. For example, at one of the elementary schools where we will place student teachers, the teachers and student teachers will use action research to develop new curriculum and methods of authentic assessment.

Our goal is to develop within each school and across sites, including between the schools and university, a community of learners who are engaged in developing, documenting, evaluating, and disseminating their efforts to rethink and reform schooling and teaching. We are aiming to analyze and change not only classroom practices but the way we talk about schooling and the way schools are organized. For example, one positive outcome of the AFT project is reflected in changes in discourse. Teachers engaged in organized, teacher-led discussions unlike those that typically occur in schools. They discussed, for example, varying views of multicultural education, debating whether multicultural education should emphasize teaching about different cultures or attempting to understand and respond to the cultures of the African American, Latino/a, and White working class students. And student teachers were encouraged by the teachers to raise questions about and develop new teaching and evaluation methods.

What the teachers did not have control over—the scheduling of classes and planning times, including the option of block scheduling—undermined the possibility of real collaboration and school reforms. But, because of recent administrative and structural changes in the school, including plans for the creation of four schools-within-the-school, they will have more control during the upcoming school year.

What we, university and school faculty, have learned from attempting to collaborate with teachers in undertaking action research is that such projects are worthwhile only when educators are able to not only reflect on and change the teaching practices within their own classrooms, but also explicitly engage in examining and changing how they talk about education and the organizational structure of their classrooms and school. To do less limits educators to minor changes within their own classrooms. We also have learned how difficult it is to develop the kind of structured relationships required for such collaboration. The schools are attempting to support teachers by providing the space and time to engage in collaboration and to make programmatic changes beyond the classroom. At the university level we are restructuring our program so that seminars led by faculty from both institutions can occur in schools. This chapter does not describe a program that has achieved its aims, but a program that is struggling to put all the parts together: to connect practice and theory, to link schools and universities, and to use action research as a way of directing the analysis and reform of teaching and schools.

11

What Happens When a School District Supports Action Research?

Cathy Caro-Bruce & Jennifer McCreadie

In 1990, 10 staff members of this school district sat around a table intensely discussing their action research questions. The two facilitators, feeling the excitement and uneasiness that come with stepping into unfamiliar territory, encouraged, probed, and reassured the eight elementary school teachers as they worked through the process of inquiring about their topics. Another 12 middle school teachers and 12 elementary principals participated in action research the following year. In 1992–93, we were joined by four additional facilitators, and almost 40 elementary and middle school teachers were split among four action research groups. Over 40 teachers became action researchers during 1993–94, and 10 facilitators led five groups.

How did action research grow in this district? How can a district support and sustain a large number of teachers and principals interested in participating in this experience? Several critical elements have nurtured the growth of classroom action research in the Madison Metropolitan School District, and the implications may be helpful to other districts interested in establishing an active action research program. In this chapter, we will describe the background and context of how action research has grown in the district; the organization and process being used to help teachers and principals work on their questions; the value of the experience as perceived by the participants; and some lessons we have learned about implementing classroom action research in our school district. This is Madison's story, but aspects of it could easily apply to other districts.

The Madison Metropolitan School District is located in Madison, Wisconsin, the state capital and home of the main campus of the University of Wisconsin. This is a city where education has been valued and supported by the community. With approximately 24,000 students, the district has 29 elementary schools, nine middle schools, and four high schools. The teaching staff comprises approximately 2,100 elementary, middle, and high school classroom teachers.

BEGINNINGS

Classroom action research did not arrive in Madison for the first time in the fall of 1990. Rather, commitment, patience, and making the most of opportunities contributed to its development over time. For 2 years, beginning in 1985, a staff development specialist in the district sought funding to try this idea. She had heard about action research at a teacher center conference and thought it would be an interesting and stimulating staff development activity. After justifying the use of a pocket of research money to fund released time (to pay substitute teachers), she embarked on this independent project. Seven teachers from kindergarten through high school participated the first year, five teachers during the second year. Although teachers felt the experience was worthwhile, as with many initiatives, it was seen as this individual's project.

When this staff development specialist left the district after the second year of action research, she hoped that what she had begun would be sustained. At this stage, a partnership was born, which continues, bringing together the authors of this chapter, a staff development specialist and the coordinator of research and evaluation for the district. In the fall of 1987, with a little knowledge, a strong inclination, a collection of books and articles, and notes from the previous facilitator, we designed a 6-hour course to introduce district staff to the concept of teachers researching questions important to them. We thought that if we could build some knowledge of and interest in the process, teachers would sign up when money could be found to support them. When just two people registered, we canceled the workshop.

During the 1987–88 school year, we presented information about action research to a district leadership group and to elementary principals. Action research was met with mild interest, and several suggestions were made for possible sources of money for released time, which we felt was essential to attract and sustain participants. We went to the schools where special money had been allocated to support racial integration. Teachers were interested in action research, but their money had already been designated for other projects, and they were hesitant to take on yet another commitment.

At the same time, some dramatic changes in the demographics of the school district's student population were being recognized. Dialogue increased among staff about trying to meet the needs of more diverse, more challenging students. Teachers were finding that what used to work in their classrooms was no longer appropriate or successful. Some district funds were directed toward schools with high levels of special needs. In the beginning, the efforts were designed by individual schools, but it became apparent that district resources had to be organized more effectively. Minority student achievement became a district priority. Continuing to seek funding, we talked with principals at schools that had minority student achievement grants, but their money was committed to other efforts. Our determination and search were eventually rewarded, however.

For 2 years, the district had been supporting a project called "Cultural Differences and Classroom Strategies." Elementary school teachers had been participating in this effort to help teachers increase the repertoire of instructional strategies they used to meet a variety of needs of students from different socioeconomic and ethnic backgrounds. The third year of this project (1990–91) was to be spent helping teachers to implement the ideas they had been discussing and to learn what was making a difference to students' success in school. Action research had the potential to enable teachers who had participated in the Cultural Differences and Classroom Strategies project to explore these ideas more deeply. The Cultural Differences and Classroom Strategies planning committee supported the idea and allocated funds for the project.

Finally, there was a source of funding and an organizational connection to action research. The budget would cover the cost of substitute teachers for a total of 6 full days of released time (a combination of half- and full-day meetings), materials (notebooks, references, and journals), and printing (handouts and final report).

THE ACTION RESEARCHERS

In the spring of 1990, we described action research to all elementary principals and asked them to encourage teachers to consider participating. Information and an application form were sent to all elementary teachers in the district (about 800). Eight teachers applied, and they became our first group. We felt that we were finally on our way, although at the time it was not clear what that meant.

The 1990–91 year was a learning experience every step of the way. At times, it seemed that we were barely staying ahead of the group. Numerous hours were spent planning the next session, analyzing what took place at the previous session, and continuing to educate ourselves about action research. But the time was invaluable in what we learned.

We learned, for example, that if teachers settled on a question too quickly, they might narrow their focus and choose topics that might not sustain their interest over the year. Yet, if they did not decide on a question after several meetings, the likelihood of completing a quality project within the time frame was lessened. Journals, we discovered, cannot be a required activity. For some teachers, it was a helpful way to record their thinking over time; for others, it was merely a task to be completed and to feel guilty about when they didn't. We learned the value of having more than one teacher from a school participate in the group. When back at their schools, these teachers could talk about their questions and were able to support each other through various stages of their projects. As we learned more about the action research process, we gained confidence in what we were doing.

We began to look ahead to the following year. Since we had worked with a group of elementary teachers, we thought it would be worthwhile to offer this opportunity to middle school teachers. We were curious about whether middle school teachers would be interested in this kind of experience, and how it might differ from our work with elementary teachers. At about that time the Cultural Differences and Classroom Strategies budget was cut in half. With that decision went half the funding for released time for teachers. However, what initially seemed like a blow later turned into an opportunity.

At a middle school principals' meeting, we described classroom action research and asked the principals to support one or two teachers from their school budgets (e.g., Minority Student Achievement, Talented and Gifted, School Improvement Planning funds). If they would commit half of the costs for each teacher, the Cultural Differences project budget would cover the other half. The response was enthusiastic. Principals indicated that many teachers were attempting to look at their instruction and curriculum from different perspectives, and the principals appreciated the importance of supporting those efforts.

A casual comment by the assistant superintendent for secondary education during our presentation to a meeting with middle school principals took action research into an exciting and entirely new direction for our district. As she watched principals become enthusiastic about the possibilities, she announced, "We should have action research for administrators, and I already have my question!" Everyone chuckled, and we smiled and promised to "follow up with you on that suggestion." What resulted from that brief exchange was the formation of the school district's principals' action research group. The assistant superintendent for elementary education followed up by writing a memo encouraging principals to participate. He discussed it with each principal as he met with them for their conferences at the end of the year. We believe that his personal contact and encouragement were persuasive. Although skeptics in the district told us there was no way a group of principals would participate, when the application forms were returned, 14 principals had signed up. The 1991–92 action research groups ultimately consisted of a classroom action research group of 12 middle school teachers from seven middle schools and a principals' action research group of 12 elementary principals.

AN ACTION RESEARCH CULTURE

Teachers' and principals' action research has gradually become part of the culture of the Madison Metropolitan School District. During the winter of 1992, a panel of teachers and principals shared their action research questions and experiences with the Education Committee of the Board of Education. The presentation was designed to inform the Committee about this project, but also to start to build a financial commitment to action research. The response was enthusiastic, with one committee member asserting, "This should not be a question of how can we let people participate in action research, but how can we not have *everyone* doing this!" It was time to look ahead to the next year (1992–93).

Having facilitated a small group of elementary teachers the first year, and recognizing that we were novices at what we were doing, we thought it would be appropriate to offer the experience to another group of elementary teachers the following year. When we discussed this with our group of middle school action researchers, they responded, "But we've been talking this up at our school," and "I know other middle school teachers who are interested in participating."

It was time to rethink the direction for action research in the district. It was apparent that this project had moved beyond the pilot stage and needed to be integrated into the future directions of the district. After several discussions with the assistant superintendent for instruction, it was decided to offer classroom action research to elementary and middle school teachers. When 41 applications were returned, we were overwhelmed! This number represented teachers from 11 elementary schools and seven middle schools. The only way that we could support so many teachers in this process was to involve more facilitators. A few teachers dropped out during the summer, but with the addition of teacher-facilitators, the district still had to support half the costs for 40 teachers.

It had become clear that interest in action research was growing through a combination of factors, including publicity sent to all district teachers and administrators, encouragement from principals, informal discussions with past participants, and dissemination of the write-ups of teachers' work to the schools.

ORGANIZATION AND PROCESS

The structure and process we use with our action research groups have been developing along the way and we expect that they will continue to evolve. The two of us work as a team, representing staff development and research and evaluation in our district. This combination of interests and backgrounds is a strong partnership for action research. We bring the skills, knowledge, and experience of our separate specialties to our groups, and we learn from each other. Through our collaboration, we feel that we gain as much and have at least as much enthusiasm for action research as any group member. However, by the third year, we came to feel that it was time to share the leadership, because of both the increasing numbers of participants and our desire that action research not be dependent on individuals. The two of us enjoy working together and appreciate the support of a colleague in planning and conducting the process, so we suggested that pairs of teachers facilitate two of the groups, while we would lead the other two groups. We shared with other facilitators all of our references and materials about the structure, process, and organization of this project, but encouraged flexibility and adaptation to suit their own styles and the needs of their groups. We are pleased to see the kinds of change and innovation other facilitators and their groups bring, and are excited about this new level of involvement in action research.

Goals and Expectations

As we began to facilitate action research, based on experience with other groups, we established three general expectations for all participants: (1) that they would attend meetings regularly; (2) that they would participate in discussions; and (3) that they would write about their projects. These expectations have proven to be valid and we have continued to use them. Attendance and discussion are part of the responsibility of any team or group member. They are also the kind of investment that yields maximum benefits from the process. The importance of writing has been affirmed over and over and will be discussed later.

Goals of the action research project in this district have continued to be that:

- Each participating teacher will identify the problem or question s/he will pursue.
- Participating teachers will be encouraged to examine and assess their own work and then consider ways of working differently.
- Participating teachers will work collaboratively with each other, with course facilitators, and with other staff members in their schools.

Action research in our district is a process that takes the full school year (or sometimes more) from beginning to end. We start by getting to know each other, introducing the process of action research and the structure of the meetings, distributing materials, and explaining our expectations. The materials distributed include a binder, a journal notebook that we don't require but recommend that everybody at least try, articles, copies of other teachers' reports, and handouts ranging from a list of group members to a project time line to tips for giving constructive feedback. Participants have told us that they perceive us as organized, nonthreatening, and enthusiastic, and that they appreciate the opportunity the district is providing them. During early sessions, we present some information and resources. We are quite talkative and directive in the first meeting or two, after which we draw the participants into more active roles and eventually diminish our own roles.

The Group Process

The group support and interaction that occur throughout the year are an integral part of the action research process. We believe that group members need to feel at ease with each other in order for this to be successful. Therefore, we begin the year, and early sessions, with informal "warm-up" activities in which people gradually get to know each other and become more comfortable with the group. Over the course of the year, meetings vary according to topic and stage in the process, but the basic structure allows for each member to have 10 to 15 minutes to talk about his/her question and get support, encouragement, references, and suggestions from the rest of the group. At every meeting, participants share their questions, concerns, frustrations, and progress. This process enables all participants to become interested and involved in each other's projects. We emphasize the need to facilitate others' learning by asking questions that help individuals to think more deeply or in different ways about their questions rather than just offering solutions to problems they present. Participants are creative and thoughtful in their interactions with colleagues. The generosity, caring, and investment of individuals in each other's projects are apparent.

We agreed that our second-year groups of 12 to 15 were too large. Dividing each group into two discussion groups deprived members of the opportunity of being involved in everyone's research. Based on 2 years of experience, we felt that 8 to 10 was the optimal group size, which we confirmed in the third year. This group size allows every participant significant opportunity to participate, while still exposing all to a range of topics and issues.

Through a variety of articles and readings, including examples of action research done by teachers in Madison and elsewhere, our action researchers begin to get a sense of what action research is and can be. This enlightenment may come during the first meeting but more often takes longer. After two or three meetings, most participants have an initial grasp of action research. Some participants feel constrained by traditional research paradigms. These can be intimidating, even aversive to some teachers, while they are comfortable and desirable to other participants. Visits to the group meetings by previous years' action researchers give new participants the opportunity to hear what others' experiences have been and to ask questions about concerns or interests. Other resource people are invited to visit meetings as requested by the group members or as they seem worthwhile to us. Examples of such visitors include faculty members from the University of Wisconsin who can share their experiences with action research at other institutions and sites, and action researchers from elsewhere.

Finding the Right Question

Beginning with general topics of interest, participants develop possible questions to pursue. Through a series of exercises, participants generate criteria for "good" action research questions. Participants each write a question about some topic of interest, which is not necessarily the question they will end up with. Then each participant reads a question aloud and the group listens carefully without comment. Based on writing their own questions and listening to others, participants generate criteria for "good" action research questions. Groups fairly consistently suggest certain characteristics. Such criteria include a question that: is clear and concise; is "doable" or manageable; will yield observable or measurable evidence; is meaningful to the action researcher and others; will make a difference to the researcher and others; has some tension and cannot be answered yes or no; and will sustain the researcher's interest or passion over the course of the year. The group and facilitators help each member to refine individual questions, a process that can happen almost instantly or take months.

The group is introduced to a variety of research methods so that participants can make informed choices about data collection techniques that suit their questions. Triangulation, gathering data from a variety of sources using a variety of methods over time, is stressed to help the participants choose approaches for gathering their own data. We emphasize that the data-gathering methods chosen should be relatively easy for the researcher to use in the course of normal classroom activities with the resources available, as well as appropriate to the question being asked.

Throughout the action research process, participants discuss problems, issues, concerns, insights, and observations emerging from their inquiry. The process can be never-ending as action researchers iteratively plan, act, observe, reflect, plan, act, and so on. However, we do require that they pull together their experiences in this project and their findings to date at the end of the year. In the course of the year's meetings, we schedule considerable amounts of "work" time in which action researchers do library research, read, develop data gathering instruments, analyze data, confer with colleagues—whatever is most useful to them at the time. They eventually come to the struggle of analyzing data, making sense of the muddle, and, finally, write about their questions, inquiry, and findings.

But I Haven't Written a Paper Since I Was an Undergraduate . . .

Although writing a report is intimidating to some action researchers, it is a clear expectation of this project from the start. We emphasize that they will have plenty of support and help from us and from each other as we progress through the year. Group members are generally excited about the opportunity to read or hear about other teachers' research, and recognize the importance of their own contributions. While we encourage alternative means of communicating about action research projects, written reports are still an expectation, and they are the most widely disseminated form of information about the inquiry conducted. Participants in action research enjoy the opportunities it gives them to be learners, as well as to be respected and sought as professionals and experts with knowledge and experience to offer. Creating and disseminating reports enhances the professional image and self-concept of these educators. But this is not the only reason for writing. We have found that participants feel proud of the accomplishment of completing their projects and have a greater sense of closure after writing reports than before. Some participants also feel that they come to a sense of clarity or understanding through writing that they did not achieve earlier in the process, even though they had already learned from their action research and reached some findings or conclusions. While writing may not be intrinsic to action research, the participants and facilitators in this project have seen enough benefits to warrant the continuing expectation of a written report. Despite this emphasis on writing and reports, it is also clear that this is often a starting point for further reflection and not a conclusion in any sense.

The Value of Action Research

At some time during each meeting, we ask participants to give us oral or written feedback about the process. This evaluative information helps us to identify needs of individuals and the groups and to modify plans, if necessary, to meet those needs. At the end of the year, participants share with us their perceptions about the value, effectiveness, and substance of action research and about its applicability to their work.

Action researchers in this district have conducted systematic inquiry into questions or issues that are important and meaningful to them. They report that they have become more reflective in their practice. They have grown professionally, developing a greater sense of efficacy and professionalism. They also have learned that their experience and expertise are valid and valued. Group members have pursued their questions independently or with partners, but have had the interest, resources, and support of a whole group of colleagues as they pursued their inquiry. Their questions have led to more questions and to further inquiry and learning. Some teachers have found that when they shared their projects with their students, the students became involved and contributed meaningfully to the research.

We are now gathering data from past action research participants about their retrospective perceptions of the experience and the influence that experience has had on their teaching practice. We hope to trace some of the effects that ripple out from action research participants to their colleagues, their students, and their practice beyond the initial year of involvement.

CONCLUSIONS, OR LESSONS LEARNED (SO FAR) ABOUT IMPLEMENTING ACTION RESEARCH IN OUR SCHOOL DISTRICT

It takes time and effort for a district to embrace action research. While this may not be true in many other settings, some people in this school district are reluctant to support an activity that has a perceived connection to the research of university settings. Some participants need time and different experiences to let go of their negative impressions of traditional research. Some struggle with this problem the entire year, and those who are not participating in action research find it even more difficult. In our district, commitment to action research has grown through sharing the experiences of past participants, making presentations to a variety of groups, holding informal discussions at individual schools, and learning about action research in other professional contexts.

Finding a meaningful context to which action research can be connected is critical. Unless teachers and principals perceive that what they will learn will make a significant difference in the success of their students, the chance of people wanting to become involved is minimal. Connecting the themes of action research to district and personal priorities and future district directions is necessary.

Moving action research from the initiative of individuals to a district commitment is essential. While it is crucial for districts to support pilot projects and encourage risk-taking among their staffs, finding funds and trying to convince others of the worth of new efforts is time- and energy-consuming. When the leadership of a district decides that action research is an important direction, it shifts from the ownership of individuals and then can be evaluated in the context of district priorities.

Funding released time for teachers to do action research results in teachers feeling valued and renewed. It is hard to overestimate the importance of giving teachers time away from their classrooms to meet and talk with their colleagues about issues that are important to them. Mostly, teachers spend many hours in late afternoon or evening classes working on their own professional growth. While the action research meeting time did not have the same kind of impact on principals because they do have regular opportunities to meet as a group, the principals spoke often about the importance of creating time to discuss meaningful issues with their colleagues, away from their buildings. (The opportunity to earn credits from the district for professional advancement, from the state to meet recertification requirements, and from the university is another incentive and reward for participating in action research.)

Sharing the costs with the school leads to increased commitment and interest by principals. When principals started sharing the cost of released time, they more actively supported teachers pursuing action research questions. They were also more willing to designate funds, knowing the district was contributing to expenses.

The more layers of support, the more likely action research will succeed. The layers of support for participants in the action research process include the group of colleagues from around the district in their action research group, another teacher-participant from the same school, past participants from other groups, and facilitators working with individuals. Facilitators of the action research process have found support from their collaborative efforts with co-facilitators, University of Wisconsin professors, colleagues elsewhere, and other action research facilitators. These different layers have all served a variety of purposes in strengthening the process, the skills, and the quality of the experience of all those involved.

THE FUTURE

Action research has a strong base of support in this district, including its incorporation into the district's strategic plan, *Madison Schools 2000*. As of the end of the 1992–93 school year, about 100 teachers and principals have participated in action research projects in the district and the number is growing. We don't know how many more undergraduates, student teachers, cooperating teachers, supervisors, and active professionals have been involved in or touched by action research through university programs.

One of the possibilities we envision for the future is a Madison area action research network. Staff members from the school district and university faculty members formed a partnership to organize and support the first Madison Area Action Research Network Conference in the spring of 1993, at which area teachers, student teachers, and principals presented their work to colleagues. Interest in building an action research network was discussed at that conference. We are eager to explore with others ways of disseminating the action research experience and findings. We also look forward to a time when several studies will have been done on the same topic, building bodies of practitioner knowledge in specific areas.

We plan to continue to meet with other action research facilitators, in our project and beyond. We hope to encourage more action researchers to become facilitators of action research, and we are happy to share our experiences with others who want to start action research groups or projects. Other groups we would like to see emerge include action research groups within schools, as well as action research on a single topic or question, either within or across schools. Two special topic groups were formed for 1993–94: re-structuring the ninth grade and technology in the curriculum. We would like to see a group of action researchers continue beyond the current framework of one year, ending with a report. Group members could represent mixed grade levels, roles or responsibilities, and topics or subject areas. Madison high school teachers haven't yet had an opportunity to form an action research group, but we hope they will become involved soon. Principals and other administrators should have further opportunities to conduct action research in this district. Others may suggest topics, in addition to those we can imagine. The possibilities are endless.

We hope that the concept of action research will evolve in this district, both with our involvement and independent of us. We believe that it has tremendous potential to stimulate the professional growth of those involved, to acknowledge and create teachers' individual and collective knowledge and wisdom, to solve problems and enhance instructional practice, and to provide leadership in the profession.

12

The Role of the Collaborator
in Action Research

Eduardo Flores & Susan Granger

This chapter is an attempt to share an ongoing discussion regarding the role of "collaboration" in an action research group. The project the authors worked on is described in Chapter 5 of this volume. This chapter focuses exclusively on the role of the "collaborator," a role that we found (and still find) problematic.

Both authors took a course in action research offered by two professors (the editors of this volume) at SUNY Buffalo during the spring semester of 1991. Graduate students who were enrolled in the course were required to engage in action research on their own educational practice, as teachers or administrators or counselors. Neither of us was working in education at that time, and we were asked by the instructors to participate with them in an action research group examining their practice in teaching the course.

We understood that the focus of action research was the educational practice of the researchers, and in this case we were affected by that practice as students. Furthermore, both of our professors were engaged in "emancipatory action research," as described by Kemmis and McTaggart (1988), where it is explicitly stated that research is on *the practice of the members of the group*. This was obviously not our case. Therefore, it wasn't clear to us what our role would be in the group.

After our first meetings as an action research group, we assumed the name of "collaborators" in an effort to make sense of our role and to differentiate it from that of our professors, who were the "practitioners" in the group. It made sense, at least intuitively, that our participation in the group was useful, as students affected by the practice of practitioners. However, in what way our participation was useful, and to what extent, were issues that continued to haunt us throughout the project and after our participation ended.

Once the project ended, we decided to revisit the collaborator issue. This chapter addresses this issue from our particular perspective as students and "collaborators" in a project that was not related to our own practice. An additional factor should be made explicit at this point. After the project was completed, while Sue remained in Buffalo, Eduardo moved to northern Mexico. Our discussion on the issue of collaboration continued at a distance, via mail and e-mail, fax and phone calls. This gave our communication a perspective, which the chapter tries to convey to the reader, that is different from meeting and discussing these issues face to face.

This leads us to a final consideration regarding how this chapter is structured. Although we both believe that our understanding of action research has improved, and that the collaborator in an action research project has a useful and meaningful role, we consider that the *process* by which we arrived at these conclusions also contributes significantly to understanding how action research plays out in practice. In consequence, instead of writing this chapter only in terms of our conclusions, we have tried to convey a sense of how our discussion progressed. We have used a "letter" format not as a literary device, but to highlight the fact that our discussion was at a distance, in writing, and discontinuous, and as a way to exemplify how action research takes place.

In summary, the chapter addresses the issue of the collaborator as someone who engages in action research focused on the practice of others within the group, not on his or her own practice, but who is, however, directly affected by that practice. The letter format exemplifies how the discussion between the authors, who were separated by 3,000 miles and in two different countries, took place, and progressed from an intuitive sense that our role as collaborators contributed in some way to improve educational practice, to our explicit understanding of this contribution and of the value of incorporating collaborators in an action research group.

Dear Eduardo,   7/25/92

Where to begin? Perhaps I should start with my initial conception of working as a collaborator in trying to create a critical community of equal voices in the class [the action research group's thematic concern; see Chapter 5]. I remember the first few weeks trying to sort out what "our" intended goals were for this project. In fact, I don't think I really viewed the goals as mine at all at that point, but rather, I believed I was going to be doing what was necessary to get my grade for the course. For my part, I thought that the professors had a specific agenda for me and I would simply abide by it. That seemed reasonable. It was difficult and confounding for me to think in terms of action research, critical communities, and collaboration. I had no knowledge or experience with these concepts and so to think that I could contribute to this research project in some significant fashion was beyond my belief. I remember wondering if you were feeling the same way, although somehow I had the impression that you had more experience with these concepts.

Not understanding the process of action research, I was sure the professors had a clear plan of action for this project. All my faith, or call it ignorance, was wrapped up in helping the professors to successfully create a critical community. I didn't question too much at first because of my position as "the student." Furthermore, this was their project, not mine. It wasn't until several weeks into the project that I realized a role for myself, to some extent, and I began to question what we were doing and whether it was possible.

I knew from the beginning you were skeptical. That was evident in some of your comments. I was impressed because you too were just a student but you felt confident enough to assert your reservations in the face of the professors' concerns. It was interesting to see how we both moved to a middle ground somewhere in the process. For me, I believe I worked through some of the power dynamics that were present and I believe that Susan and Bob definitely encouraged that. Had I not thrashed that problem out I would not have internalized a meaningful role for myself. Additionally, though, I think the process of becoming committed to this project stimulated in me a degree of ownership which undoubtedly changed the significance of it for me. I'll talk further about these changes at some other point. Since we've got much to discuss and presumably limited space, I'll yield the next page or two to you. I am curious to know though, what your initial perceptions were and how you saw yourself move toward a middle ground. Can you share a little of that with me?

Sincerely,
Sue

Dear Sue,   8/6/1992

Thinking back, I consider I was on the opposite side coming into the project. I was almost finished with the literature review for my dissertation, which is about action research. So, I had been reading a lot about it, and not only the emancipatory action research version, but many others. When we started, I was suffering from information overload, and part of the overload included a number of critiques and arguments that academics are so fond of; extolling the virtues of one approach toward action research, many times at the expense of other forms. This made me very skeptical about what we were doing. Going back to my journal, the following problems seem to stand out.

First, as an action research group, the four of us should be the first to be or become a "critical community." This involved a common concern regarding our own practice, and to some extent to come to an explicit agreement in terms of how we were going to work together. In addition, I believed (and continue to believe for that matter) that in order to work in this fashion members of the group need to know each other. I brought this notion up again and again throughout the semester. What I saw at the beginning was very different. Although Bob and Susan shared some concerns regarding their own practice, you and I did not have this concern at all about our practice (which was nonexistent) or about theirs. As we met for the first sessions, I couldn't find any evidence that we were trying to agree on how to work together. Susan and Bob had the procedure fairly worked out (or so it seemed), and we were just moving along. Finally, we really didn't know each other. Although I had been working with Bob for the past 2 years, as a student and as an advisee, I had only spoken to Susan briefly before the semester began, and I met you at our first session. How could we work together as a critical community if we hardly knew each other? You don't go up to a total stranger at first and tell them that you don't agree with what they are saying, especially if you know you are going to continue working with them for some time. You don't know how they are going to react. And in this case, we were also two students working with two professors who were, at the time, teaching a course in which we were enrolled. All the power dynamics enculturated into us from 16 + years of schooling would not disappear overnight.

Second, and this is more of a personal "accident," after many years of considering that my role as an educator and as a professional allowed me to treat people as objects of research (as a "good" researcher should), I had returned to the position that led me to choose education as a profession in the first place: a deep conviction that people should be treated, always, as people. To treat a person as an object of study requires that I be detached from what I study, and that I am allowed to do something to him or her and systematically observe what comes out of it, as long as what I do is methodologically correct. But if people are always subjects, this cannot apply. As subjects they should never be objectified, regardless of how "valuable" the cause. And when we began working together I kept hearing, "What are we going to do *with* the class?" which sounded very much like "What are we going to do *to* the class?"

Finally, many questions about the whole idea of action research itself kept surfacing; questions regarding how the process itself worked, to what extent the process helped to improve practice, or our knowledge of practice, or the conditions under which practice took place—if it really did all these things at all. At some point I felt I was just participating in one more academic fad in education.

In sum, I considered I was involved in an activity designed to improve my practice, although I had none, and expected to openly discuss my ideas on that practice with a group of people I hardly knew (two of whom were on my dissertation committee). Furthermore, we were using a methodology of which I had serious doubts and which I had never seen in action. No wonder I was skeptical!

It was in the process of sorting out these doubts and in working together and starting to know the group, that I arrived at the middle ground you mentioned. While you were moving from total trust in Susan and Bob's unquestioned "expertise" to a more critical stance in terms of what we were doing, I was moving from a completely skeptical (hyper-critical?) position of total mistrust to a critical stance, too. Testing our assumptions against reality, which I believe is the cornerstone of critical thought, led us both to question our previous assumptions and find that something wasn't quite right. What we were doing wasn't "perfect." But, from my perspective, what we were doing wasn't a total sham. It was only after seeing how we worked as a group concretely, not as an idea but in real practice, that many of the doubts I mentioned above began to disappear. I agree that this was possible to a great extent because Bob and Susan were open to critique from the very start, especially the first time you and I decided to voice our doubts about the project. I believe that this was the point where we really started to act as a critical community, and it was then that we began to have an equal voice. It wasn't so much that Bob and Susan weren't allowing us to speak out. I think we were reticent. Although we knew we had an equal voice right from the start, it took us about 6 weeks to finally use it. Would you agree with this? And if you do, maybe we could try to sort out what it was that Bob and Susan did or didn't do that made us finally speak, and what it was that didn't allow us to speak out earlier. I think that these questions are important if we want to understand the role of a collaborator in an action research project, especially a collaborator who has no practice, but is affected by it.

Sincerely,
Eduardo

Dear Eduardo,   8/17/92

This is really a nice experience. Keeping this project alive through our writing is quite satisfying and I am enjoying analyzing our parts in it and recording them in this fashion. I briefly talked about ownership earlier, and undoubtedly, my sense of it toward this project has contributed greatly to my comfort and commitment to this exercise. Perhaps this is a good time to explore how I gained that sense of ownership.

Most definitely, it did take time to feel somewhat at ease working with Susan and Bob. Not that either had ever given any indication of being in a superior position, but as you mentioned earlier, our conditioning cannot be changed overnight and that operated heavily on me at first. I acted the only way I knew to act around professors—deferential and subordinate. Yet, I didn't want to be in that position, and I knew Susan, and Bob weren't feeding into that insecurity because they were depending on me to assist them in their research. Still, it was hard to overcome. I think the turning point came when we decided that each of us would write our rationales defining what critical communities meant to us individually. After struggling the first several weeks with the uncertainty of my role, I realized that my contribution, in the form of my rationale, lent something meaningful to the project. I began to feel some sense of working together toward a common objective with you, Susan, and Bob in a way that I hadn't felt up to that point. My optimism ebbed and flowed, however. While there were many times I was certain that my participation was essential to the process, there were also times when I wondered how much, and to what end. I don't think this tension ever disappeared and I struggle with it even now.

As the project progressed, I believe that I began to look at how I was benefiting from it, besides simply ending up with a grade and graduate school credit. The essence of Bob and Susan's research meant something to me, if not in an immediate practical sense, at least in a philosophical sense. The intent to create critical communities in a classroom was, and continues to be, important to me. As we wrestled with different definitions of critical communities, and how exactly we could create one, if we could at all, I was benefiting. I knew that someday these same issues and problems would come up for me and I would be able to draw on this experience in the interest of my own students. At the same time, I was serious and intrigued by Bob and Susan's research. I was committed to it and believed I had a stake in it—my own personal stake apparently. Furthermore though, Susan and Bob's continued solicitation and acceptance of my suggestions and ideas felt empowering to me, and I suppose, to some extent, stimulated my participation.

Having said all of that, there were times when I felt alienated from what I was doing. Whether this alienation came from some personal insecurity or from the cynical side of me questioning whether actual collaboration and ownership can really exist under such circumstances, I am not sure. Susan and Bob had everything to gain or lose from this undertaking. You and I, by chance, became involved in their research and only peripherally did we have a claim in it. We could have easily bluffed our way through it and have been done with it, but I don't think that happened, at least for me it didn't and I don't think it did for you either. We became rather committed and I think that, despite some of our evident reservations, we felt a sense of obligation in seeing the project through. Correct me if I am wrong.

During these feelings of detachment, I used to wonder if my contributions were really essential or even heard. Susan and Bob were the "experts," drawing on their own knowledge and experiences of action research and critical communities. Their ideas sounded good to me. I didn't feel quite competent to make suggestions. Their language was well versed. I remember sitting in some of the meetings thinking: "What's going on here?" "What are they saying?" I tended to be overwhelmed by Susan and Bob's strategies. How was I collaborating, I asked myself. Then there were times when I was simply tired and jaded. I wondered if it was at all worthwhile or possible. The comfort for me, however, was that it wasn't mine to worry about. Susan and Bob took full responsibility.

So, was I a true collaborator? Did I have an equal interest and share in the research and is that essential to collaboration? Undoubtedly, Susan and Bob were more passionate and consistent in their efforts because this research was significant to them. I attached a different sense of importance to it, however. Help me with this for a bit Eduardo. You were pretty good at breaking through the extraneous things and getting to the point. I look forward to hearing your point of view.

Sincerely,
Sue

Dear Sue,   8/28/1992

I have also been grappling with the idea of collaboration. Was I a collaborator or not? Or, as you have put it, a TRUE collaborator. I believe we are both trapped in a way in feeling that we have to determine if we were true collaborators or not throughout the ENTIRE semester. If this is the case, then it is obvious that we were not. Our "group's" thematic concern, which was centered on how to improve "our" practice in order to create a critical community of equal voices, was in fact Susan and Bob's concern. You and I were involved in the project for different reasons, none of which had to do with this concern. We came in as students, taking a graduate research course for credit, trying to find an acceptable arrangement to continue in the course even though we didn't meet the requirement of having an educational practice to improve. Lacking such a practice and having our own lives, as a married full-time doctoral student with a one-year-old son and a fellowship running out (in my case) and a single full-time professional pursuing a graduate degree part-time in a field not directly related to your work (in your case), the idea of creating a critical community was not on the top of our list of priorities. In addition, in my case, I was more concerned about measuring up to and working in the future with these two professors who were going to sit on my dissertation committee. In your case, this project could be an option for meeting the requirements for your master's degree.

It is reasonable to say that if we did in fact share Bob and Susan's concern at the outset, it was after they told us what their concern was and after they had planned how we were going to work as a group, and not before. At least in my case, the *idea* of creating a critical community had never crossed my mind until we met for the first time as a group, and to be honest, it was no concern of mine until after 5 or 6 weeks into the project.

However, if we consider our view at the end of the semester, we have a different picture. I think both of us agree that at some point in the middle of the semester, this previously alien concern regarding critical communities and the importance of equal voices became a real concern. It affected us, as students at that time, and began to make us reconsider our own role as future educational practitioners.

This leads me to a different view of our role as collaborators. We can, of course, reconceptualize our role and say that we began as observers, detached from the action research project, and talk about how we became "collaborators" with Bob and Susan in their project to improve their practice. But for some reason this idea does not sound quite right. It comes out as if true collaboration is a state one reaches where one shares a concern deeply with others. It takes away the doubts, the questioning, the redefinition that I feel is necessary if one is really critical. Critique starts with constantly reviewing our own ideas, testing them over and over again against reality, but also against ourselves. I really can't get myself to say that I am a collaborator or I am not, that I am in a state of grace or I have fallen from grace.

Therefore, although I recognize that we eventually were collaborating with Susan and Bob, I also consider that they were collaborating with us in working out our concerns as future teachers, as present students, as members of the action research team who considered themselves novices. And just as we had, and still have, doubts and questions regarding our role, they also went through the same process, wondering what *we* were talking about, being confused about the direction the project was taking, discouraged or elated by what we were doing. In being critical, uncertainty is at the core of what we do. If not, we would be smug and happy knowing that we hold the "truth," and that would go against the entire action research process.

This may seem a digression, but bear with me. I consider that the best evidence that we were true collaborators is the fact that we continue to question our own motivations and concerns regarding our efforts as a group. Collaboration lies in our disposition to do so, as well as the kind of behaviors we exhibit. In our case, we can say that we did not share Susan and Bob's concern. And for that matter, we still don't, just as Bob and Susan may not share the same concern exactly. This is not the point in terms of collaboration. I consider that it is not necessary to share the same concern to collaborate. What needs to be shared is the disposition to work together. And if nothing else, this disposition was present, right from the start.

Of course, this leads to a whole different interpretation of how and why we worked together. Were we manipulated into collaborating by Susan and Bob? Were we pressured into doing so by our different positions as instructor/ student, or advisor/advisee? And if this wasn't the case, what was it that led us to find relevance in a concern that we hadn't found relevant in the first place? Maybe our discussion should be focused more on what it was that made us move from observer to participant to collaborator. What do you think about all this anyway?

Sincerely,
Eduardo

Dear Eduardo,   9/30/1992

I'm not sure if I fully understand what you are suggesting about the extent of our positions as collaborators, but I think you are right in saying that we are trapped trying to come up with a specific definition or role for ourselves in this project. At this point, I am beginning to think that we need to get beyond that whole mind set of questioning to what extent we were collaborators and look in terms of the way in which we collaborated. I think this is what you are saying, but I don't want to put words in your mouth.

You asked what led us to move throughout the stages of this project. I think that besides the aforementioned reasons, such as credits and requirements, there is a philosophical appeal that we were, and are, trying to reckon with. Granted, we had some problems with how and why we should proceed with such a maneuver, but I think our rationales (which are discussed in Chapter 5) speak to the importance and value of our undertaking. The value in creating critical communities was different for each of us. Yet, it was also similar in many respects.

For me, one of the most important things about creating critical communities in a classroom is allowing for the thoughtful expression of students' ideas and insights. But, as you have suggested, and I do agree, sharing and expressing ideas with "strangers" isn't an easy thing. Do you recall how awkward it was initially in our "common group" of collaborators in the course [a group formed in the action research course described in Chapter 5 by six students taking the course who were not practitioners]? At first, you and I were viewed as "experts" in the group and were looked to for the "answers" because we were working with the professors, the "ultimate authorities." (Does this sound similar to our initial feelings toward Susan and Bob?) There was an assumption that we must "know" things about collaboration, even though we were struggling with it ourselves.

Furthermore, we didn't know each other in this common group. You and I knew each other, and Nancy and Norma knew each other, but basically we were a group of strangers struggling with the concept of collaboration. The exchange of ideas did seem to come easier as the weeks went by, however, and I think that aspect addresses your contention about trust. Do you remember when our group was discussing the question on how we wanted to function and go about sharing as a group? Building trust and having mutual respect were two common goals that we all agreed were necessary for the functioning of our group. Not surprising, right? We, as a group, never really had common goals to work towards though, except for our final presentation, and that was flimsy at best.

I don't think that our role in this common group could ever be considered as collaboration, in the sense that you and I were in Susan and Bob's project. While our common group met weekly and discussed "collaboration," it never had the same feeling for me that I eventually got working with Susan and Bob. While groups who work together might desire elements of trust and respect, I don't think these elements by themselves, nor the fact that a group is working together, necessarily make the members collaborators.

The kinds of thoughts and actions that took place in our planning sessions depended on all of us working together toward the same goals—that of creating a critical community of equal voices in a graduate course. In spite of our philosophical questions and concerns, our (I mean you, Susan, Bob, and myself) primary goal was set in motion and we all worked toward that end. In your last letter you said you didn't think it was necessary for people working together to share the same concerns. I am assuming that you are not equating concern with goal. Concern to me suggests perhaps a philosophical dilemma, such as why we are trying to create a critical community rather than the goal of creating a critical community. If that is what you are suggesting, I might agree.

As difficult as this struggle was for me in coming to this point, I am glad of the opportunity to deal with it. I don't think people struggle with something unless there is a meaningful reason to struggle with that "thing." In this case, I can say with absolute certainty that this process did mean something to me. Not only did it give me a foundation for attempting to create "critical communities" in my own practice, it also allowed me the opportunity to be a participant in a critical community whose actions affected me. And I had a voice in this process.

Sincerely,
Sue

Dear Sue: 10/7/1992

You put it quite clearly in your last letter. I think it is better to move on and discuss how we contributed as collaborators. I will try to summarize our ideas on collaboration that emerge from our discussion. In doing so, when I refer to our group, I am thinking of Bob, Susan, you, and me.

We can say that initiating a project is not a prerequisite for collaboration. Our situation is a clear example of that. Along the same lines, a shared concern at the beginning of a project is not a prerequisite either. This makes sense to me, both logically and intuitively. A concern is sometimes difficult to articulate. Our experience with the group makes this particularly evident. Our first task as a group was to grapple with our individual concerns, to try to include them in one shared statement of what we intended to do. Moreover, we can say that it *must* continue indefinitely while the group is working as such. In consequence, a first characteristic of collaboration is to constantly question if individual concerns and the group's concern are relevant or not to the project, and if actions are in fact congruent with the group's stated concern, both in terms of practitioners and those affected by this practice, the collaborators.

This constant questioning does not limit itself to form. I don't think either one of us is talking about the kind of questioning that merely serves the purpose of mutually reassuring us that we are doing the "right thing." To collaborate involves questioning our own individual approach to the project, and articulating it as clearly as possible to other members of the group. It also involves adopting a stance that actively requires other members of the group to respond to our questions in a manner that is comprehensible to the collaborator. To question with the intent of seeking *clarity*, not reassurance.

It seems possible to consider that a collaborator in an action research group may in fact adopt a position that is in open opposition to that of others. For example, a student might consider that creating critical communities of equal voices in classrooms is not a valid enterprise of educational practice. This position doesn't seem to contradict the idea of a shared concern. Collaborators in the group may share a concern with the topic, but how they approach their concern may be rooted in opposing positions regarding how such a concern should play out in practice. In this situation, we can see how clarity does in fact have a more important role. Consider our initial doubts and questions. At first each one of us may have been looking for reassurance from Bob and Susan regarding our roles. It wasn't until we wrote our rationales, and expressed our differences in outlook, that the need for reassurance gave way to a demand for clarity. I believe that if Susan or Bob, instead of trying to grapple with these inconsistencies, had told us not to worry, that we would understand eventually, then you and I would have simply tuned out of the project and gone through the motions to get the semester over with.

This leads to a second characteristic of collaboration in an action research project, that of retaining one's individuality while collaborating with the group. As we discuss what we did, I consider that we haven't lost ourselves in a complete *we*. We are a group, but we are also Sue and Eduardo and Bob and Susan, each concerned in terms of our relationship with the project, as one who affects it or is affected by it, each with our own struggle to understand what we are doing as a group. This may run against the idea that a collaborator's first responsibility is for the team or group of which s/he is a member. But this doesn't hold true for an action research group, not in our case at least. What makes our shared concern relevant is the fact that educational practice derived from the group's work affects us all, although in very different ways. When a teacher improves his/her practice, it not only affects him/her, but also his/her students, parents, other faculty members, the community. What we did had an effect on our class, not only on us.

I know that this idea opens up the entire notion argued by Kemmis and McTaggart (1988) that members of an action research group must focus on their own practice. This affected our thinking deeply throughout the entire semester, to the extent that our final class presentation with our common group, "the collaborators" group as we called ourselves, was called "action research without practice," a notion with which you and I are still struggling. At least in our case, yours and mine, what we did affected us directly as students in Bob and Susan's action research course. This was not the case with the other members of our common group (Nancy, Norma, Kim, and Zee). They were complete outsiders. They were not affected by the practice of others. Our only shared concern was to get the course over with, and this we did.

Finally, our discussion centers around the power dynamics created by our roles as student/professor, advisee/advisor, novice/expert, male/female, foreigner/national, etc. I believe it is important to mention because I cannot imagine an action research group where collaborators are included, people affected by the educational practice of others, where these and/or similar dynamics do not take place and affect the work of collaborators and practitioners alike.

Considering our work as a group, we could easily (and mistakenly) adopt the view that power dynamics were not a factor to consider. From the outset, Bob and Susan were very open and encouraged us to express our ideas. The focus of our discussions as a group were on clarification, not on agreement or reassurance. We tended toward consensus on the process, but all ideas and positions were subject to critique. All of us were able to express our thoughts in our own voice, even if our ideas led the group to change its original assumptions (and this happened a number of times during the semester). We can say that there is no evidence of explicit behaviors from any one of us to force the group to adopt our views by taking advantage of a superior power position. I would even assure that none of us *intended* to exercise power over other members of the group to achieve a particular purpose.

Yet you and I felt an underlying tension when we worked as an action research group, and continue to feel it now writing this chapter edited by Bob and Susan, which is brought out precisely because we are working as a critical community and not as a complacent one. As we continue to allow each other an equal but different voice, as we force ourselves to really listen to what those other voices are trying to say, and not gloss over them, the different power structures that operate in our twentieth-century world try to take hold. Now it is editor/writer, as before it was student/professor. Our different academic backgrounds, which limit our views of the world instead of enhancing them, reinterpret what that other voice is saying so it can "fit" into our view of what is "valuable" knowledge and what is not. Our professional and personal interests, which require us to "do" certain things to prove our worth, such as publishing an article, receiving a degree, using our time to meet or write instead of playing with our children, set the time and the pace that we devote to our projects. Even though you and I are 3,000 miles apart and have other projects and activities at hand, here we are writing a chapter for a book that has very little to do with our lives at this juncture, even though the conditions in which we are writing it are far from "optimal," to use a very administrative term.

Our standing as "experts" in a particular task (writing, expressing ideas, working with a group, analyzing) structures how we work, relinquishing our responsibility in certain matters to the "other experts." It was interesting to note that at one point during the semester Bob and Susan couldn't meet because they were going to the American Educational Research Association (AERA) annual meeting. So you and I took a week "off." The experts at scheduling our work decided that we wouldn't meet, and we simply accepted the fact, uncontested. Because we identified ourselves as "novices" at the outset of the project, we didn't speak out even though we were "allowed" to do so. The issue of trust may be a factor, but the entire notion of being allowed to speak in itself rests on an underlying structure of power that both of us accepted as a given, although conceptually we were "equal." After we raised this issue I feel we were granted the role of "experts" on collaboration in the group, and we took on the role, and still do. This is our chapter (Sue and Eduardo's chapter) on collaboration, although it was a group concern. In this discussion Bob's and Susan's voices are mute, not because they have nothing to say, but because we the "experts" on collaboration have not even bothered to let them in on the discussion.

So even if all of us are willing (and we are) to be a critical community, an action research community, and allow our voices to be heard on equal ground, and even if we make a concentrated and constant effort to achieve this purpose, at some point these power dynamics hinder the process and must be contemplated by all members of the group, collaborators and practitioners included, from time to time. How they can distort an action research project and lead it in different and unintended directions is evident from the examples above. That this didn't occur (and who knows if it really didn't occur?) in our project was due to the fact that we were constantly bringing it up. However, when we worked with "the collaborators" on our final presentation for the course, we weren't able to move beyond the role of "experts" that Kim, Zee, Nancy, and Norma "bestowed" upon us. In consequence, that group died as a "critical community" the second the course ended, if it ever was a critical community at all.

I am not suggesting that an action research group should try to eliminate all power dynamics (which we both believe is impossible anyway). Rather, they should be brought into the open and included in the group's discussion by the collaborator, as they help the group understand and improve their individual practice.

How did the power dynamics play themselves out in our group? It is true that both of us, at first, were silent, and much of our silence can be accounted for by how we perceived our roles compared to Bob and Susan. But when we started to articulate our positions (doubts and all) clearly, roles were altered. Recounting our experience, we see that our role as *students* became a powerful role when we took it seriously. What the practitioners did was contingent on our own position of students, of *collaborators*. This aspect is important, because power will always play a role in practice, and in the context in which practice takes place. If we consider power relations as an essential feature of social life, and not as an obstacle to be eliminated, it is necessary to play out these roles and even take them to the extreme while discussing how to improve practice.

I consider that we were finally viewed as equals by Bob and Susan not be-cause we had the same roles, but precisely because our roles were *different*, repre-senting traditional power positions that affect educational practice every day. As educators, we may be thoroughly committed to improving our practice and the conditions in which practice takes place. But to do this students also need to be willing, they must also share a concern for improvement. What happens if stu-dents do not want to be a part of it?

We brought up this point, as students who were part of the process and the other recipients of the "benefits" of Bob and Susan's practice. Our contribution, at that point, was to bring up the fact that some students could be equally com-mitted as Susan and Bob *not* to be a part of a critical community of equal voices in a graduate setting. What then? It was at this point, I believe, that we were viewed by ourselves and by Bob and Susan as real equals, because we stopped depending on them and started to contribute something new that opened up the discussion to further ideas on improving their practice. This was the point where I think we began to work as a group with a shared concern.

Sincerely,
Eduardo

CONCLUSION

We conclude, on the basis of our discussion, that the role of the collaborator in an action research project has characteristics that seem to run against the tradi-tional connotation of the word "collaborator." In the face of ambiguity, a collabo-rator's role is to seek clarity, not reassurance, although this may increase ambigu-ity. The collaborator needs to remain an individual, and not "blend" in one cohesive unit called a "team" or "group." Finally, whereas one would think that it is necessary to adopt an equalized role of collaborator for all members of the group, our discussion appears to indicate that the action research collaborator should in fact emphasize his or her own individual role as he or she illustrates power relationships that are an essential component of practice.

The implications of this atypical characterization of "collaborator" should be considered by an action research group that includes those affected by prac-titioners as equal partners. Ambiguity, individuality, and difference are the princi-pal contributions of an action research collaborator to the group to which she or he belongs, although these attributes definitely need a closer look, both conceptu-ally and practically.

We also recognize that these conclusions are the product solely of our discussion, and need to be brought up with others engaged in action research. This chapter does not pretend to be the last word on collaboration, but the first tentative words on a discussion that should continue if it is considered relevant by others. We recognize that it generates many questions and few, if any, answers.

What we have tried to present in this chapter, using an expression coined by Susan Noffke, is a "photograph" of our project. It only shows a particular part of it, but one we think is important in terms of the issue of collaboration. When we began our discussion of the project, our notion of "collaborator" was that of an outsider, not directly involved in the process because it did not regard his or her practice. The collaborator helped out, doing what others did, sharing a common purpose. Our discussion has led us to radically revise this notion, stressing the fact that a collaborator's role should stress ambiguity, individuality, and difference in order to keep the critical aspect of the community alive. This we believe is a useful role in practice, and one that should be taken into consideration.

13

The Institutionalization
of Action Research

The California "100 Schools" Project

Allan Feldman

My purpose in writing this chapter is to come to a better understanding of my role as a field coordinator and facilitator of action research within a national effort to reform the way in which science is taught in the United States. I begin by describing the origins of my involvement in this enterprise and the structure of the California site for this reform effort, the "100 Schools" Project. I then present two interwoven narratives: one a story of my part in the project as field coordinator and facilitator, and the other a story of my interactions with three teachers involved in action research in their schools. The final section of the chapter consists of a more traditional academic analysis of my evolving conception of action research and my role as facilitator, drawing on my experience and understanding (as well as others' understanding) of action research.

SCOPE, SEQUENCE, AND COORDINATION
AND THE 100 SCHOOLS PROJECT

Scope, Sequence, and Coordination (SS&C) is an attempt to create a major overhaul of the way that science is taught in order to extend scientific literacy to all students. The mechanism for this reform is the replacement of the current U.S. model of teaching each science in turn, typically, biology, chemistry, and then physics (the "layer cake model"), with a sequential and coordinated model. Each of four subjects (physics, chemistry, biology, and earth and space science) would be taught each year with a high level of coordination among the topics in each subject, and then in successive years the same concepts would be revisited at higher levels of abstraction. The California version of the reform, the 100 Schools Project, one of five state efforts, is under the direction of the State Department of Education. It focuses on the high school years, with teachers acting to initiate, develop, and implement incarnations of SS&C science that are peculiar to each of the more than 100 secondary schools involved.

Action research was written into the original proposal to the National Science Foundation (NSF) to serve several functions: first, to review the curricula developed for the quality of conceptual relationships in the science topics addressed, and for developmental appropriateness; second, to learn how students integrate scientific ideas in abstract settings; and third, to serve as a means of formative evaluation to allow all of the participants in all the schools to benefit from successes and avoid failures (CSDE, 1989).

TWO NARRATIVES: SPRING AND SUMMER 1991

I joined the California SS&C project during the winter of 1991 to serve as field coordinator of the action research component. By that time the project included over 100 high schools and an additional 100 or so feeder middle schools and junior high schools. Our first task in the action research component was to begin to disseminate information about action research. The component director, Fred Goldberg, and I developed and sent to the hub coordinators, who served as intermediaries between the state and the schools in their regions, a packet of information about action research, including a proposal form. I began to attend hub meetings to talk with teachers about action research, answer their questions, and solicit proposals. After extending the deadline because of a poor initial response, we received 20 proposals, of which all but two were accepted. Seventeen of these proposals came from teachers in high schools. Although the schools were distributed throughout the state, most were clustered in the two major metropolitan areas of Los Angeles and San Francisco.

In this chapter I focus on three of the action research fellows with whom I worked, Bill Miller, Robert Doyle, and Penny Young.[1] They were selected because my interactions with them provide an opportunity to see the effects of my actions as a facilitator in a variety of situations. Both Miller and Young teach in the major urban centers of the state, and they not only have had many years of teaching experience but have been recognized as educational leaders. Although Doyle has taught for just a few years, he can no longer be considered a novice. And while some of the constraints on Miller and Young could be attributed to economic and political factors within their districts, Doyle teaches in an area that is experiencing development and growth.

The Spring: An Introduction to the Action Research Fellows

Bill Miller. Bill Miller retired from the armed forces before beginning a second career as a science teacher. He teaches in an urban school that is designated as an alternative academic high school. Although there are no entrance requirements, students are expected to be committed to preparing for postsecondary education.

Miller is the site coordinator for the SS&C project in his school and one of the feeder middle schools.

In his proposal Miller wrote the following response to the item, "Describe what problem or problems you would be interested in addressing as an action research project":

> Of the many fascinating problems that I see ahead for our implementation of SSC [SS&C] beyond the ninth grade, I believe that the curriculum of the tenth grade ISC [Integrated Science Curriculum] poses both the greatest challenge and the most opportunity for assessment. I would want to address planning the tenth grade curriculum as my Action Research Project.

To the next item, "Describe your initial ideas about how you would go about solving that problem," he wrote:

> I would use my grant money [$500] to gather the [combined departments of the high school and middle school] together for as long as the money lasts and let all of us determine how we want the curriculum to expand on the past year's learning. We would have to determine how much we want to expect our tenth graders to learn and how much we would pass into the eleventh grade.

Miller's proposal has a number of features common to many of the proposals. It focuses on a problem that he and his department already face—the development of a curriculum for the next year's implementation of SS&C. He foresaw the problem of needing to plan a totally new curriculum while engaged in teaching a new curriculum. Therefore he decided to try to use the process of action research to help the department engage in the curriculum development process.

Robert Doyle. Robert Doyle is in his fifth full year of teaching but only his second of teaching science. He left a Ph.D. program in biology at a University of California (UC) campus to become a teacher. Despite his significant experience as a biology researcher, he told me:

> Teaching is what I really like to do. I wasn't happy as a research scientist. I wanted to get back into the classroom, that's what I really enjoy . . . this was research for the sake of getting a publication. I would rather be doing something that I got some personal gain from [interview 10/17/91].

He teaches at a crowded high school in a rapidly growing suburb in southern California. As with just about all communities in that region, the population is highly diverse racially, ethnically, and socioeconomically. There are large numbers of new immigrants, and a large Hispanic community that had its origins in the region's agricultural roots. A new high school will open next year in order to relieve the crowding and Doyle will join that faculty.

The science department at his school had already decided to be a part of the 100 Schools Project by the time Doyle joined the faculty, and as he taught his first full year of science he became intrigued by the nature of the reform.

> It's an alignment of what I think should be done in a science class and my impression of how science should be taught, with a more thematic, more hands on, more conceptual approach. So I expressed interest in it [SS&C] and began going to the hub meetings and then offered to teach the Natural Science II, which is our second year [interview, 10/17/91].

Doyle became interested in becoming part of the action research component after I attended one of the hub meetings and made a presentation about the possibilities of doing action research. His interest was aroused because he was seeking ways to evaluate his teaching and to share ideas with other teachers. In addition, he saw action research as a way of "improving my teaching in the classroom, improving the type of course that the students are receiving, the type of instruction, [and] making it more interesting and relevant to them" [interview, 10/17/91].

In the statement of purpose that he included with his proposal he told of his concern for education that will result in a scientifically literate population and how available curriculum materials did not meet the needs of the SS&C courses developed at his high school. He is concerned not only with meeting the goals of SS&C, which he finds very desirable, but also with the constraints of the *Science Framework for the California Public Schools* (1989) and the entrance requirements for the University of California system. He is also concerned with the transportability of the instructional packets from site to site so that teachers from the 10 or so schools in the hub can profit from the task that he has undertaken.

Penny Young. Penny Young teaches in the largest school district in the state. The room in which she has taught for the past 15 years is a "temporary" classroom moved to the site from another school. The view through the doors is of the parking lot where teenagers dressed in black and white clump together in groups of three or four. On the day I came to meet her, Young asked me whether I had noticed the color scheme, which I had. She told me that they were the colors of the Los Angeles Raiders football team and the colors of the largest gang in the area. The presence of the gangs has a significant effect on the school. For example, a student who had been enrolled in Young's class, but never attended, had been shot and killed just 2 days earlier on the periphery of the school grounds.

In addition to her duties as a teacher, teaching four classes with three different preparations, Young is the science department chair and the site coordinator and co-hub coordinator for the 100 Schools Project, teaches the methods course in science teaching at one of the UC campuses, and is on the district textbook selection committee. Despite all these commitments, she decided to participate in the action research component.

In her proposal for an action research project, she wrote:

> How does one assess for conceptual learning? Are we really designing our assessments to test what we have taught? Should a pretest be given? Is it right to compare students in these classes with ones in Biology and Chemistry? If not, is their work of equal quality and value? Is "hands on activities based learning" really more meaningful to the students? Is it cost effective?

Of the proposals that we received, Young's was the only one that suggested the importance of normative issues. She is concerned about the meaning of a comparison between "life science" students and biology students—a difference that is as much ethnic and racial as it is academic. She is also concerned about the value of the work, that is, she is quite aware of the worth given to accomplishment in traditional science courses. She worries whether success in SS&C classes will be seen by others as having the same societal value.

The Summer: Reformulating Problem Statements

While reading through the proposals submitted by the action research fellows, it became apparent to the project staff that the problem statements were too broad and unfocused to be accomplished in 1 year. Soon after the proposals were accepted, I telephoned the action research fellows to discuss their proposals. I asked them to reformulate their problem statements and to send a copy to me. Miller's reply was a more detailed statement of the problem and an additional page-and-a-half of methodology. He added that he had learned that there would not be enough money available to write new curriculum for SS&C and that his school would not implement the tenth grade course in 1991–92. He ended with the question, "What can be done . . . with no funding for extensive planning?"

I responded to Miller by focusing on his reworded problem statement and his more detailed methodology. I missed the importance of his statement regarding lack of funding.

As with Miller, I followed up with a telephone conversation with Doyle, suggesting ways in which he could reformulate his proposal, but I did not receive anything from him before the end of the summer.

My exchange with Young was more complex. After I spoke with her, I received her reformulated action plan and a letter. Her new problem statement reiterated, but in greater detail, her concerns about assessment of her primarily minority students. She raised questions about her students' ability to communicate in written English and the effect that has on their apparent comprehension. She asked herself whether she should give oral quizzes, whether she should prepare a glossary of science terms, and whether more time should be spent teaching writing skills. And, she questioned her own teaching: Whether she is covering the material that she is testing for and whether she is asking the right questions in the right way.

I responded to Young's reformulated plan by first recognizing the significance of the questions that she had raised. I then made some suggestions as to how she might develop short-term and long-term action plans. But before I sent Young these comments, I attempted to address other issues that she raised in her letter. In it she wrote of her concern that she was taking on more than she could do well. She asked me to remember that she was a full-time teacher, department chair, and co-hub coordinator.

In part, I answered with:

> Do not be concerned at this time about the amount of work that the action research project will entail. This is a very new project and it is important for us to figure out the best way to do it. The point of the project is to improve what you are doing and to share that with others.
>
> Please stick with the project so that we can benefit from your experience of having so many responsibilities and trying to do an AR project.

Fortunately, Young did not receive this condescending note until much later because I had an inaccurate summer address for her.

THREE ACTION RESEARCH PROJECTS

At the beginning of the academic year an Action Research Conference was held as a training workshop for the action research fellows. Some time was set aside for them to discuss their projects with each other and to receive reactions and critique from the other action research fellows and the component staff. From the evaluations it appeared that, in general, the action research fellows found the training sessions very useful, and the discussion session especially helpful. They left to go back to their schools filled with enthusiasm about action research and about their projects.

Miller. I next spoke to Miller on September 19, when he told me that he was "up to his eyeballs in courses and kids," but was keeping his research notebook,[2] talking with the SS&C teachers, and "getting ideas about what was going on" in the school. During the next few weeks we arranged through e-mail my visit to his school to observe a class or two and have a long discussion about his project. The reasons I gave for this visit were threefold: for me to get some idea of the context within which he works; for him to report to me on his progress; and, most important, for me to provide help through suggestions and critique. Several of the action research fellows voiced a fourth purpose—that I was visiting them in order to "check up" on their work. Although I did not view my visits in this way, it is possible that my visits served as reminders that it was time to "get back to work."

I was unable to sit in on an SS&C class because of scheduling problems, but I was able to observe one of Miller's traditional science classes.[3] After the visit and our discussion about his project, I wrote:

> 10/10—Miller is concerned that he does not have enough time to do the research project that he proposed. They [Miller and the other science teachers] are finding it very time-consuming to write the curriculum for the tenth grade, which they are implementing as soon as they write it.
>
> He has a lot of projects going on. Besides his teaching, being site coordinator, and writing curriculum, he has been working on [statewide] assessment. . . .
>
> He feels that there is a great lack of resources [to allow for the teachers to expand past the ordinary demands of the school].
>
> He would like to be a half-time teacher, use the afternoon to build next year's curriculum. Instead he's teaching five classes and has two different preparations. There is a conflict with physical resources. They need more equipment and supplies because all the classes are doing the same thing at the same time.

Miller had begun to find his participation in the project as an action research fellow as untenable. Shortly after our meeting, he sent a letter to the component director withdrawing from the project and returning the honorarium check that he had received.

Doyle. In my first conversation with Doyle before visiting his school, he informed me that he was keeping his research notebook and that he would make a presentation at the next hub meeting in order to encourage interest in his project. On October 13, he told me that very few people had attended the first hub meeting and that he was therefore not able to get the word out about his project to collect and evaluate instructional materials.

On October 17 when I visited his school, I observed two SS&C classes and spent some time with the science department chair. Later, Doyle told me that he was having difficulty setting up the curriculum exchange. As a result of few people attending the hub meeting, he decided to limit the scope of his project. He would focus on his primary objectives:

- developing his own thematic lessons
- asking people to contribute their own lessons at hub meetings every 6 weeks
- establishing sharing sessions at the hub meetings

In addition to exchanging materials, he wanted the teachers to evaluate them in terms of UC requirements and how well they work with the students. In effect, his thinking through of his project resulted in his decision to eliminate student evaluations of the curricular materials. I suggested that he try to develop a core group of teachers to work on this with him and that he make sure to telephone people about coming to the meetings.

The next time I spoke with Doyle he was still having difficulties setting up the exchange mechanism, in part due to his lack of time to follow through in the way he desired. He was nearing completion of his master's thesis and found that a great deal of his time and energy was going into that task. As a result he was not getting the response to the exchange idea that he had hoped. He had begun to think about a new focus for his project. Since the problem seemed to be in establishing contact with all the teachers in the hub, he thought he should put his effort into the state computer network (CSUnet). This interest had arisen partly from his designation as the hub communication specialist, a position that was originated after the state project leadership found that the teachers in the project needed more help and encouragement to go on-line.

As we talked about his new plans, we speculated why his original plan had not worked. I suggested that he investigate that question in order to find out why something as useful as an exchange network was difficult to establish. He replied that he would try to get some information at the next hub meeting, either through interviews of individual teachers or through focus groups.

Young. I have had a great deal of contact with Young through the academic year because of her status as a hub coordinator. She has been to all of the statewide meetings and has also attended a national SS&C meeting. As a result, we have had several informal conversations about the larger project and her immediate concerns, which relate to her teaching context.

I began plans to visit Young at her school, but in one of her first e-mail messages, she wrote: "My SSC class is very discouraging. I am ashamed to have anyone visit. Give me another week or two maybe I'll see it in a more positive mood" (e-mail, 10/21/91). I responded (again by e-mail):

My job is to help you get un-discouraged. I seem to be pretty good at that. I will not be able to get to your school until sometime in December. How late is too "late"? I know that you go off session for a while. Let me know your schedule. I will call you soon.

Not too late turned out to be December 11, just before the beginning of a lengthy period when school was not to be in session because of a new year-round schedule. I observed one class, spent some time with Young in the afternoon, and then attended a hub meeting that began in the late afternoon and went through dinner.

During our conversation, Young and I were constantly being interrupted by students and other teachers as she attempted to attend to her many responsibilities. Her concerns went back and forth between the problems that teachers were having in her district and the problems associated with teaching in the inner city. For example, when we were discussing how she could organize group work in order to encourage participation by as many students as possible, she asked:

> What do you do with the kids who are there half the time? The attendance rate is never the same. . . . That's the biggest problem. Let's say your project runs for three days, I might have one kid there two days, and one kid who's never there, one day, or another three days, or half a period, or "I forgot it at home" [interview, 12/11/91].

Her concern for the teachers emerged in statements that reflected both demands on teachers and new structural changes in the schools. At one point she said, "I know we're not going to keep the same program because we've had all these changes." These changes included a 4-½% pay reduction, the elimination of preparation periods and substitute teachers, and a district policy that had resulted in the midyear transferring out of a bilingual earth science teacher who had been an integral part of the SS&C program.

She told me that "the teachers here are really devastated" [interview, 12/11/91] and later went on to talk about her co-hub coordinator.

> Teachers are getting so run down, she [the co-hub coordinator] said that she is so tired, she's teaching 200 students a day, she's trying to go to all these meetings . . . these teachers, the good ones, are going to be physically beat to death. Yesterday I went to a meeting, I didn't get home 'til 9:00 last night. I have this [hub] meeting today, tomorrow I have to be at the Board at 8[a.m.] to work on all these textbooks. I still have lesson plans for tomorrow, I can't talk to you anymore [interview, 12/11/91].

But before she dismissed me, she asked, "Am I doing anything?" I replied with a comment about how teachers are involved on the grass-roots level in this reform. Her response was, "But they don't let us do anything." When I asked her to elaborate, she modified her statement: "They let you do things but there's no money, let's put it that way" [interview, 12/11/91].

Doyle and Young continued to work on their action research projects as their busy lives continued. Doyle completed his action research report while finishing up his master's thesis, and Young was writing hers as Los Angeles was in the turmoil of racial riots. Their reports are part of a collection of 15 reports by action research fellows published and disseminated throughout California (Feldman, Mason, & Goldberg, 1992).

REFLECTIONS AND ANALYSIS

In this section I try to come to a understanding of what transpired during the year as I served as a facilitator of action research. First, I examine the way that my conception of action research has changed. I then contrast my conception with the definition of action research held by the developers of the 100 Schools project and the various conceptions of research held by the action research fellows. These differing conceptions and the structure of the statewide implementation of SS&C have resulted in problems associated with the timetable for the action research projects, the isolation of the action research fellows from one another, and contradictions of control (McNeil, 1988). I look at each of these in turn and conclude this section by discussing modifications in the ways that I would act as facilitator and field coordinator in year two of the action research component.

Conceptions of Action Research

My conception of action research has changed and evolved as I have worked with teachers involved in a variety of action research projects. I initially saw it as a process that results in the action researchers becoming better at what they do and gaining a better understanding of the contexts in which they work. So when school teachers engaged in action research, their practice improved and they gained a better understanding of their educational situations.

My understanding of action research has derived from this operational definition. First, I view it as a self-developmental process because the primary goal of this research is the improvement of practice and not the generation of new propositional knowledge, whether local or more universal. This does not differ significantly from the way in which John Elliott (1991) has written about action research as

> developing the practitioner's capacity for documentation and judgment in particular, complex, human situations. It unifies inquiry, the improvement of performance and the development of persons in their professional roles. (p. 52)

Although the generation of knowledge is not primary, there is the goal that the teachers would gain a better understanding of their practice and that that understanding can be shared with others.

A second aspect of action research arises from its self-developmental nature. Teachers seek to develop their practice because they want to provide a better educational experience for their students. Therefore, action research is an ethical process that is deeply rooted in the moral aspects of teaching (Elliott, 1991). The moral nature of the process is reflected in teachers' choices of projects to undertake: projects that improve their practice or their situations in order to better the educational situations for their students or peers.

This definition has resulted in a discrepancy between how I see action research and the way it has been defined as part of the California SS&C project. The principal investigators of the project wrote action research into their proposal so that university faculty and secondary school teachers could "learn more about the curricular and instructional implications of SSC" (CSDE, 1989). They saw this statewide component as consisting of "a host of coherent and coordinated, locally designed action research studies that will get results directly into the hands of classroom teachers" (CSDE, 1989, p. 4). Furthermore, they envisioned that "action research will contribute an ongoing feedback loop to all schools in the SSC reform in a way that teachers from other departments can utilize information about what works and why" (CSDE, 1989, p. 15).

I call this vision of action research *institutionalized* action research, in the sense that an organizational institution has been created and given legitimate status in order to promote a cause, in this case the implementation of SS&C in California. This differs from the forms of action research in which teachers engage in the process in order to improve their teaching and to gain a better understanding of their educational situations. That is, institutionalized action research focuses not on the development of the participants but on the development of the program. In the 100 Schools action research component, there is a purpose that supersedes the immediate goal of improvement of practice and the longer-term goal of generating knowledge—that is, to implement SS&C and/or to evaluate that implementation.

In this project, however, the action research component had as its primary function the research agendas of university researchers and policy makers, namely, the implementation of the SS&C reform through the generation of knowledge about science learning and careful program assessment. Given these agendas, the conception of action research was of teachers working with university researchers to explore the ways in which science is learned and to assess the implementation of the reform. The teachers' roles would be to assist the university researchers in their inquiry in order to get a closer look at schools and to return the findings to the teachers in a more timely manner. That is, the teachers' part in the research process would be to increase its efficiency.

There also was a discrepancy between my conception of action research and that of the teachers.[4] It appears as if knowledge of two research perspectives contributed to the ways that the teachers thought about action research: scientific research and evaluation research. These teachers, all of whom are science teachers, have received at least some training in scientific research methods. Although most have not had the opportunity to do formal research in the sciences, they have been initiated into a culture that values the "scientific method." The second perspective, that of evaluation research, is ubiquitous in the public school systems. With the growth of state and federally mandated and funded programs, school districts have been required to keep detailed records of the enactment and efficacy of these programs. The focus of the first perspective is on "What do we know?" while that of the second is "What can we show?"

For at least several of these teachers, action research was a way to demonstrate that their SS&C-type programs were more effective than traditional science courses. And, for these science teachers, the way to do that was through some quantitative comparison. In the most ambitious project of this sort, a teacher used two different pre- and posttests; a comparison of attendance and grade data; and student, parent, and teacher interviews to evaluate the program at his school. While he was able to demonstrate that the program was meeting its goals, he was disappointed that he was not able to show that the students were learning more science and were more motivated to study science than those in traditional classes (Gilbert, 1992). What he was seeking was some evidence that what he had done had a positive effect on students – that students were learning what was asked of them "better" than they would have in traditional classes. This "need to know" (Feldman, 1994), and the teachers' training in the sciences, were important factors in shaping their projects.

On the other hand, my goal was for them to look carefully at their own work – their actions – and to "get smarter" about their practice through that look. But for many of these teachers, and others for whom I have acted as an action research facilitator, this "need to know" has kept their lenses focused on their students.

The Timetable

The institutionalization of the action research shows up in several other ways. The first is the requirement that it fit within the larger project's timetable. The 100 Schools project had received initial funding for 3 years. In order to reach as many teachers and schools as possible, it was decided that there would be three sets of action research fellows,[5] each of whom would complete his or her proposed project within 1 academic year. The decision to limit each action research fellow's work time in this way was due in part to the organizational constraints of the larger project. Whether the decision was due to the institutionalization of this action research or to the influence of tradition on the staff, or some combination of the two, the teachers found themselves with a timetable that required them to submit proposals for action research before they had a clear understanding of the nature of action research or sufficient experience with implementing SS&C to be able to identify potential projects.

This situation worked against my goal of the action research being self-developmental. In order for the teachers themselves to identify projects or goals that focused on improving their practice, it was important for them to have had some experience as a basis for determining what it was that was problematic about their practice. My observations, however, suggested that the converse was not true: Experience with the project did not ensure self-developmental goals. Some of the action research fellows had at least 1 year of experience with the implementation of SS&C in their schools and hubs, but their proposals were written in the same instrumental manner as the others. In other words, engaging in a practice does not necessarily lead to being self-critical of that practice.

How then can I encourage teachers to focus on their own practice? First, if the teachers were to be identified as action research fellows independently of their possible research projects, then there would be an opportunity for them to look critically at their own practice in order to identify *starting points* (Altrichter, Posch, & Somekh, 1993) for their research and to assess whether they have the resources to attempt a specific project. If my interactions with the action research fellows had proceeded in this way, it is possible that some problems might have been avoided. For example, Miller might have been able to identify a starting point for a project that was more embedded in his practice. For Doyle, who has many personal and professional commitments, but is not as burdened as some of the other teachers, this process could have given him the time to work another half year with the implementation in his school and hub to find a more appropriate starting point. In fact, that is what he has done, after first articulating a different project. It became clear to him that one of the biggest problems that he and his colleagues had was one of communication. Once he had identified this problem, he began to seek ways to improve communications and to understand the forces that act against facile communications, whether in person, telephone, or electronic mail.

Young's situation was more complex. For while the others have been working within the moral framework of education, she was the only action research fellow who had clearly articulated her ethical stance. Her original proposal arose from the problems she saw in assessing nontraditional students in nontraditional ways, and she is immersed in a situation that is filled with discrepancies and dilemmas that are institutional and societal in nature. In order for her to successfully meet her goal, she needed to tackle institutional problems, such as the lack of time and resources for teachers, and the societal problems that result in large numbers of youths turning off to the school systems. In such situations the problems that I face in my role as an action research facilitator also grow. This has led me to recognize the importance of a critical dialogue between the action research fellow and the facilitator in order to sort through the multitude of issues to identify those with which the teacher has the resources to be effectual.

Isolation

The action research fellows in the 100 Schools project have found themselves for the most part isolated from both the other action researchers and me. This isolation has been due in part to the institutionalized nature of the action research and can be traced directly to the expansion of the California SS&C project to more than 100 schools. In the original proposal, there were to be two or three action research fellows at each of 10 sites. With the expansion of the number of sites but without a proportional increase in the budget for action research, the action research fellows were distributed throughout the state. Although most are clustered in the two large metropolitan areas of Los Angeles and the San Francisco Bay area, these areas are large and congested. In addition, there are teachers considerably north of San Francisco and south of Los Angeles. As a result of these separations, they have for the most part been independent actors.

Two major problems have arisen from this isolation. The first is that the action research fellows have felt that the problems encountered in their projects, such as lack of time and other resources, are unique to each of them. The second is that they have not been able to get critical feedback from the other action research fellows and from me in a regular and timely manner to enable them to move ahead on their projects. They are missing colleagues who can view their activities in similar ways, offer sympathetic ears, and give critical feedback and advice when needed. In other words, what appears to be missing is a *community* of action researchers, or what Lave and Wenger (1991) call a "community of practice" with "a set of relations among persons, activity, and world, [and] over time" (p. 98) within which knowledge of action research, science teaching, and SS&C could be generated and shared.

Although the group never again met as a whole, there were two types of opportunities for subgroups to meet and discuss their situations in order to foster the development of a community of practice. The first was a chance for teachers in each of the two state geographical regions to meet. However, several of the action research fellows were recognized as leaders in other areas within the reform effort and facilitated meetings that were scheduled concurrently with the action research meeting. The second type of opportunity was at state or regional SS&C meetings. The constituency of these groups changed because attendance at the meetings depended on individual resources for travel. So even though there were these opportunities to meet during the academic year, the composition of the group varied from time to time, which impeded the formation of a community of practice.

Both the need for this sort of community and the difficulty that I had in fostering its development suggest that it is important for the action research component to have built into it some mechanism for regular regional or local meetings of fellows throughout the academic year. The action research fellows have found it useful when this has occurred; it appears that in my role as field coordinator and facilitator I must find ways to encourage more regular meetings.

Contradictions of Control

The institutionalized nature of action research within the 100 Schools project leads to another consideration. Elliott (1991) has warned that "there are signs that action research has become hijacked in the service of technical rationality" (p. 52). The result can be, as he suggests, a re-emergence of "hierarchicalized, specialist functions to control and regulate primary practice" (p. 55). This possibility is indicative of the contradictions that can exist between action research as a humanistic, personal process and the goals of large institutions.

The goals of the California 100 Schools project cause even larger contradictions. When seen as a government initiative, the project appears to be another top-down reform effort relying on center–periphery information transfers and control. However, the project is structured so that much of the curriculum development, including long-term planning of courses over several years (coalitions of sixth–eighth grade feeder schools with ninth–twelfth grade high schools are not uncommon) and day-to-day microplanning, is done by classroom teachers. In addition, the type of teaching encouraged by the reform and the California science framework is thematic, hands-on, and student-centered. This sort of teaching requires the teacher to have a fair amount of autonomy. These contradictions are visible in Young's comments. She is aware of the contradiction between the autonomy provided to her by the state in her multiple roles of hub coordinator, site coordinator, and classroom teacher, while at the same time being quite aware of the restrictions placed on her ability to act by the constraints of underfunding for both her project activities and her teaching. Although not as apparent, this same problem was related to Miller's withdrawal from the action research project.

As field coordinator and facilitator, I need to be aware of these contradictions. There is a tension that arises between the more micro goals of individual action researchers and the instrumental goals of the project directors. Therefore, while starting points are being identified and research methods are being chosen, the requirements of the larger project must be kept in mind. Questions such as

- How does this action research project help to implement the reform?
- How will a report of this project help teachers and others to implement the reform?

must be asked when starting points are identified, if the action research is to serve the larger project. If these questions and concerns become the only criteria for whether an action research project is acceptable, there is the danger that projects will not focus on the concerns and needs of the teachers. As field coordinator and facilitator for the statewide project, my actions need to reflect both the goal of successfully implementing SS&C and that of aiding the action research fellows to reach their own goals, while not interfering (too) negatively with their work as teachers and their private lives.

CONCLUSION

In this chapter I have tried to come to an understanding of my involvement with teachers engaged in action research as part of a statewide reform effort in science education—the California Scope, Sequence, and Coordination Project. My efforts have been directed primarily at helping teachers come to a better understanding of their involvement in the project and how that relates to the idea of doing research in schools on their practice, and at helping them to determine appropriate methods for their inquiries. The way that I have developed my understanding has been to take a close look at my interactions with three of the action research fellows and to analyze how our interactions were related to the structure of the reform effort itself and how action research was conceptualized within it.

The first teacher, Miller, withdrew from the action research component. This should not be seen as a reflection of his abilities or commitment as a teacher, school leader, and researcher. He continues to be a dynamic leader within his school and in the statewide effort. Rather, his withdrawal from the project serves to highlight the need for better coordination of the demands of action research with teachers' work and lives. The second, Doyle, has attempted to bring together the efforts of teachers at several sites in order to develop better programs at all the schools in his hub and to improve the efficiency of the instructional design process. His frustrations serve to model the problems of communication throughout the action research component. Finally, Young's situation served to remind me of how the reform process in general, and the action research process in particular, are tied to the contexts of individual schools, school districts, and communities.

As a result of this reflection and analysis, I plan to modify the way I act in this role. In this chapter I have suggested some of the ways in which I will do so. First, I will try to encourage more meetings of groups of action research fellows. This might happen through special gatherings, or at hub meetings, or at other meetings of the California SS&C project. Second, I will try to remain aware of the contradictions of control that I have identified above and help the action research fellows to be cognizant of them. The third modification concerns the way in which the new action research fellows are selected. As I go to hub meetings around the state, I will talk with teachers about both the advantages of action research and the need to make an assessment of resources before making a commitment to a project. I also will try to make it clear that although the component staff would like the teachers to have an idea of the type of problems that they would like to be involved in and ways in which they could begin to address those problems, their focus can change as their experience with SS&C in their settings causes them to be aware of specific problems, dilemmas, or discrepancies that can serve as starting points for action research.

NOTES

1. The teachers asked me to identify them by pseudonyms. I will use pseudonyms but refer to them by their surnames following the convention used to refer to academic authors.

2. The action research component's staff had decided that it would be useful for the action research fellows to keep reflective journals of their experiences doing action research. I met resistance from other science teachers when I discussed with them the idea of journal keeping. I realized that while reflective journal keeping seemed to be out of the culture of science, keeping a research or laboratory notebook was deeply embedded within the syntactic structure (Schwab, 1978) of the disciplines. Therefore we decided to encourage the action research fellows to keep *research notebooks* in which they keep track of their actions and their thoughts re their actions or the results of those actions.

3. In retrospect, that was probably a mistake. There was no need for me to see him teaching that class, and it might have led him to see me in more of an evaluative role.

4. To try to come to an understanding of another person's conception can be thought of in some ways as an act of mind reading. To attempt to develop a composite image through reflection on conversation and observation approaches folly. My claim is not that I am providing the reader with an accurate image of what these teachers have been thinking, or that I am giving them "voice." What I am attempting is to identify some ways of thinking about research that I believe affected the ways in which the teachers engaged in their projects and the ways in which I interacted with them.

5. Because of the way in which the funds were released, there were only 2 years of the action research cycle.

14

Action Research and
Supportive School Contexts

Exploring the Possibilities for Transformation

Robert B. Stevenson

Significantly, nearly all the case studies of action research reported in this book took place within the supportive context of specific programmatic structures (e.g., graduate classes, funded projects) that were external to the setting in which the action research was conducted. External support was neither a criterion of editorial selection nor a random accident. It is, however, a reflection of one kind of support that seems crucial if educational practitioners are to engage in research on their own practice.[1] This point is reinforced in the preceding chapters by several authors (see, for example, Bronson and Soffer, Chapters 7 and 8, respectively) who experienced considerable difficulty in sustaining their action research projects when supporting structures were no longer in place. Their experiences are not surprising, of course, given the highly demanding professional lives of teachers and school administrators and the absence of both structural arrangements and cultural norms to encourage educational practitioners to engage in action research.

Yet educational practitioners regularly reflect on and work to improve their practice. Action research has the same intent: It seeks not to replace what practitioners normally do, but to enhance the way they do it by helping them work through the problems they encounter. However, "action research is not a set of practices that can be packaged and brought *into* the worklives of educational practitioners" (Noffke, 1992, p. 4). It offers a means of making efforts to study and improve one's practices and the situations in which they occur, more systematic, more rigorous, and more collaborative.

In order to sustain such efforts, however, at least two conditions would seem to be necessary. First, as Feldman and Atkin (Chapter 9, this volume) argue, a conception and a methodology of action research are needed that are "embedded in teachers' practice" and that match "the temporal and spatial flow . . . of teaching" (pp. 133–134). However, a methodology is required that also is distinct from the procedures of practice itself since, as a research process, it must offer something beyond our existing level of understanding (Winter, 1989). These two sets of demands create a dilemma: Methods (of planning, data collection, and analysis) that are low in intrusiveness with respect to the flow of teaching are likely to parallel practice and be low in systematic rigor (and therefore difficult to justify as "research"), while methods that are highly rigorous are likely to be highly intrusive on practice and demand other forms of support (e.g., time, resources). In order for action research to involve procedures that are different from (i.e., additional to) one's practice, the work and workplace of schools must be transformed so that educational practitioners possess the supporting conditions to regularly engage in action research. This means that if action research is to become "self-sustaining," then internal forms of support need to be cultivated to gradually replace a reliance on the external support structures that are inevitably withdrawn.

In this concluding chapter, I examine the possibilities of developing school cultures and structures that support ongoing action research activities as a regular part of professional practice. In particular, I focus on the role that action research itself might play in constructing these internal conditions of support and thereby transforming the school workplace. Before exploring these transformational possibilities, I briefly review the conceptual issues of the purpose and goals of action research and methodological procedures that are both rigorous and relevant. After arguing for a conception of action research that embraces a concern for improving one's educational situation and for a methodology that incorporates principles of rigor that differ from traditional positivistic research, I address the issue of creating cultural norms and structural conditions that support the practice of action research. Central to this discussion is the argument that school cultures and structures are shaped in part by the individuals who work within them and that action research can help reconstruct a school environment that is supportive of sustaining its own ongoing practice without depending on external support. In addressing these issues I draw substantially on the case studies presented in the preceding chapters, but also on my experiences in conducting action research, teaching action research, and collaborating with others engaged in action research.

CONCEPTUAL ISSUES OF MOTIVES, MEANINGS, AND METHODS

Different versions of action research are evident in both the literature and practice (and to some extent in the preceding chapters). For some writers and action researchers, the single purpose of action research is the improvement of individual practices. In other words, action research is seen as offering a vehicle for self-development. For example, in the Interactive Research and Development projects of the late 1970s and early 1980s, the purpose of engaging teachers in collaborative action research was to help them become more competent practitioners by acquiring traditional research skills and habits of inquiry (Tikunoff & Mergendoller, 1983). This orientation to action research reflects a concern that practitioners master a discrete set of practices or techniques, but does not address their consideration of the goals or ends of teaching.

Although Lawrence Stenhouse maintained this focus on "professional self-development" (Noffke, 1992), his work represents a second conception of action research in emphasizing the role of teachers in making professional judgments about both the means and ends of instruction. Stenhouse and other British scholars (e.g., Elliott, 1978, 1991) argued the need for developing an understanding of one's educational intentions, as well as actions, and for monitoring the congruency between those intentions and one's classroom actions. Rather than only leading to more technically competent practices, Stenhouse believed that action research should contribute to the development of teachers' practical theories of teaching by improving the coherence of those theories through a focus on understanding the relationship between intentions and practices. This is similar to Atkin and Feldman's argument that action research should help teachers become wiser about their practices and get better at moving toward goals they value. Implicit in this conception is the dual and related purposes of improving understanding of practice as well as improving practice itself.

A third conception of action research, and one preferred by the editors of this book, encompasses the threefold purpose of improving one's practice, one's understanding of practice, and—most important in the context of this chapter—the situations in which those practices are carried out (Kemmis & McTaggart, 1988). In this version there is a concern for the social and institutional structures that shape teaching and schooling. In other words, this conception recognizes that contextual factors influence curriculum, teaching, and educational change and therefore includes the broader conditions in which educational practices take place. Besides reflecting inwardly on one's own intentions and actions, reflection and analysis are also directed outwards toward the situations circumscribing one's practice. Thus, action research is viewed as being concerned not only with understanding and transforming educational practices, but also with understanding and transforming educational situations. Furthermore, the purpose of such a transformation is to create not only a better (i.e., more effective) educational system, but also one that is "characterized by justice, equity, caring, and compassion" (Zeichner & Gore, Chapter 2, this volume, p. 20). This conception suggests that action research itself can play a role in contributing to the construction and reconstruction of school cultures and structures that support and help sustain action research as a regular practice in schools. I return to this question later in the chapter.

METHODOLOGICAL DISTINCTIONS FROM
TRADITIONAL RESEARCH

Action research is not distinguished by particular methods or techniques of data collection, but its general methodological process is quite different from other forms of research. As the case studies in this book clearly illustrate, it involves a recursive or spiraling process of cycles of planning, acting, observing, and reflecting. So instead of collecting data in order to act, the action researcher is studying the intentions, consequences, and circumstances of the actions he or she has taken, as well as using the information to influence further actions. Besides these differences, there are also many similarities to more traditional research, especially to interpretive or naturalistic research. For example, as data are systematically collected and analyzed, the initial research question may be clarified or revised in light of the data, and reflection on and analysis of data determine subsequent (actions and) kinds of data to be collected.

The rigor of action research, however, is not derived from particular techniques of selecting, gathering, or analyzing data. In fact, its methodological standards are still evolving, as the chapters in this book illustrate. Winter (1989), for example, argues that action research has "a *different* conception of 'rigor' than that which characterizes positivistic research" (p. 37). Instead, according to some writers, rigor is derived from the coherence of justifications of proposed actions and the coherence of the interpretations (from observation and reflection) of the consequences and circumstances of actions (Carr & Kemmis, 1986). In the first instance, the articulation and reasoned justification of one's educational intentions, are intended to reveal the reasons for one's professional actions and to enable those reasons to be subject to critical scrutiny (by oneself and others). Underlying these intentions are the individual's beliefs (e.g., about teaching and learning, education and schooling, students and subject matter), values, and commitments (e.g., to particular goals for oneself as an educator and for students, and to a broader notion of the educational and social good) (Oberg, 1986). The particular beliefs and values behind one's professional decisions and actions must not only be identified, but must also be justified. "Beliefs are warranted if they are borne out in practice or in theory" (Oberg, 1986, p. 8), but values should be internally consistent and reflect a commitment to moral and ethical principles (such as equity and caring).

In regard to developing coherent interpretations, Winter (1989) offers an intriguing approach. He proposes the two principles of reflexive and dialectical critique as ways of redefining the processes of observation and reflection. Reflexive critique begins with making "modest" judgments or claims about a professional interaction from an account of that interaction (collected from observations, interviews, or documents). Questions then are raised about these claims by identifying alternative (or neglected) interpretations. The intent of this reflexive critique is to "open up lines of argument and discussion" (p. 44) by showing that, since a knowledge statement or claim is grounded in interpretive judgments, other possible interpretations need to be critically examined and therefore a modification of the original claim can be considered. Dialectical critique is intended to provide a principled method of data analysis by subjecting observed phenomena to a "critique." This entails a search, first, for a unity of meaning among separate and diverse elements, and, second, for internal contradictions within and between those elements. Several epistemological assumptions underlie both reflexive and dialectical critique. The first is that the classroom or school context is too complex to be described in only one way: Multiple events are happening and there are multiple ways of interpreting those events. Second, theories (and the ideas derived from theories) enlarge our vision by directing our attention to important aspects that would otherwise go unnoticed and by providing alternative frames for reinterpreting our experiences (Prawat, 1991). Finally, assumptions and judgments should be examined in two realms: the private and the public (or, in Prawat's terms, in "conversations with self" and "conversations with others," p. 742). In other words, intentions (including the underlying beliefs and values) and interpretations of actions and the consequences and circumstances of those actions need to be voiced and tested in internal dialogue or reflection and in dialogue with "critical friends."

CULTURAL AND STRUCTURAL CONDITIONS
FOR SUPPORTING ACTION RESEARCH

What kinds of conditions are likely to support practitioner involvement in a form of action research that is characterized by the goals and methodology described above? This question can be examined by considering two sets of distinctions that emerge from the conceptualization presented. The first concerns the focus of reflection and analysis in the action research process: whether it is directed *internally* toward one's intentions and actions, or *externally* toward the context in which one's practices take place. The second distinction involves the contextual realm in which internal or external reflection is carried out: *privately* as an individual action or internal dialogue with oneself, or *publicly* in dialogue or collaboration with others. The four categories that result from these distinctions should not be viewed as mutually exclusive, but rather as mutually constitutive where there is continual movement back and forth among them. Beginning with an inward or internal focus in the private realm, I examine in turn the conditions likely to support reflection and analyis within each of these categories.

An Internal Focus in a Private Context

What conditions enable practitioners to articulate the intentions that underlie their actions and to critically self-examine both those intentions and the consequences of their actions? Identifying and justifying one's intentions, making knowledge claims for testing against alternative claims, and examining relationships among sets of ideas and beliefs for their differences and interdependence, first demand certain dispositions of action researchers, such as "a commitment to improve practice, a willingness to question practice and to entertain alternatives, a willingness to take responsibility for their actions and intentions, [and] faith in themselves as a source of improvement" (Oberg, 1986, p. 11). Such commitment and volition are influenced by personal histories, educational and career experiences and perspectives, and prevailing norms in one's professional subculture and in the general school workplace.

Institutional norms and structures not only influence an individual's disposition to experiment with new practices and to engage in internal reflection, but also determine whether or not time and space are available for engaging in the kind of careful and thoughtful planning (of new actions) and reflection implied by the processes that have been described. For example, as a school principal, Elizabeth Soffer (Chapter 8, this volume) was in an advantaged position to create supportive conditions to enable her to pursue her action research endeavors, but she still experienced problems in finding time for planning actions and collecting and analyzing data on the consequences of those actions.[2]

As well as the time and disposition, a language for reflecting on and critiquing practice and for generating and assessing alternative possibilities is also needed. In examining models of peer coaching to try to find one that captured the intentions of her staff development practice, Catherine Battaglia (Chapter 6, this volume) became uncomfortable with the "emphasis on the observer's ability to name and label instructional decisions" (p. 76) in a technical or behavioristic model of coaching. The language used in this task revealed to her the behavioristic assumptions about teaching that were embedded in this model and helped her recognize an inconsistency with her constructivist beliefs about teaching and learning. Having become alerted to the significance of language, Battaglia continued to struggle for a conceptual vocabulary that adequately represented a form of coaching practice that reflected her philosophy and intentions. When she studied her field notes and journal entries, the concepts of focus, engagement, and accountability emerged as categories that provided a new language for scripting questions and a framework for developing "the kind of reflective dialogue [she] was striving to achieve" (p. 86). Her experiences indicate the importance of developing both a language for expressing assumptions, beliefs, ideas, and value commitments, and an analytical framework for guiding reflection, critique, and the search for alternative possibilities for practice. Without a language of critique for examining educational claims and an ability to articulate alternatives, the result can be a willingness to accept the status quo (Gitlin, 1990). Thus, a language and framework for institutional critique and the generation of alternative institutional possibilities are important for collectively reflecting on the context in which one works and the ways that context might be transformed.

An Internal Focus in a Public Context

Private internal reflection also should be accompanied by shared reflection with others. Just as dialogue within the scholarly community is viewed as the most important mechanism for validating knowledge claims (Prawat, 1991), dialogue with action research colleagues provides a means of testing reasons for educational actions and interpretative judgments about the consequences of those actions. Making the internal focus of reflection public requires a supportive environment in which one can speak one's authentic voice and take professional risks. Stephen Corey in his post–World War II work at the Horace–Mann Lincoln Institute at Columbia University stressed the importance of building personal relationships of trust, respect, and understanding among those engaged in action research through "free discussions" (Noffke, 1992). Trust must first be established if teachers are expected to adopt a critical stance toward each other's beliefs and practices. The kinds of relationships envisioned might be described as a collegial community characterized by norms of caring and constructive critique where personal support is balanced with "hard-nosed deliberation about present practice and future direction" (Little, 1990, p. 520).

In such a community, members should be able to raise critical questions and express alternative possibilities of interpretation and action, and "still feel a sense of acceptance and belonging" (Stevenson and co-authors, Chapter 5, this volume, p. 64). In other words, not only are mechanisms needed for allowing multiple voices to be heard, but also a norm of critical inquiry has to be established in which people constructively challenge each other's intentions, understandings, and actions. Of course, the open expression and questioning of deeply held beliefs and sacred practices creates the potential for considerable conflict. Moderate levels of conflict, however, have been found to contribute to the development of integrative agreements, whereas the desire to avoid conflict can undermine efforts to reach such agreements (Little, 1990).

Collaborative work on action research is obviously dependent on creating opportunities for extensive and intensive professional interactions, as well as institutional norms of collaboration. Even when organizational arrangements provide opportunities for collaborative work, such work also must be valued within the organization. Although the teachers with whom David Hursh (Chapter 10, this volume) worked had a common planning time, they spent much of their time and energy defending this time in response to continual threats from the administration to take it away. This lack of administrative support for a common time conveys a clear message that the practice of teaching, and the improvement of that practice, is an individual, rather than a collaborative, activity. Thus, a condition for public reflection and analysis involves challenging traditional assumptions about how teachers should spend their time and redefining their work to include working with colleagues.

Collaborative planning and reflection also require appropriate ways or methods of working together. Battaglia (Chapter 6, this volume) found that developing a new language of cognitive coaching provided a way that helped her generate "fluid, reflective discussions" (p. 86) with the teacher whom she was coaching. She, and several other authors in this volume, also found that it was important to familiarize their colleague(s) with the process of action research in order to develop a shared language and understanding of the goals and methods of their project. Creating collective school and personal histories has been suggested as another way of establishing a shared frame of reference and identifying common points of struggle (Gitlin, 1990). The point is that shared referents (of language, processes, or histories) for capturing and discussing the complexity of educational intentions and practices must be "preferred over idiosyncratic perceptions" (Grimmett & Crehan, 1992, p. 64).

An External Focus in a Private Context

In reflecting outwards in the private realm, attention focuses on both the institutional and broader social context in which one's educational practice takes place. As well as scrutinizing one's beliefs and values (both privately and publicly) in relation to one's practices, the first task is to examine one's values in relation to those of the organization and culture in which one works. This includes the material conditions and cultural norms of the immediate workplace, as well as wider societal influences. Critical reflection also addresses the way in which one's practices are shaped by institutional norms and structures.

Institutional norms and values were important impediments to conducting and sustaining action research in several cases described in this book. School norms, especially of control, conformity, and practicality, were identified as significant obstacles to preservice teachers' action research efforts (Brunner, Chapter 3; Schuyler & Sitterley, Chapter 4). Student teachers, for example, were pulled toward the "norms, practices, and operating procedures of their schools" (Schuyler & Sitterley, p. 57), which usually conflicted with the critically reflective approach to teaching they, or their university supervisors, were trying to develop. And as student teachers they had rather limited power to combat, or especially transform, these norms and structures.

In order to question and deliberate on these institutional influences, a language and framework of institutional critique are needed. One framework for guiding planning, data collection, and analysis that we have used in teaching and collaborating on action research is the three "registers" of "language and discourse," "activities and practices," and "social relationships and organization," discussed in Kemmis and McTaggart's *The Action Research Planner* (1988). Within each of these registers, questions are posed in relation to three dimensions: historical and contemporary usage, contestation, and institutionalization.[3] For example, a teacher engaging in an initial analysis of historical and contemporary social relationships and organizational structures, might ask: How did the current relationships between teachers and administrators in this school evolve? Or how does the cellular organization of classrooms lock me into particular forms of teaching?

An External Focus in a Public Context

The matrix of registers and dimensions is most comprehensively completed in the public realm where multiple voices can help illuminate and broaden understanding of the contextual influences on educational life. As Stevenson and co-authors (Chapter 5, this volume) argue, the creation of a democratic community of equal but diverse voices among practitioners engaged in action research can provide the beginnings of a vehicle for developing such understandings across differences in age, gender, race, ethnicity, education, power, and politics. In contrast to the dominant beliefs in schools that educational practices are ahistorical and apolitical, we need to establish a norm of thoughtful, public examination of how educational goals and practices are historically shaped by institutional and sociopolitical contexts. As Hursh (Chapter 10, this volume) argues:

> The particular educational practices, discourses, and organizational structures that become institutionalized are neither inevitable nor natural but are outcomes of ongoing political, ethical and philosophical struggles over schooling. (p. 143)

He explains how tracking became the accepted organizational response to dealing with the increasingly diverse student population that resulted from southern and eastern European immigration and the enforcement of compulsory attendance. Yet, Hursh maintains, other responses to this situation are conceivable, such as heterogeneous classrooms where more emphasis is placed on cooperative learning. Such an alternative approach, however, demands a different way of talking about the goals of education, the assumptions about students and society, and a different way of organizing schools.

Although, in teaching action research, we have emphasized the importance of reflecting on and analyzing the situational conditions circumscribing one's practice, many practitioners conducting an action research project (especially for the first time) tend to focus almost exclusively on their own technical competence and on developing improved practices within existing constraints (Stevenson, 1991). This focus on individual competence deflects attention from the conditions in which educational practice, and action research, take place. By not making the constraints themselves a subject of inquiry and possible transformation, we are left with a depoliticized approach to action research and an acceptance of current institutional and social arrangements.

Questioning and challenging these arrangements is clearly a political and conflict-ridden task that is most effectively tackled collectively rather than individually, although many action research efforts are highly individual. It demands a "collective confrontation with the school's fundamental purposes [and] with the implications of the patterns of practices that have accumulated over time" (Little, 1990, p. 531), and a collective commitment to developing organizational forms that enable faculty to engage in the collaborative pursuit of "best" practices. This commitment is more likely to develop when teachers recognize that they require each other's participation in order to confront institutional practices and arrangements. In other words, teachers are dependent on one another for successfully coping with and negotiating the inevitable power struggles over competing values and interests that arise when existing arrangements are challenged.

Paradoxically, a condition for publicly problematizing institutional structures is structural arrangements that enable faculty to meet for such a purpose. Furthermore, particular structural conditions can both enable and inhibit institutional critique. Brunner (Chapter 3, this volume), for example, describes how structural features of the school, together with characteristics of both her biographical history and the broader sociocultural context, "interacted at times to impede and at times to facilitate my attempts to develop an empowering practice" (p. 37). In any educational situation there is a complex and dialectic relationship between contextual factors and the promotion or impediment of improved practices, including the practice of action research.

To summarize the four categories, critical action research attempts to integrate internal or self-reflection on an individual's intentions, practices, and the consequences of those practices, and external reflection on the structural and historical forces that shape those intentions and practices and the circumstances in which they occur. This ongoing reflection, and subsequent revised planning and actions, should take place in conversations with both self and others. The conditions that promote these kinds of reflection include individual and collective commitments to improving educational practices, a language and analytical framework(s) for self and institutional critique, a caring community in which personal support is balanced with critical inquiry (including constructive critique), institutional norms of collaboration, and structural arrangements that provide time and space for the intensive collaborative work involved in action research.

TRANSFORMING SITUATIONS TO SUPPORT ACTION RESEARCH

The way to approach the task of transforming school workplaces to establish the kinds of norms and conditions that support action research is governed to a large extent by whether or not institutional cultures and structures are viewed as being constructed externally to and independently of the people who work within the institution. If they are seen as developed externally, then appropriate workplace conditions must be in place *before* practitioner research can be conducted. In other words, the institutional norms and arrangements that govern teachers' work must be manipulated, presumably by policy makers and administrators, to enable teachers to pursue action research projects.

However, collaborative norms should not be viewed as something to be manipulated directly, but should evolve from within the group of teachers who are working together. The values, such as mutual trust, caring support, and constructive critique, that underlie the kind of collaborative norms that sustain action research have to be nurtured rather than imposed. Therefore, administrators, in initiating efforts to support "bottom-up" action research, can create the conditions in which teachers try to work collaboratively, by reinforcing the underlying values and providing both moral support and specific opportunities for groups to meet. However, administrators should avoid deliberate efforts to manipulate directly teachers' practices and behaviors. According to Grimmett and Crehan (1992), this indirect approach, which they term "organizationally induced collegiality," can "evolve into a truly interdependent culture in which the teacher reflectively transforms his [or her] classroom experience" (p. 76). They emphasize that, while administrators can influence the workplace of teaching, teachers make the ultimate choices about collaboration, both before and during the structuring of collegial activities. Furthermore, since the beliefs and values that underlie the norms of collegial interdependence and experimentation constitute the basis for normative action, organizational arrangements should be loosely structured (Grimmett & Crehan, 1992). Therefore, the transformation of practices is linked to the transformation of the organizational structures in which the practices are enacted.

These last two points suggest an alternative view, namely, that school norms and structures are in part socially constructed by the members of the school. Stated another way, although educational practices are shaped by the organizational and larger sociocultural context in which teachers work, as members of a school social system teachers and the practices to which they are disposed also shape the social system. Practices and contexts are dialectically constituted. But this perspective raises the question: How can existing relationships and structural arrangements be reconstructed by teachers with the support of school administrators? And, furthermore, what is the role of action research in first critiquing and deconstructing existing institutional values, norms, and structures that impede action research, and then reconstructing values, norms, and structures that promote ongoing projects, by practitioners? Put simply, the transformation of school cultures and structures becomes part of the concern of action research endeavors.

Significantly, when a collaborative group of practitioners work together on action research projects, they can create a new system of norms and structures in place of the regular school system and essentially can behave differently (Oja &

Smulyan, 1989). In other words, "new structures and norms can be substituted for existing ones and can be tested to determine their value" (Oja & Pine, 1987, p. 111). However, there is also a natural tendency for teachers to form reference groups with like-minded colleagues who hold similar beliefs and value similar practices. Not only does this limit the questioning of taken-for-granted assumptions and the generation of alternative possibilities within the group, but it also can create, or reinforce, within the school discrete subcultures that hold opposing sets of beliefs and values and pursue correspondingly contradictory practices. If action research groups isolate themselves from the rest of the school, they may transform their understandings but they are unlikely to transform school-wide (or even their own classroom) practices and structures.

More important, reconstituted norms and structures are likely to endure only if they become legitimated within the organization. So while collaborators or "critical friends" from outside the school, such as university faculty (see Chapters 10 and 13, this volume), can play a significant role in helping action research groups try to transform cultures and structural arrangements, ultimately such changes must be accepted by the other members of the school community.

The school community embraces a complex structure of interrelated roles and relationships. Part of this structure is a division of labor in roles of "teacher," "student," "administrator," "counselor," and "parent," with the relationships among these roles defined historically by structures that delineate particular positions of power and authority (Kemmis & Di Chiro, 1987). In the first instance, the existing hierarchy of power relationships means that administrative support is particularly important in transforming organizational norms and structures. For example, the principal can support or undermine the group's autonomy and ability to experiment with new practices and to work collaboratively. This does not necessarily mean that administrators must be members of any action research group, although they may be important collaborators or form their own action research group. A balance needs to be struck between maximizing the group's autonomy to pursue concerns that are most meaningful to its members and maintaining close ties to the administration without subjugating control so that resources and support can be mobilized (Oja & Smulyan, 1989).

Second, since any educational practice involves relationships between people in different roles, practices cannot be changed independent of these relationships and structures. Therefore, other members of the school community need to (at least gradually) become participants in action research groups. This participation should strive to build more collaborative relationships among all players in the educational enterprise. To sustain itself, action research must be about helping individuals become more conscious and critical of their agency in restructuring their relationships in particular and in the processes of educational change in general (Kemmis & Di Chiro, 1987).

CONCLUSION

Problems of sustaining action research activities in schools are not significantly different from the problems of developing and sustaining innovative educational practices in general. Existing educational practices are shaped by the historical, cultural, and structural characteristics of the context in which they take place, as well as by the biographies, skills, and dispositions of the practitioners who implement them.

> The work of a school, a classroom, or a whole education system is a product of history: the product of a set of struggles between real people, real ideas, real ways of working and real ways of organising the work. But people are not just pawns or products of history; through their struggle, they are also the producers of history. Changing education is a matter of engaging in an organised struggle towards better educational ideas, better educational practices, and better social relationships and forms of organisation for education. (Kemmis & Di Chiro, 1987, p. 117)

Action research provides a systematic or organized process to help people who are continually working for better forms of educational life. Yet as an educational practice itself, and one that is intended to problematize institutionalized practices (and structural arrangements), the creation of a new orthodoxy by institutionalizing a particular form of action research must be avoided. Instead, action research also must be subject to continual critique as part of the struggle for better forms of educational inquiry and transformation. This volume of explorations in action research is, in part, presented in an effort to further that struggle. The intent, after all, is to be practically critical in order to improve our educational practices, our understanding of those practices, and the circumstances in which they take place.

NOTES

1. There are examples of "grass-roots" action research efforts that have been carried out without any external support, but I would argue that most of these efforts involved extraordinary individuals and/or atypically supportive school environments. However, I also acknowledge that since the editors of this book are based in a university, our knowledge of action research in schools is biased toward projects that have relied on external support.

2. Her difficulties, however, are not surprising given that the role of the principal has evolved into the demanding position of manager of a large and complex organization.

3. I have presented these registers and dimensions as a nine-celled matrix.

References

Altrichter, H. (1988). Inquiry-based learning in initial teacher education. In J. Nias & S. Groundwater-Smith, (Eds.), *The enquiring teacher: Supporting and sustaining teacher research* (pp. 121–134). London: Falmer Press.

Altrichter, H., Posch, P., & Somekh, B. (1993). *Teachers investigate their work: An introduction to the methods of action research*. London: Routledge.

Apple, M. W. (1993). *Official knowledge: Democractic education in a conservative age*. New York: Routledge.

Bastian, A., Gittell, M., Greer, C., & Haskins, K. (1986). *Choosing equality: The case for democratic schooling*. Philadelphia: Temple University Press.

Beckman, D. (1957). Student teachers learn by doing action research. *Journal of Teacher Education, 8*(4), 369–375.

Berlak, A., & Berlak, H. (1981). *Dilemmas of schooling: Teaching and social change*. New York: Methuen.

Beyer, L. (1988). *Knowing and acting: Inquiry, ideology, and educational studies*. London: Falmer Press.

Biott, C. (1983). The foundations of classroom action research in initial teacher training. *Journal of Education for Teaching, 9*(2), 152–160.

Block, B. (1993). *Independent study report: Marshall video project*. Unpublished manuscript, University of Rochester, Rochester, NY.

Boomer, G. (1987). A case for action research in schools. In D. Goswam & P. Stillman (Eds.), *Reclaiming the classroom: Teacher research as an agency for change* (pp. 4–13). Montclair, NJ: Boynton/Cook.

Brennan, M., & Noffke, S. E. (1988, April). *Reflection in student teaching: The place of data in action research*. Paper presented at the annual meeting of the American Educational Research Association, New Orleans.

Britzman, D. P. (1991). *Practice makes practice: A critical study of learning to teach*. Albany: State University of New York Press.

Calderhead, J. (1989). Reflective teaching and teacher education. *Teaching and Teacher Education, 5*(1), 43–51.

California Science Curriculum Framework and Criteria Committee (1989, October). *Science framework for California public schools* (interim ed.). Sacramento: California State Department of Education.

California State Department of Education. (1989). *California scope, sequence, and coordination: A model of statewide leadership and support*. Sacramento: Author.

Carr, W., & Kemmis, S. (1986). *Becoming critical: Education, knowledge, and action research*. London: Falmer Press.

Clark, C. (1988). Asking the right questions about teacher preparation: Contributions of research on teacher thinking. *Educational Researcher, 17*(2), 5–12.

Clift, R., Houston, W. R., & Pugach, M. (Eds.). (1990). *Encouraging reflective practice in education: An analysis of issues and programs*. New York: Teachers College Press.

Clift, R., Veal, M. L., Johnson, M., & Holland, P. (1990). Restructuring teacher education through collaborative action research. *Journal of Teacher Education, 41*(2), 52–62.

Cochran-Smith, M. (1988). A new assignment for student teachers. *Harvard Education Letter, 4*(4), 3.

Cochran-Smith, M. (1991). Learning to teach against the grain. *Harvard Educational Review, 67*, 279–310.

Cochran-Smith, M., & Lytle, S. (1993). *Inside/outside: Teacher research and knowledge.* New York: Teachers College Press.

Corey, S. (1953). *Action research to improve school practices.* New York: Teachers College Press.

Corey, S. (1954, January). Hoping? Or beginning to know? *Childhood Education, 30*(5), 208–211.

Cornbleth, C. (1990). *Curriculum in context.* New York: Falmer Press.

Costa, A., Garmston, R., & Lambert. (1988). Evaluation of teaching: The cognitive development view. In S. J. Stanley & W. J. Popham (Eds.), *Teacher Evaluation: Six prescriptions for success* (pp. 145–172). Alexandria, VA: Association for Supervision and Curriculum Development.

Coulter, R. P. (1989). To know themselves: The transformative possibilities of history for young women's lives. *History and Social Science Teacher, 25*(1), 25–28.

Crittenden, B. (1973). Some prior questions in the reform of teacher education. *Interchange, 4* (2–3), 1–11.

Cruickshank, D. (1987). *Reflective teaching.* Reston, VA: Association of Teacher Educators.

Curwin, R. L., & Mendler, A. N. (1988). *Discipline with dignity.* Washington, DC: Association for Supervision and Curriculum Development.

Delpit, L. (1986, November). Skills and other dilemmas of a progressive black educator. *Harvard Educational Review, 56*(4), 379–385.

Dewey, J. (1933). *How we think.* Chicago: Henry Regnery.

Di Chiro, G., Robottom, I., & Tinning, R. (1988). An account of action research in a tertiary context. In S. Kemmis & R. McTaggart (Eds.), *The action research planner* (3rd ed., pp. 133–143). Geelong: Deakin University Press.

Dreikurs, R. (1968). *A new approach to classroom discipline: Logical consequences.* New York: Harper & Row.

Duckworth, E. (1987). *The having of wonderful ideas.* New York: Teachers College Press.

Elliott, J. (1978). What is action research in schools? *Journal of Curriculum Studies, 10*(4), 355–357.

Elliott, J. (1985). Educational action research. In J. Nisbet & S. Nisbet (Eds.), *Research, policy, and practice: World yearbook of education* (pp. 231–250). London: Kogan Page.

Elliott, J. (1987). Educational theory, practical philosophy and action research. *British Journal of Educational Studies, 35*(2), 149–169.

Elliott, J. (1991). *Action research for educational change.* Philadelphia: Milton Keynes/Open University Press.

Elliott, J., & Adelman, C. (1973). Reflecting where the action is: The design of the Ford Teaching Project. *Education for Teaching, 92*, 8–20.

Ellsworth, E. (1989). Why doesn't this feel empowering? *Harvard Educational Review, 59*(3), 297–324.

Fagan, W. T. (1989). Empowered students; empowered teachers. *The Reading Teacher, 42*, 596–606.

Fals Borda, O., & Rahman, M. A. (1991). *Action and knowledge: Breaking the monopoly with participatory action research*. New York: Apex.

Feiman-Nemser, S., & Floden, R. (1980). *A consumer's guide to teacher development*. East Lansing, MI: Institute of Research on Teaching.

Feldman, A. (1994). Erzberger's dilemma: Validity in action research and science teachers' need to know. *Science Education, 78*(1), 83–101

Feldman, A., Mason, C., & Goldberg, F. (Eds.). (1992). *Action research: Reports from the field, 1991–92*. San Diego: Center for Research in Mathematics and Science Education.

Fenstermacher, G. (1986). Philosophy of research on teaching: Three aspects. In M. Wittrock (Ed.), *Handbook of research on teaching* (3rd ed., pp. 37–49). New York: Macmillan.

Foshay, A. W., Wann, K. D., & Associates. (1954). *Children's social values: An action research study*. New York: Bureau of Publications, Teachers College.

Fosnot, C. (1989). *Enquiring teachers, enquiring learners: A constructionist approach for teaching*. New York: Teachers College Press.

Foucault, M. (1978). *The history of sexuality: Vol. 1. An introduction*. New York: Vintage Books.

Foucault, M. (1984). On the genealogy of ethics: An overview of work in progress. In P. Rabinow (Ed.), *The Foucault reader* (pp. 340–372). New York: Pantheon Books.

Freire, P. (1972). *The pedagogy of the oppressed*. New York: Herder & Herder.

Fullan, M., & Hargreaves, A. (Eds.). (1992). *Teacher development and educational change*. London: Falmer Press.

Gilbert, D. (1992). Evaluation of SS&C laboratory science at Millikan High School. In A. Feldman, C. Mason, & F. Goldberg (Eds.), *Action research: Reports from the field 1991–92* (pp. 53–104). San Diego: Center for Research in Mathematics and Science Education.

Gitlin, A. D. (1990). Educative research, voice, and school change. *Harvard Educational Review, 60*(4), 443–466.

Gore, J. (1991a). Practicing what we preach: Action research and the supervision of student teachers. In B. R. Tabachnick & K. Zeichner (Eds.), *Issues and practices in inquiry-oriented teacher education* (pp. 253–272). London: Falmer Press.

Gore, J. (1991b). On silent regulation: Emancipatory action research in preservice teacher education. *Curriculum Perspectives, 11*(4), 47–51.

Gore, J., & Zeichner, K. (1991). Action research and preservice teacher education: A case study from the U.S. *Teaching and Teacher Education, 7*(2), 119–136.

Grant, C. A., & Zeichner, K. (1984). On becoming a reflective teacher. In C. A. Grant (Ed.), *Preparing for reflective teaching* (pp. 1–19). Boston: Allyn & Bacon. Cited in G. J. Posner (1989). *Field experience: Methods of reflective teaching* (2nd ed.). New York: Longman.

Greenfield, T. B. (1982, Winter). Against group mind: An anarchistic theory of education. *McGill Journal of Education, 17*(1), 3–11.

Grimmett, P. P., & Erickson, G. (Eds.). (1988). *Reflection in teacher education*. New York: Teachers College Press.

Grimmett, P. P., & Crehan, E. P. (1992). The nature of collegiality in teacher development. In M. Fullan & A. Hargreaves (Eds.), *Teacher development and educational
change* (pp. 56–85). London: Falmer Press.

Grundy, S. (1982). Three modes of action research. *Curriculum Perspectives, 2*(3), 23–34.

Gutmann, A. (1987). *Democratic education.* Princeton: Princeton University Press.

Handal, G., & Lauvas, P. (1987). *Promoting reflective teaching: Supervision in action.*
Philadelphia: Milton Keynes/Open University Press.

Heidegger, M. (1962). *Being and time.* San Francisco: Harper & Row.

Henderson, J. (1992). *Reflective teaching: Becoming an inquiring educator.* New York:
Macmillan.

Holly, P. (1987). Action research: Cul-de-sac or turnpike? *Peabody Journal of Education,
64*(3), 71–99.

Holmes Group. (1990). *Tomorrow's schools.* East Lansing, MI: Author.

Hursh, D. (1988). *Becoming teachers: Preservice teachers' understanding of school and society.*
Unpublished doctoral dissertation, University of Wisconsin–Madison.

Hursh, D. (1993, April). *Developing reflective practitioners: Collaborating within and across
educational institutions.* Paper presented at the annual meeting of the American Educational Research Association, Atlanta, GA.

Hursh, D. (1994). Reflective practice and the culture of schools. In W. Ross (Ed.),
Reflective practice in social studies (pp. 69–76). Washington, DC: National Council for
the Social Studies.

Jensen, K., & Walker, S. (1989). *Towards democratic schooling: European experiences.* Philadelphia: Milton Keynes/Open University Press.

Journal of Teacher Education. (1989). Critical reflection in teacher education: Practices
and problems [Special issue], *40*(2).

Joyce, B., & Showers, B. (1988). *Student achievement through staff development.* New York:
Longman.

Kemmis, S., & Di Chiro, G. (1987, Spring). Emerging and evolving issues of action
research praxis: An Australian perspective. *Peabody Journal of Education, 64*(3), 101–
130.

Kemmis, S., & McTaggart, R. (Eds.). (1988). *The action research planner* (3rd ed.).
Geelong: Deakin University Press.

Ketcham, R., Meiklejohn, D., Julian, J., Fetsko, W., Zalewski, P., & Julian, M. (1988).
Participation in government: Making a difference. Littleton, MA: Copley Publishing
Group.

Kliebard, H. (1986). *The struggle for the American curriculum: 1893–1958.* London:
Routledge & Kegan Paul.

Kozol, J. (1991). *Savage inequalities.* New York: Crown.

Lacey, C. (1977). *The socialization of teachers.* London: Methuen.

Lackey, D., & Walker, S. (1994). Blizzards, E-Mails, FAXes and phones. A collaborative
issue of *Democracy & Education, 8*(4) and *Hands On: A Journal for Teachers, 48,* 2–3.

Lanier, J., & Little, J. W. (1986). Research on teacher education. In M. Wittrock (Ed.),
Handbook of research on teaching (3rd ed., pp. 527–569). New York: Macmillan.

Lave, J., & Wenger, E. (1991). *Situated learning: Legitimate peripheral participation.* Cambridge, UK: Cambridge University Press.

Liston, D., & Zeichner, K. (1990). Action research and reflective teaching in preservice teacher education. *Journal of Education for Teaching, 16*(3), 235–254.

Liston, D., & Zeichner, K. (1991). *Teacher education and the conditions of schooling: A social reconstructionist perspective.* New York: Routledge.

Little, J. W. (1990, Summer). The persistence of privacy: Autonomy and initiative in teachers' professional relations. *Teachers College Record, 91*(4), 509–536.

Lucas, P. (1988). An approach to research-based teacher education through collaborative inquiry. *Journal of Education for Teaching, 14*(1), 55–73.

Madison Metropolitan School District. (1992). *Classroom action research.* Madison, WI: Author.

Martin, R. (1991). The power to empower: Multicultural education for student teachers. In C. E. Sleeter (Ed.), *Empowerment through multicultural education* (pp. 287–297). Albany: State University of New York Press.

McCarthy, C. (1986). Teacher training contradictions. *Education and Society, 4*(2), 3–15.

McNeil, L. (1988). *Contradictions of control: School structure and school knowledge.* New York: Routledge.

Mies, M. (1983). Towards a methodology for feminist research. In G. Bowles & R. Duelli-Klein (Eds.), *Theories of women's studies* (pp. 117–139). London: Routledge & Kegan Paul.

Nelsen, J. (1987). *Positive discipline.* New York: Ballantine Books.

New York State Education Department. (1985). *Participation in government: Tentative syllabus.* Albany: Author.

Noddings, N. (1984). *Caring: A feminine approach to ethics and moral education.* Berkeley: University of California Press.

Noddings, N. (1986). Fidelity in teaching, teacher education, and research for teaching. *Harvard Educational Review, 56*(4), 496–510.

Noffke, S. E. (1989, March). *The social context of action research.* Paper presented at the annual meeting of the American Educational Research Association, San Francisco.

Noffke, S. E. (1990). *Action research: A multidimensional analysis.* Unpublished doctoral dissertation, University of Wisconsin–Madison.

Noffke, S. E. (1992). The work and workplace of teachers in action research. *Teaching and Teacher Education, 8*(1), 15–29.

Noffke, S. E. (1994). Action research: Towards the next generation. *Educational Action Research, 2*(1), 9–21.

Noffke, S. E., & Brennan, M. (1988, April). *The dimensions of reflection: A conceptual and contextual analysis.* Paper presented at the annual meeting of the American Educational Research Association, New Orleans.

Noffke, S. E., & Brennan, M. (1991). Student teachers use action research: Issues and examples. In B. R. Tabachnick & K. Zeichner (Eds.), *Issues and practices in inquiry-oriented teacher education* (pp. 186–201). London: Falmer Press.

Noffke, S. E., & Zeichner, K. (1987). *Action research and teacher thinking.* Paper presented at the annual meeting of the American Educational Research Association, Washington, DC.

Oberg, A. (1986). *Teacher development through reflection on practice.* Paper presented at the annual meeting of the American Educational Research Association, San Francisco.

Oja, S. N., & Pine, G. J. (1984). *Executive summary: Collaborative action research. A two year study of teachers' stages of development and school contexts.* Washington, DC: National Institute of Education.

Oja, S. N., & Pine, G. J. (1987, Winter). Collaborative action research: Teachers' stages of development and school contexts. *Peabody Journal of Education, 64*(3), 96–115.

Oja, S. N., & Smulyan, L. (1989). *Collaborative action research: A developmental approach.* London: Falmer Press.

Park, P., Brydon-Miller, M., Hall, B., & Jackson, T. (1993). *Voices of change: Participatory research in the United States and Canada.* Westport, CT: Bergin & Garvey.

Parnes, S. (1976). *Guide to creative action.* New York: Scribner.

Pateman, C. (1989). *The disorder of women.* Stanford: Stanford University Press.

Perrodin, A. (1959). Student teachers try action research. *Journal of Teacher Education, 10*(4), 471–474.

Posner, G. J. (1989). *Field experience: Methods of reflective teaching* (2nd ed.). New York: Longman.

Posner, G. J., Strike, G., Hewson, P., & Gertzog, W. (1982). Accommodation of a scientific conception: Towards a theory of conceptual change. *Science Education, 66,* 211–227.

Prawat, R. S. (1991). Conversations with self and settings: A framework for thinking about teacher empowerment. *American Educational Research Journal, 28*(4), 737–757.

Robottom, I. (1988). A research-based course in science education. In J. Nias & S. Groundwater-Smith (Eds.), *The enquiring teacher: Supporting and sustaining teacher research* (pp. 106–120). London: Falmer Press.

Roethke, T. (1961). The waking. In T. Roethke, *The collected poems of Theodore Roethke: Words for the wind* (p. 124). Bloomington: Indiana University Press.

Ross, D. (1987). Action research for preservice teachers: A description of why and how. *Peabody Journal of Education, 64*(3), 131–150.

Ross, D., & Kyle, D. (1987). Helping preservice teachers to learn to use teacher effectiveness research appropriately. *Journal of Teacher Education, 38*(2), 40–44.

Rudduck, J. (1985). Teacher research and research-based teacher education. *Journal of Education for Teaching, 11*(3), 281–289.

Rudduck, J., & Hopkins, D. (1985). *Research as a basis for teaching: Readings from the work of Lawrence Stenhouse.* London: Heinemann.

Sagor, R. (1992). *How to conduct collaborative action research.* Alexandria: Association for Supervision and Curriculum Development.

Saphier, J., & Gower, R. (1987). *The skillful teacher.* Carlisle, MA: Research for Better Teaching.

Schön, D. (1983). *The reflective practitioner: How professionals think in action.* New York: Basic Books.

Schön, D. (1987). *Educating the reflective practitioner.* San Francisco: Jossey-Bass.

Schön, D. (1988). Coaching reflective teaching. In P. P. Grimmett & G. Erickson (Eds.), *Reflection in teacher education* (pp. 19–29). New York: Teachers College Press.

Schwab, J. (1978). Education and the structure of the disciplines. In I. Westbury, & N. J. Wilkof (Eds.), *Science, curriculum, and liberal education: Selected essays* (pp. 229–272). Chicago: University of Chicago Press.

Sergiovanni, T. J. & Starratt, R. J. (1993). *Supervision: A redefinition.* New York: McGraw-Hill.

Shor, I., & Freire, P. (1987). What is the dialogical method of teaching? *Journal of Education, 169*(3), 11–31.

Shujaa, M. (1994). *Too much schooling, too little education: A paradox of black life in white societies.* Trenton: Africa World Press.

Shulman, L. (1987). Knowledge and teaching: Foundations of the new reform. *Harvard Educational Review, 57*(1), 1–22.

Shumsky, A. (1958). *The action research way of learning.* New York: College Bureau of Publications, Teachers College Press.

Sirotnik, K. (1990). Society, schooling, teaching and preparing to teach. In J. Goodlad, R. Soder, & K. Sirotnik (Eds.), *The moral dimensions of teaching* (pp. 296–328). San Francisco: Jossey-Bass.

Sleeter, C. E. (1991). Introduction: Multicultural education and empowerment. In C. E. Sleeter (Ed.), *Empowerment through multicultural education* (pp. 1–23). Albany: State University of New York Press.

Smyth, J. (1989). Developing and sustaining critical reflection in teacher education. *Journal of Teacher Education, 40*(2), 2–9. Cited in B. Wellington, The promise of reflective practice. *Educational Leadership, 48*(6), 4–5.

Somekh, B. (1989). The role of action research in collaborative enquiry and school improvement. In B. Somekh, J. Powney, & C. Burge, *Collaborative enquiry and school improvement* (Bulletin 9A of the Classroom Action Research Network). Norwich: University of East Anglia.

Stenhouse, L. (1975). *An introduction to curriculum research and development.* London: Heinemann.

Stevenson, R. (1991). Action as professional development: A U.S. case study of inquiry-oriented inservice education. *Journal of Education for Teaching, 17*(3), 277–292.

Taba, H., & Noel, E. (1957). *Action research: A case study.* Washington, DC: Association for Supervision and Curriculum Development.

Tabachnick, B. R., & Zeichner, K. (Eds.). (1991). *Issues and practices in inquiry-oriented teacher education.* London: Falmer Press.

Tabachnick, B. R., & Zeichner, K. (in press). Using action research to support conceptual change teaching in science. In M. Watt & D. Watt, *Action research and the reform of mathematics and science instruction.* New York: Teachers College Press.

Takata, S. R. (1991). Who is empowering whom? The social construction of empowerment. In C. E. Sleeter (Ed.), *Empowerment through multicultural education* (pp. 251–271). Albany: State University of New York Press.

Tikunoff, W. J., & Mergendoller, J. R. (1983). Inquiry as a means of professional growth: The teacher as researcher. In G. Griffin (Ed.), *Staff development.* Eighty-second yearbook of the National Society for the Study of Education (pp. 210–227). Chicago: University of Chicago Press.

Valli, L. (1990a). Moral approaches to reflective practice. In R. Clift, W. R. Houston, & M. Pugach (Eds.), *Encouraging reflective practice in education: An analysis of issues and programs* (pp. 39–56). New York: Teachers College Press.

Valli, L. (1990b, April). *The question of quality and content in reflective teaching.* Paper presented at the annual meeting of the American Educational Research Association, Boston.

Valli, L. (1992). *Reflective teacher education: Cases and comments.* Albany: State University of New York Press.

Van Manen, M. (1977). Linking ways of knowing with ways of being practical. *Curriculum Inquiry, 6*, 205–228.

van Oech, R. (1983). *A whack on the side of the head.* New York: Warner Books.

van Oech, R. (1986). *A kick in the seat of the pants.* New York: Harper & Row.

Weiler, K., & Mitchell, C. (1992). *What schools can do: Critical pedagogy and practice.* Albany: State University of New York Press.

Weiner, G. (1989). Professional self-knowledge versus social justice: A critical analysis of the teacher-research movement. *British Educational Research Journal, 15*, 41–51.

Weis, L., & Fine, M. (1993). *Beyond silenced voices: Class, race, and gender in United States schools.* Albany: State University of New York Press.

Wellington, B. (1991, March). The promise of reflective practice. *Educational Leadership, 48*(2), 4–5.

Winter, R. (1987). *Action research and the nature of social inquiry.* Aldershot, UK: Avebury

Winter, R. (1989). *Learning from experience: principles and practice in action research.* London: Falmer Press.

Wood, G. H. (1989). Whatever happened to the social studies? *International Journal of Social Education, 4*(1), 55–59.

Wood, P. (1988). Action research: A field perspective. *Journal of Education for Teaching, 14*(2), 135–150.

Young, I. M. (1990). *Justice and the politics of difference.* Princeton: Princeton University Press.

Zeichner, K. (1991). Contradictions and tensions in the professionalization of teaching and the democratization of schools. *Teachers College Record, 92*(3), 363–379.

Zeichner, K. (1992a). Conceptions of reflective teaching in contemporary U.S. teacher education programs. In L. Valli (Ed.), *Reflective teacher education: Cases and comments* (pp. 161–193). Albany: State University of New York Press.

Zeichner, K. (1992b). Rethinking the practicum in the professional development school partnership. *Journal of Teacher Education, 43*(4), 296–307.

Zeichner, K. (1992c, September). *Personal transformation and social reconstruction through action research.* Paper presented at the international meeting of the Classroom Action Research Network, Worcester College, Worcester, UK.

Zeichner, K. (1993a). Connecting genuine teacher development to the struggle for social justice. *Journal of Education for Teaching, 17*(1), 5–20.

Zeichner, K. (1993b, February). Traditions of practice in U.S. preservice teacher education programs. *Teaching and Teacher Education, 9*(1), 1–13.

Zeichner, K., & Tabachnick, B. R. (1991). Reflections on reflective teaching. In B. R. Tabachnick & K. Zeichner (Eds.), *Issues and practices in inquiry-oriented teacher education* (pp. 1–21). London: Falmer Press.

Zeichner, K., & Teitelbaum, B. (1982). Personalized and inquiry-oriented teacher education. *Journal of Education for Teaching, 8*, 95–117.

About the Editors and the Contributors

Susan E. Noffke is a former elementary and middle school teacher. She is currently Assistant Professor of Curriculum & Instruction at the University of Illinois at Urbana-Champaign. Her recent publications include Action Research: Towards the Next Generation in *Educational Action Research* and Personal, Professional, and Political Dimensions of Action Research (to appear in the 1995 *Review of Research in Education*). Her research has focused both on the historical and contemporary practices of action research internationally and on the intersections of social research and social advocacy.

Robert B. Stevenson is Associate Professor in the Department of Educational Organization, Administration, and Policy at SUNY-Buffalo. His publications have appeared in *Journal of Curriculum Studies, Journal of Education for Teachers, Journal of Staff Development, Teaching and Teacher Education*, and *British Journal of Sociology of Education*. His teaching and research interests focus on professional or staff development and school reform and change. Specifically his research includes ways of supporting practitioners' critical inquiries into their own practices, the influence of the structure and culture of secondary schools on curriculum and teaching practices, and student perspectives on schooling.

J. Myron Atkin, a former science teacher, has served on the faculties of the University of Illinois at Urbana-Champaign and Stanford University. His current major projects include a 12-country study of innovations in science, mathematics and technology education sponsored by the Organization for Economic Cooperation and Development and the continuing study of local, interinstitutional alliances to improve science education.

Catherine Battaglia is a Staff Development Specialist for the Niagara Falls City School District, Niagara Falls, New York and an educational consultant and speaker in private practice. Her areas of interest include cognitive science, Whole Language, student assessment, and all aspects of teacher professional development. The material included in this book represents ideas that have since formed the basis for her doctoral work in Social Foundations of Education at SUNY-Buffalo.

Gregory Bronson teaches high school social studies at Lockport (NY) High School. He coaches football and women's basketball, and enjoys sports and his family.

Lynn Brunner completed her teacher certification program and is currently a doctoral student in Sociology of Education at SUNY-Buffalo. Her academic interests lie in the area of the creation of working conditions for teacher empowerment.

Cathy Caro-Bruce is a Staff and Organizational Development Specialist for the Madison, Wisconsin Metropolitan School District. Jennifer McCreadie was formerly with the MMSCD and is now Supervisor of Research, Evaluation and Assessment for the Indianapolis Public Schools. Together they developed and coordinated classroom action research in the Madison schools. They continue to find the collaborations between staff development and research and evaluation stimulating and exhilarating.

Allan Feldman is Assistant Professor of Science Education at the University of Massachusetts at Amherst. His interests include seeking ways to better understand what it means to teach and to be a teacher, and helping teachers to improve their practice and their educational situations through action research.

Eduardo Flores is Assistant Professor in the School of Management at ITSM-Chihuahua Campus in northern Mexico. His areas of interests include action research and organizational change.

Jennifer M. Gore is Senior Lecturer in Education at The University of Newcastle, New South Wales, Australia, where she teaches sociology of education, curriculum theory, gender studies, and subjects on power and pedagogy. She is author of *The Struggle for Pedagogies* and co-editor of *Feminisms and Critical Pedagogy*. Her current research is an empirical investigation of the functioning of power relations in a range of pedagogical sites.

Susan Granger completed her masters program in 1992 at SUNY-Buffalo. She is currently working in child protection for the Erie County Department of Social Services.

David Hursh is Assistant Professor and Chair of the Teaching and Curriculum Program at the Warner Graduate School of Education and Human Development at the University of Rochester. His interests include educational reform at the school and university levels, critical theory and pedagogy, and action research.

Pat Schuyler is a doctoral candidate in Social Foundations of Education, with a minor in Teacher Education, at SUNY-Buffalo. She is a former high school teacher who has worked in university teacher education and in nonformal education. She is completing her doctoral dissertation on teacher education in Venezuela. Her research interests include a comparison of teacher education in Venezuela and Cuba.

David Sitterley is a doctoral candidate in the Department of Educational Organization, Administration and Policy at SUNY-Buffalo. He is presently teaching at Zhenghou University in China. His dissertation topic addresses conceptions of professionalism among inservice and preservice teachers.

Elizabeth Soffer is an elementary school principal for the Pittsford Central School District in Pittsford, New York. She is a doctoral student in philosophy of education concentrating in the area of moral education and theory. Her interests as an administrator have been critical thinking, conflict management, learning styles and developmentally appropriate education.

Kenneth M. Zeichner is Hoefs-Bascom Professor of Teacher Education at the University of Wisconsin-Madison and a senior researcher with the National Center for Research on Teacher Learning, Michigan State University. His recent publications include Connecting genuine teacher development to the struggle for social justice in *Journal of Education for Teaching* and Action research: Personal renewal and social reconstruction in *Educational Action Research*.

Index

Accountability, 85–88
Action research
 action cycles and, 78–85, 98–111, 116–123
 case study in teaching, 60–73
 change and, 3, 5–8
 collaboration among teachers in, 128, 129–130, 132–133, 146–153, 165–179
 components of, 23–24
 conceptions of, 198–200
 connecting theory and practice in, 141–144
 critical community in, 19–22, 25–26, 63–65, 70–71, 166–178
 defining, 4–5, 189–190
 democratic community in, 6, 60, 68–72, 110–111
 described, 2
 in elementary school, 115–126, 156–157
 explorations in, 8–10
 focus on own practice in, 77–78, 89–91, 128
 in high school, 95–114, 180–196
 history of, 2–4
 improving schools with, 5–8
 institutionalized, 190–195
 in middle school, 157–158
 model for, 34, 44, 58–59
 planning in, 82, 85–89, 118–119, 120, 203–204
 in preservice teacher education, 19–26, 43–59, 144–153
 principals and, 115–126, 144, 156, 157, 163, 164
 projects in, 149–151, 181–189
 relationship between university researchers and teachers in, 128–130, 165–166, 181–185
 school district support for, 154–164
 within social reconstructionist tradition, 16–22
 sustaining, 133–137
 traditional research versus, 124–126, 132, 168, 200–201

Action Research Planner, The (Kemmis & McTaggart), 204
Active listening, 86
Adelman, C., 3
African Americans, 6, 51–52. *See also* Minority students
Alienation, 170
Altrichter, H., 23, 135, 192
American Educational Research Association (AERA), 14
American Federation of Teachers (AFT), 145–153
Apple, M. W., 6
Atkin, J. Myron, 9, 127–137, 197, 199
Australia, 3–4
Authentic assessment, 144
Authority. *See also* Empowerment; Power dynamics
 of principals, 144
 of teachers, 38–39, 41

"Banking" teaching style, 38, 39–40
Bastian, A., 6
Battaglia, Catherine, 9, 74–91, 202, 204
Beckman, D., 13
Berlak, A., 54, 57
Berlak, H., 54, 57
Beyer, L., 16
Biographical context, 37–41, 44–45
Biott, C., 13
Blended classrooms, 147–153
Block, B., 149–150
Boomer, G., 29 n. 5
Brennan, M., 2, 29 n. 3, 72
Britzman, Deborah P., 36, 38, 40
Bronson, Gregory, 9, 95–114, 197
Brunner, Lynn, 9, 31–42, 204, 206
Brydon-Miller, M., 4

Calderhead, J., 14
California, 100 Schools Project, 180–196
California Science Curriculum Framework & Criteria Committee, 183

California State Department of Education
    (CSDE), 181, 190
Caring, 17–19, 20, 21
Caro-Bruce, Cathy, 10, 154–164
Carr, W., 4, 29 n. 4, 200
Child-centered schooling, 3
Clark, C., 13
Classroom Action Research Network
    (CARN), 3
Clift, R., 13, 14
Coaching, in Instructional Theory Into Practice
    Seminar (ITIP), 76–77, 79–80, 84–85,
    86, 202, 204
Cochran-Smith, M., viii, 13, 28
Collier, John, 2
Community. See Critical community; Demo-
    cratic community
Context
    biographical, 37–41, 44–45
    reflective approach and, 36–41
    sociocultural, 37, 38
    structural, 37, 40–41
Control, in action research projects, 194–195
Cooperating teachers, 34–36, 38–41, 47, 48–
    49, 144, 146
Cooperative Learning approach, 41, 76, 85
Corey, Stephen, 3, 7, 13, 62, 203
Cornbleth, Catherine, 33, 36
Costa, Arthur, 77, 82, 86
Coulter, R. P., 32, 33
Crehan, E. P., 204, 207
Critical community, 63–65, 70–71
    collaborator role in, 166–178
    in preservice education, 19–22, 25–26, 63–
        65, 70–71
Critical theory, 4
Crittenden, B., 17
Cruickshank, D., 14, 15
Curriculum development, 3–4, 182, 186–187
Curwin, R. L., 115, 117, 120

Deakin University, 26
"Defensive teaching" style, 38–39
Delpit, Lisa, 51–52
Democracy and Education, 5–6, 27
Democratic community, 6, 60, 68–72
    in Participation in Government (PIG)
        course, 110–111
Democratic education, 3–4, 8
Dewey, John, 6, 14, 43

Dialectical critique, 200–201
Di Chiro, G., 26, 208, 209
Dilemmas of Schooling (Berlak & Berlak), 54, 57
Disciplinary practice, principals and, 115–126
Dreikurs, R., 118
Duckworth, E., 16

Educational Action Research, 3
Educational reform, 100 Schools Project in,
    180–196
Elementary school, action research in, 115–
    126, 156–157
Elliott, John, 3, 29 n. 5, 62, 189, 190, 194,
    199
Ellsworth, E., 65
Empowerment
    defining, 31–33
    practices leading to, 33, 34–36
    in preservice teacher education, 34–42
Engagement, 85–88
Engrossment (Noddings), 17
Equity, 17–19, 20
Erickson, G., 14
Ethical caring (Noddings), 18
Ethic of care, 17–19, 20, 21
Experimentation, 29 n. 2
External locus of control, 117–118

Fagan, W. T., 33
Fals Borda, O., 4
Feiman-Nemser, S., 21
Feldman, Allan, 9, 10, 127–137, 130, 180–
    196, 189, 191, 197, 199
Fenstermacher, G., 13
Fetsko, W., 96
Fine, M., 6
Floden, R., 21
Flores, Eduardo, 10, 60–73, 165–179
Focus, 85–88
Ford Foundation, 145
Foshay, A. W., 3
Fosnot, C., 13
Foucault, M., 18
Freire, Paulo, 6, 33, 34

Garmston, R., 77
Gertzog, W., 13
Gilbert, D., 191
Giroux, Henry, 6
Gitlin, A. D., 202, 204

Gittell, M., 6
Goldberg, Fred, 181, 189
Gore, Jennifer M., 7, 9, 13–30, 21, 24, 29 n.
    3, 199
Gower, R., 115, 117, 118, 123
Granger, Susan, 10, 60–73, 165–179
Grant, C. A., 45
Greenfield, Thomas B., 79
Greer, C., 6
Grimmett, P. P., 14, 204, 207
Grundy, S., 2, 29 n. 4
Gutmann, A., 6

Hall, B., 4
Handal, G., 19
Hands On: A Journal for Teachers, 5–6
Haskins, K., 6
Heidegger, M., 134
Henderson, J., 14
Hewson, P., 13
High school, action research in, 95–114, 180–
    196
Holland, P., 13
Holly, P., 16
Holmes Group, 29 n. 6
Hopkins, D., 66
Houston, W. R., 14
Hursh, David, 9–10, 141–153, 142, 143, 144,
    203, 205

Individualism, 8, 16, 175
Institutional change, 19, 41
Institutionalized action research, 190–195
Instructional Theory Into Practice Seminar
    (ITIP), 74–91
    action cycles in, 78–85
    background to, 74–75
    coaching support in, 76–77, 79–80, 84–85,
        86, 202, 204
    planning in, 82, 85–89
    "practice" in, 77–78, 89–91
    reflective practice in, 77–78, 80–81, 87–91
Instrumental (technical) level, of reflective prac-
    tice, 49–51
Interactive Research and Development projects,
    198–199
Internal locus of control, 117
Interpretive level, of reflective practice, 49–51
Isolation, of teachers, 40, 44, 45, 58, 193–
    194

Jackson, T., 4
James, William, 1, 6
Jensen, K., 6
Johnson, M., 13
Journal of Teacher Education, 14
Journal writing, 185–186
    in Participation in Government (PIG)
        course, 98–99, 101
    by principals, 120, 125–126
Joyce, B., 77
Julian, J., 96
Julian, M., 96
Justice, 17–19, 20

Kemmis, Stephen, 3–4, 5, 18, 29 n. 4, 34, 41,
    44, 57, 58–59, 62, 63, 143, 148, 165,
    175, 199, 200, 204, 208, 209
Ketcham, R., 96
Kick in the Seat of the Pants, A (van Oech), 89
Kliebard, H., 3, 143
Knowledge base orientation, 4, 130–133
Kohl, Herb, 6
Kozol, J., 6
Kyle, D., 15

Lacey, C., 29 n. 7
Lackey, D., 1
Lambert, 77
Lanier, J., 21, 58
Lauvas, P., 19
Lave, J., 193
Lewin, Kurt, 2–3, 62
Liston, D., 15, 29 n. 3, 49
Little, J. W., 21, 58, 203, 206
Lucas, P., 29 n. 1, 29–30 n. 8
Lytle, S., viii, 28

Madison (Wisconsin) Metropolitan School Dis-
    trict, 23, 154–164
    beginnings of action research in, 156–157
    culture of action research in, 157–158
    implementation of action research and, 162–
        164
    preparation for action research in, 155–156
    process of action research in, 158–162
Martin, R., 32–33, 41
Mason, C., 189
McCarthy, C., 22
McCreadie, Jennifer, 10, 154–164
McDonald, Barry, 41

McNeil, L., 38, 189
McTaggart, Robin, 3–4, 5, 18, 34, 41, 44, 57, 58–59, 62, 63, 143, 148, 165, 175, 199, 204
Meiklejohn, D., 96
Mendler, A. N., 115, 117, 120
Mergendoller, J. R., 199
Middle schools, action research in, 157–158
Mies, Maria, 4
Minority students
    African American, 6, 51–52
    in blended classrooms, 147–153
    multicultural programs and, 155–157
Mitchell, C., 6
Moral education, 3
Moral relativism, 19–20
Motivational displacement (Noddings), 17
Multicultural education, 33–34, 147, 155–157

Narrative approach, 7–8, 24–26, 27. See also Journal writing
National Issues Forum (NIF) curriculum, 99–101
National Science Foundation (NSF), 181
National Teacher Corps, 19
Natural caring (Noddings), 18
Nelsen, J., 115
New York, Rochester City School District, 145–153
New York State Education Department (NYSED), 96
Noddings, N., 17–18, 29–30 n. 8
Noel, E., 3
Noffke, Susan E., 1–10, 2, 4, 29 n. 3, 60–73, 62, 70, 72, 179, 197, 199, 203

Oberg, A., 200, 202
Oja, S. N., 4, 207–208
100 Schools Project, 180–196
Organizational structures
    collaboration in, 146–153
    connecting theory and practice in, 142–144
    to support action research, 146–153, 202, 207–208

Parents, principals and, 122–123
Park, P., 4
Participation in Government: Making a Difference (Ketcham et al.), 96

Participation in Government (PIG) course, 95–114
    action cycles in, 98–111
    course changes in, 112–113
    described, 96–98
Pateman, C., 8
Perrodin, A., 13
Planning, in action research, 82, 85–89, 118–119, 120, 203–204
Posch, P., 135, 192
Posner, G. J., 13, 14, 43, 45
Poverty, 6, 44
Power dynamics, 23, 176–178
Practice Makes Practice (Britzman), 36
Prawat, R. S., 201, 203
Praxis, as term, 1
Preservice teacher education. See also Student teaching
    action research in, 19–22, 43–59, 144–153
    connecting theory , practice in, 142–144
    critical community in, 19–22, 25–26, 63–65, 70–71
    empowerment in, 34–42
    social reconstructionist approach to, 13–29
Principals
    action research by, 115–126
    authority of, 144
    disciplinary practice and, 115–126
    involvement in action research programs, 156, 157, 163, 164
Professional development. See Staff development
Progressive education, 3
Project START (University of Pennsylvania), 28
Pugach, M., 14
Punishment, 118

Racism, 44
Rahman, M. A., 4
Reality therapy, 118
Reflection in action, 13, 14–15
Reflection on action, 14–15
Reflective practice
    examples of, 33–41, 43–59
    external focus of, 204–206
    of facilitator, 189–195
    in Instructional Theory Into Practice Seminar (ITIP), 77–78, 80–81, 87–91

internal focus in, 201–204
letters between collaborators in, 165–179
levels of reflection in, 19–20, 29–30 n. 8, 49–51
in Participation in Government (PIG) course, 98–111
preparation for, 43–44
in preservice teacher supervision, 43–59
by principals, 119, 120–121, 122, 123
private context of, 201–202, 204–205
public context of, 203–204, 205–206
for student teachers, 13–29
sustaining, 133–137
versions of, 15–16
Reflexive critique, 200–201
Responsibility model, 117–118, 120
Rethinking Schools, 5–6, 27
Robottom, I., 21, 23, 26, 29 n. 1
Rochester (New York) City School District, 145–153
Roethke, T., 31
Ross, D., 13, 15
Rudduck, J., 13, 66

Sagor, R., 4
Saphier, J., 115, 117, 118, 123
Schön, D., 14–15, 135
School districts
Madison (Wisconsin) Metropolitan School District, 23, 154–164
Rochester (New York) City School District, 145–153
Schuyler, Pat, 43–59, 204
Schwab, J., 196 n. 2
Science Framework for the California Schools, 183
Scientific literacy, Scope, Sequence, & Coordination (SS&C) project and, 180–196
Self-development, 199
Self-monitoring, by preservice teachers, 13
Sergiovanni, T. J., 88
Shor, Ira, 6, 33
Showers, B., 77
Shujaa, M., 6
Shulman, L., 15, 130
Shumsky, Abraham, 3, 13
Sirotnik, K., 17, 29 n. 6
Site-based management, 6
Sitterley, David, 43–59, 204

Skillful Teacher, The (Saphier & Gower), 117
Sleeter, C. E., 31–32, 33
Smulyan, L., 4, 207–208
Smyth, J., 59 n. 5
Social justice, 3–4, 17–19
Social meliorist position, 3
Social reconstructionist approach, 16–26
distinguishing, 14–18
enacting, 18–22
to teacher education, 13–29
at University of Wisconsin-Madison, 16–26
Social studies, action research in high school, 95–114
Sociocultural context, 37, 38
Soffer, Elizabeth, 9, 115–126, 197, 202
Somekh, B., 2, 135, 192
Staff development, 4, 7, 28
connecting theory and practice in, 141–144
in Instructional Theory Into Practice Seminar (ITIP), 74–91
Standards, educational, 6
Starratt, R. J., 88
State University of New York at Buffalo, 60–73, 165–179
Stenhouse, Lawrence, 3, 62, 66, 199
Stevenson, Robert B., 9, 10, 60–73, 62, 72, 197–209, 203, 205
Strike, G., 13
Structural context, 37, 40–41
Student teaching. See also Preservice teacher education
action research in, 22–26
empowerment in, 34–42
group discussions in, 27–28, 47–49, 51–52, 54–56, 67–68
placement for, 33–34
postobservation conferences in, 46–47, 49–51, 53–54
Student voice, 62–63
in Participation in Government (PIG) course, 98–111

Taba, Hilda, 3
Tabachnick, B. R., 16, 29 n. 3, 30 n. 9, 30 n. 12
Tactics for Thinking approach, 76
Takata, S. R., 32, 33

Teacher education. *See* Preservice teacher education; Staff development; Student teaching
Teacher education associates (TEAs), 43–59
Teaching styles
    "banking," 38, 39–40
    "defensive," 38–39
Teitelbaum, B., 21
Tikunoff, W. J., 199
Tinning, R., 26
Tracking, 143–144
Transformative level, of reflective practice, 49–51

United Kingdom, 3
University of Pennsylvania, Project START, 28
University of Rochester, action research program of, 145–153
University of Wisconsin-Madison, 16–26

Valli, L., 14, 16, 142
Van Manen, M., 19, 29–30 n. 8

van Oech, Roger, 89
Veal, M. L., 13
Voice, student, 62–63, 98–111

Walker, S., 1, 6
Weiler, K., 6
Weiner, Gaby, 4, 62
Weis, L., 6
Wellington, B., 59 n. 5
Wenger, E., 193
Whack on the Side of the Head, A (van Oech), 89
Whole Language approach, 76, 144, 145
Winter, R., 65, 198, 200
Wood, G. H., 33
Wood, P., 23

Young, I. M., 8

Zalewski, P., 96
Zeichner, Kenneth M., 2, 4, 6, 9, 13–30, 15, 16, 19, 21, 24, 25, 28, 29 n. 3, 30 n. 9, 30 n. 12, 45, 49, 199